This book is dedicated
by the authors to

ALFRED WILLIAM JONES
in appreciation of his work
in preserving the history
and traditions of the

EARLY DAYS OF COASTAL GEORGIA

ERRATA

Page 11, 1st line:
    "1763" should be "1736".

Page 21, 6th line of 2nd paragraph:
    "recorded" should be "recorder".

Page 55, 1st line of 2nd paragraph:
    "mover" should be "moved".

Page 61, last line of 1st paragraph:
    "know" should be "known".

Page 101, 6th line of 2nd paragraph:
    omit the apostrophe in "Gould's".

Page 125, 5th line of 1st paragraph:
    should be "Port Royal in South Carolina".

Page 133, 2nd line of 4th paragraph:
    After "ministers" change comma to period.
    The next sentence should read: "Among the
    ministers who served this church were .. ".

Page 189, 4th paragraph:
    "her" should be "here".

Page 223, 1st line of 2nd paragraph:
    should read "Just what it means or why .. ".

Yᴏᴜ MAY WONDER why a collection of pictures was made of Coastal Georgia scenes. It happened this way.

About 1936, Margaret Davis Cate and I decided that, as many of the historic landmarks were fast disappearing, it was more or less a duty for her, as a historian, and for me, as a photographer, to take this opportunity of preserving them for posterity.

The tabby houses of two hundred years ago were falling to pieces. The slave cabins were disintegrating, roofs had fallen in, doorways were gone. But the land remained and in the cemeteries we found the history of the early settlers. Also, we were able to reach the home life of the Negroes, seeing them on the little plots of land they owned and in their native environment — unspoiled and natural. They were a lovable people, earnest, honest, and perfectly happy in their surroundings. We have tried to preserve in photographs and sketches the charm of these people, who are direct descendants of the slaves of early times and retain the characteristics of their forebears. They all tell a story — one which we do not want to lose.

Mrs. Cate, who is familiar with the life and character of the southern Negro, has been able to capture the spirit of the times as no other person could possibly do it, as she had not only the friendship but the confidence of these people.

We hope this book will fulfill the object for which it was assembled.

ORRIN SAGE WIGHTMAN, M.D., F.R.P.S., HON. P.S.A.

Dr. Wightman's wonderful pictures record for us visible evidence of our Coastal Culture. The Military Era and the Plantation Era belong to history. Each had its story and each produced its heroes. Oglethorpe and the soldiers of Bloody Marsh will never be forgotten as they give life and color to the Military Era. Neither should we forget the Plantation Era which produced a Corbin and a Neptune. Gone are the tabby walls and the way of life lived within these walls.

In writing these stories to interpret Dr. Wightman's pictures, all the knowledge gained in a lifetime of research was used. For the scores of persons who have assisted in this study throughout these years grateful appreciation is expressed.

However, especial acknowledgment is due to Miss A. Jane Macon; Miss Catherine Clark; Miss Ophelia Dent; Mrs. Ruby Wilson Berrie; Miss Mary L. Ross; Mr. Richard A. Everett; Mrs. Maude G. Lambright; Mrs. Mary Givens Bryan, Director of the Georgia Department of Archives; Mrs. Lilla M. Hawes, Director of the Georgia Historical Society; and to the Manuscripts Divisions of the Libraries of the University of Georgia and Duke University, and the Southern Historical Collection of the University of North Carolina.

MARGARET DAVIS CATE

Contents

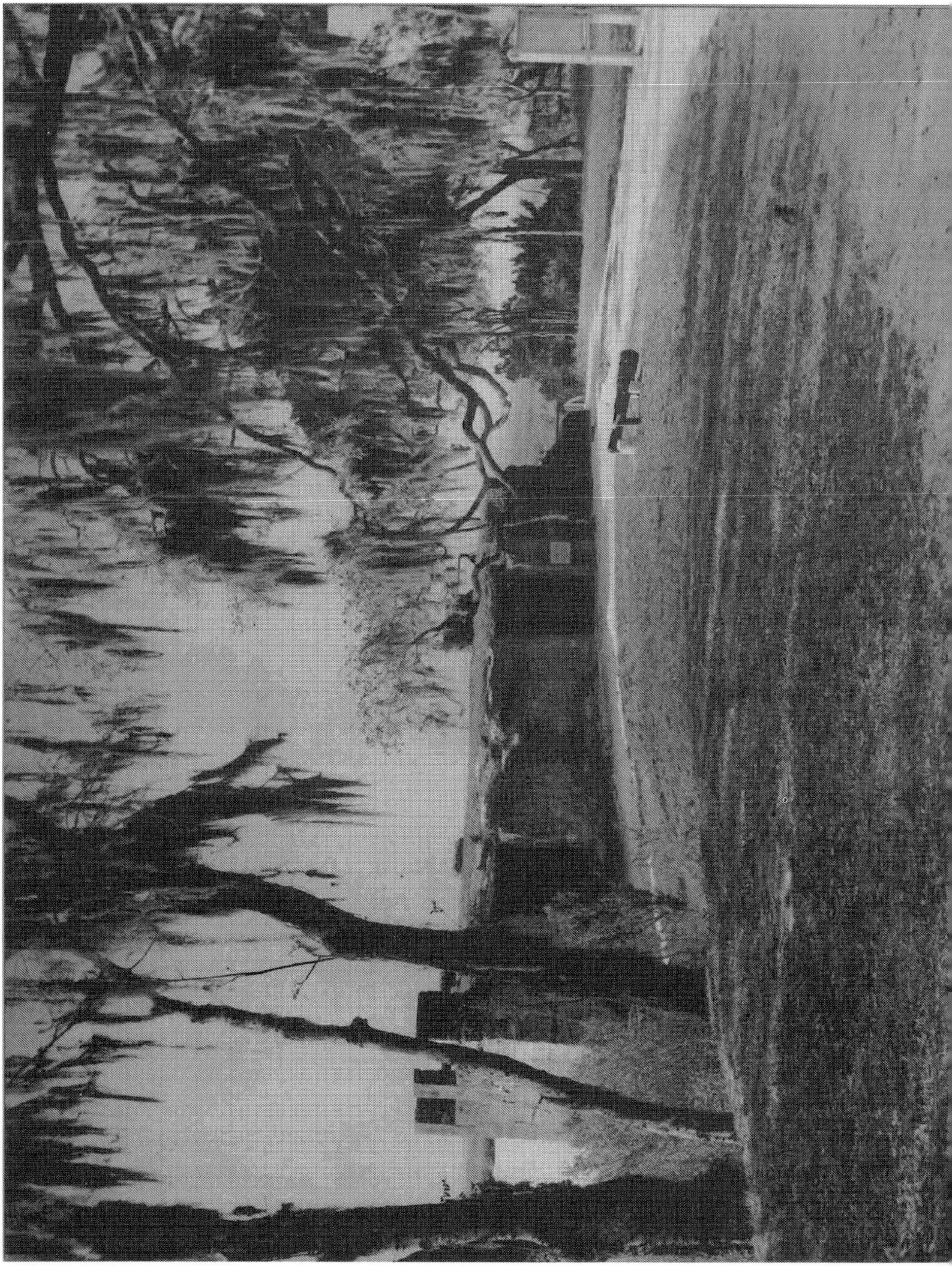

Fort Frederica, St. Simons Island, Georgia

Built in 1763 by British settlers under the direction of James Edward Oglethorpe, founder and first Governor of Georgia, Fort Frederica was the most expensive fortification built by the British in North America and became the military headquarters of this Southern Frontier for Britain's Colonies in the New World against the Spaniards in Florida.

Oglethorpe named this place Frederica in honor of Frederick, Prince of Wales, son of George II and father of George III. Augusta was named in honor of the Princess of Wales, while the naming of Cumberland Island and Amelia Island honored William, Duke of Cumberland, and Amelia, other children of the royal family.

Located on the western shore of St. Simons Island on Frederica River, a part of the Inland Waterway which was the route followed by coast-wise vessels, this site was chosen by Oglethorpe for his great fort because of its strategic position. Here the river bends and turns so that an approaching vessel would be exposed to the cannon of the fort without being able to return the fire.

Fort Frederica, a star-shaped work with four bastions and walls of tabby faced with earth on the outside, was surrounded by a moat, which was further protected by palisades. Oglethorpe wrote that in the building of the fort he followed the plan of M. Vauban, the great military engineer of France, whose work had revolutionized the art of warfare.

Inside the fort there were several buildings of brick and of tabby which were used as storehouses. The ruin of the building shown here is "all that Time has spared" of these buildings though tabby and brick foundations give evidence of the location of others.

Another fortification, Fort St. Simons, was located at the South End of St. Simons Island. A regiment of 650 British soldiers, brought over in 1738, manned both of these fortifications as well as the other forts and outposts in this area.

Fort Frederica was built for a purpose and it gloriously achieved that purpose; its defenders turned back the tide of the Spanish invaders and made this area secure for Britain.

[11]

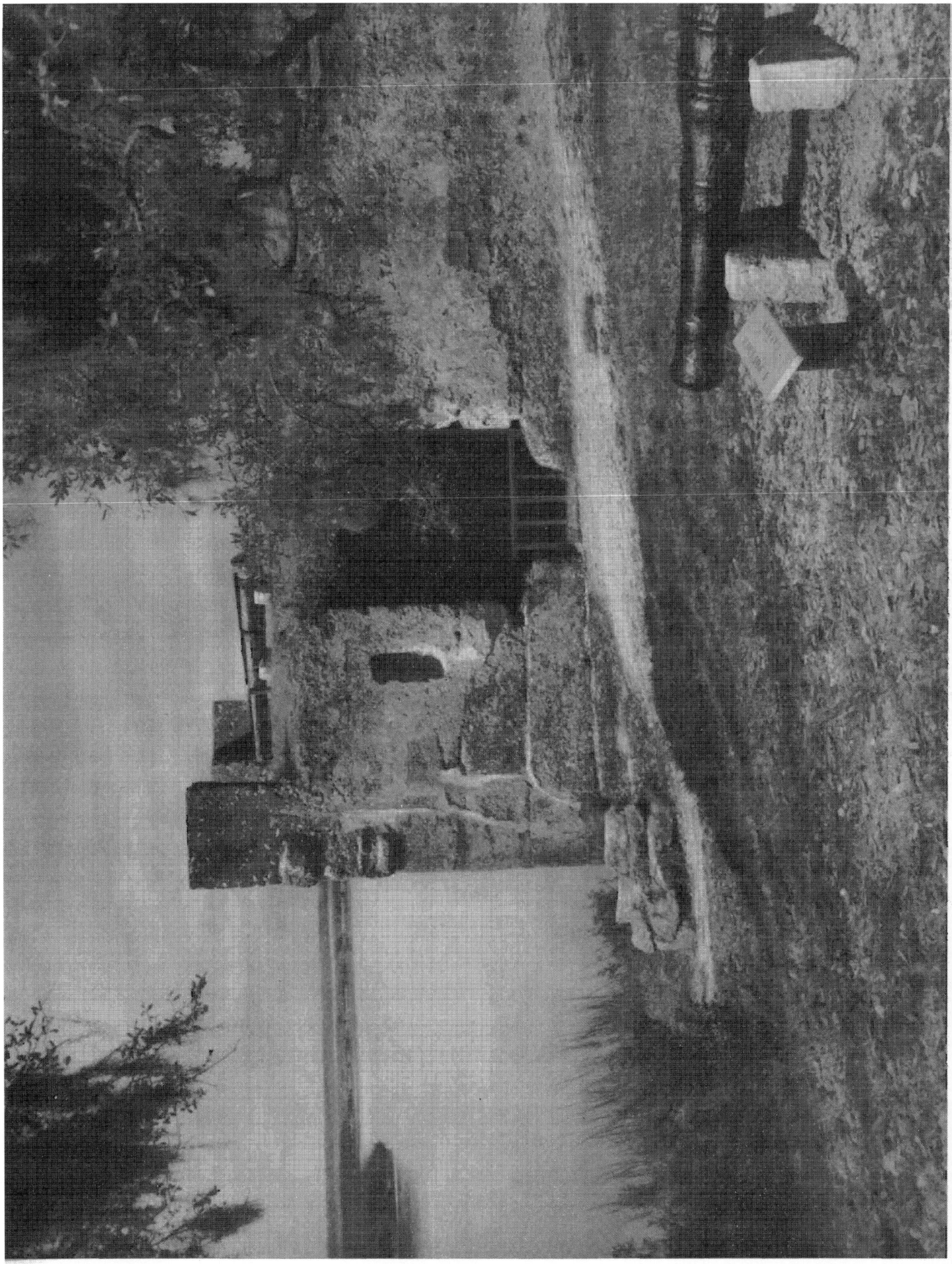

Fort Frederica in the War of Jenkins' Ear

The struggle between Spain and England for control of this southeastern section of our country was a part of the conflict which is generally known as the War of Jenkins' Ear. After the defeat of the Spaniards in the Invasion of 1742 and the termination of the war by the Treaty of Aix-la-Chapelle in 1748, the regiment of British soldiers stationed here was disbanded and Fort Frederica was abandoned.

As the houses fell into ruins, settlers from other parts of St. Simons took away the bricks and pieces of tabby to use in buildings they were erecting. The tabby walls of the Fort were sawed into blocks and used in the first St. Simons Light House. As time went on, this abandoned Frederica property came into the possession of Capt. Charles Stevens, a native of Denmark, who operated a coastwise sailing vessel on the Inland Waterway. Capt. Stevens built a home for his family on top of the building shown here. Later, the Stevens family occupied a house located a short distance east.

In 1903 the president of the Georgia Society, Colonial Dames of America, was Mrs. Georgia Page King Wilder who had been born at Retreat Plantation, St. Simons, and had known of Fort Frederica and its history all her life. Through Mrs. Wilder's friendship with Mrs. Belle Stevens Taylor, who now owned this land, Mrs. Taylor gave this building and a small piece of ground surrounding it to the Georgia Society of the Colonial Dames of America, who repaired the ruins and rebuilt this room shown in the picture. The large pieces of tabby lying on the ground were replaced in their original position and the ceiling of the room rebuilt with new brick. The other room located on the right still has its original ceiling of old English brick brought from England in 1736. So to the Georgia Society of the Colonial Dames of America goes the honor of having saved this ruin from destruction.

Through the efforts of Judge and Mrs. S. Price Gilbert and Mr. Alfred W. Jones of Sea Island, the Fort Frederica Association was organized in 1941 and funds were raised for the purchase of the lands occupied by the old Fort and the Town of Frederica. In 1947 this area was formally dedicated as Fort Frederica National Monument.

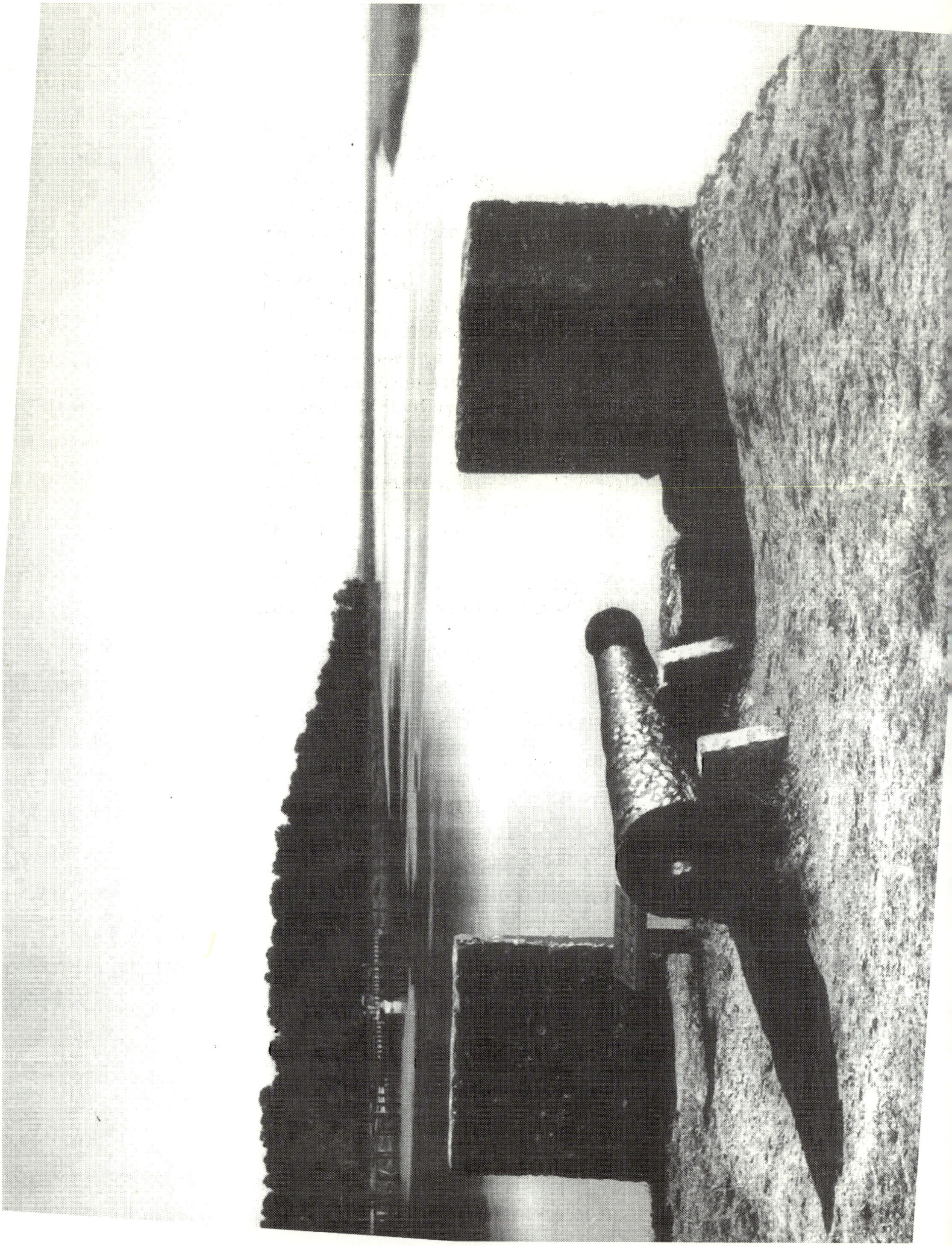

Old Frederica Cannon

This old cannon is the only one of the original Fort Frederica cannon still here. It is what was known as a twelve-pounder, the size of the cannon being determined by the weight of the cannon ball. When in use, this gun was mounted on a wooden carriage so that it could be moved from place to place. It is believed that it was never mounted on top of this building. When the Colonial Dames acquired this ruin, the cannon was on the ground near the southeast corner. In order to protect it more adequately it was placed on top of the building.

In its day Fort Frederica had many cannon. Oglethorpe's first engineer at Fort Frederica was Samuel Augspourger, a Swiss emigrant who had come to Purysburg, S. C., and from there to Georgia. Augspourger wrote that there were fifty cannon at Frederica, some of them being eighteen-pounders. His map made in 1736 (original manuscript in John Carter Brown Library, Providence, R. I.) shows the "spur work" on the river where "the cannon . . . are on a level with the water's edge, and make it impossible for any boat or ship to come up or down the river without being torn to pieces . . ." Other cannon were mounted on the bastions of the fort and at the Point Battery located on the lower part of the bluff.

Even after Fort Frederica was abandoned, a guard was stationed here to protect the place and prevent the guns from being taken away by pirates. In 1755 a dozen twelve-pounders that had been mounted in the "spur work" were removed and carried to Cockspur Island in the Savannah River where they were used to fortify Fort George. During the Revolutionary War some of the Frederica cannon were taken to Sunbury and used in fortifying Fort Morris, but this one has been here at Frederica for more than two centuries.

Fort Frederica was so well situated that the Spaniards never succeeded in attacking it, so its cannon were never fired except on special occasions, one of which was the salute to Gen. Oglethorpe when he returned from a voyage to England.

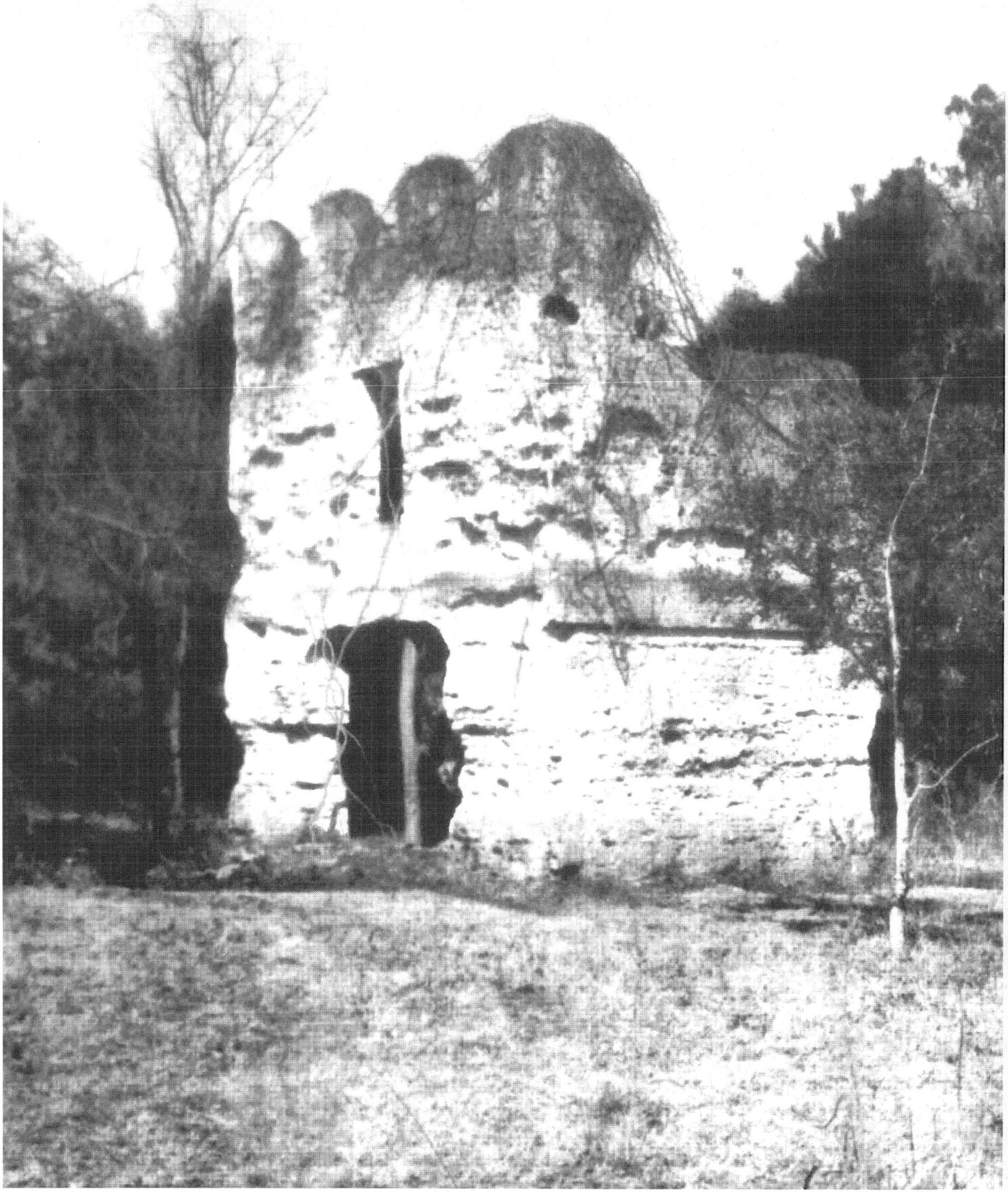

The Barracks Building

This barracks building, erected to house the soldiers of Oglethorpe's Regiment, was ninety feet square, had a shingle roof, and was built in the form of a hollow square with the rooms opening on a court yard. The only part of the building which was two stories high was this tower on the north side containing the entrance to the building.

In addition to the accommodations for the soldiers, there were facilities for the hospitalization of the troops and quarters for political prisons.

One of the famous prisoners incarcerated here was Christian Priber, who for some years lived among the Indians in the upper part of South Carolina. There he attempted to set up a communistic form of government, a Utopia which he called "Paradise," and designated himself as its Prime Minister.

In 1743 Prime Minister Priber was captured by the British, brought to Frederica, and incarcerated there. During his imprisonment the magazine at the fort exploded. With bombs flying through the air in every direction, the officer in charge threw open the doors of the prison and told the occupants to flee for their lives. When the danger had passed and the people returned to Frederica, inquiry was made as to the whereabouts of Priber whom no one had seen during the excitement. A search disclosed that the Prime Minister of Paradise had not left his prison but had stayed there taking refuge under a feather bed!

Charles H. Fairbanks, Archeologist of the National Park Service, recently excavated the area covered by two rooms of the barracks building. One of these was the kitchen in which were found pieces of dishes, spoons, and other ware used by the soldiers. A most interesting item was the brass name-plate from the gun-stock of Capt. William Horton's gun. Horton, who came to Frederica with Oglethorpe in 1736, had a plantation on Jekyll Island, and in time became an officer in Oglethorpe's Regiment, going from lieutenant to major. When Oglethorpe finally returned to England, Horton succeeded to the command of the military forces in this area.

[17]

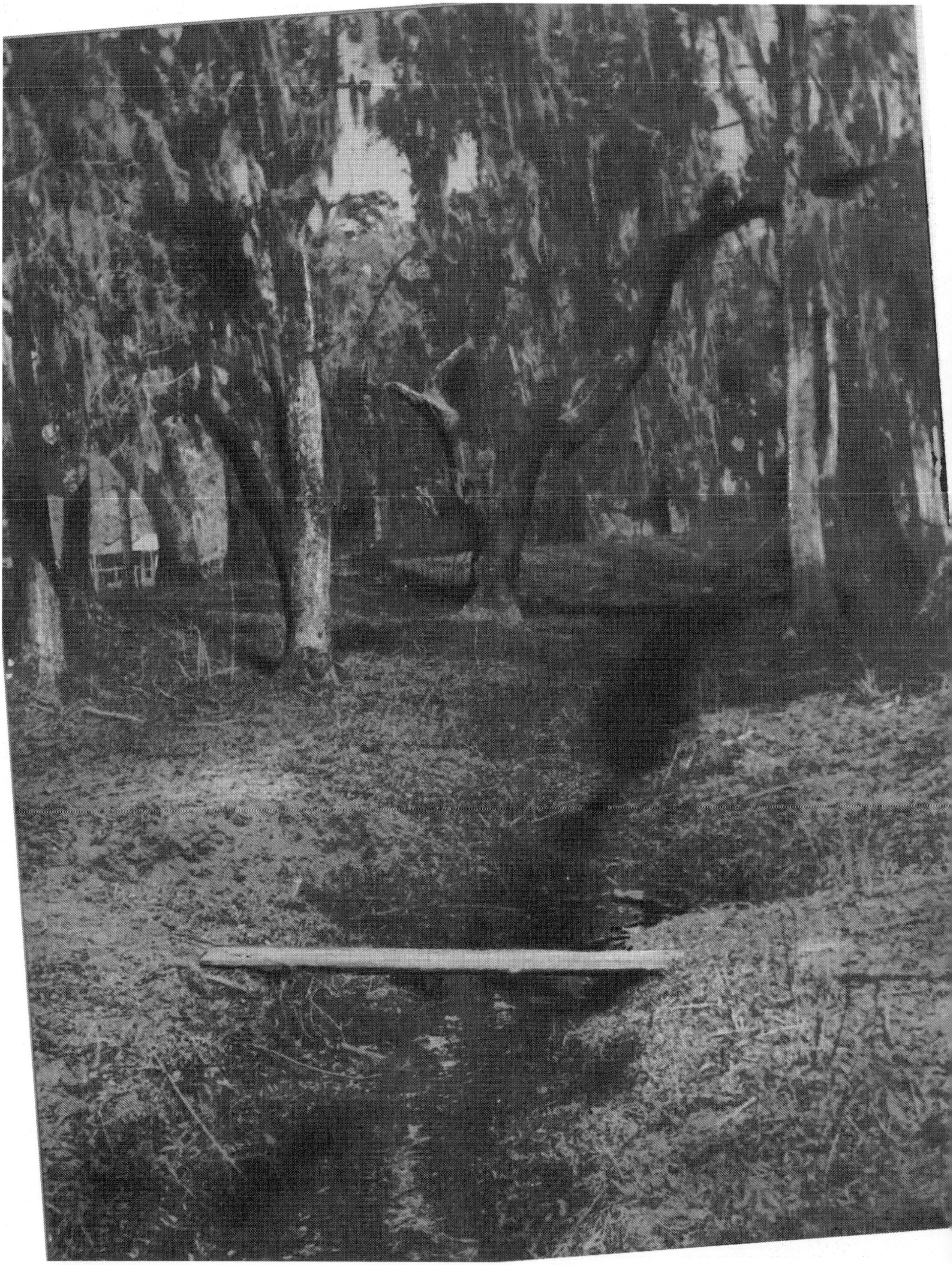

The Town Moat

Adjoining Fort Frederica on the east lay the Town of Frederica, which was half a hexagon in shape and contained eighty-four lots on which the Frederica settlers built their homes.

After the outbreak of war with Spain in 1739, Oglethorpe strengthened his defenses by fortifying the town. It was enclosed within a moat two-thirds of a mile long which was flooded by tidal water from Frederica River, the moat touching the river at either end. At the corners of the moat were bastions, on each of which was a two-story tower capable of holding a hundred men. Flanking the moat on either side were palisades while the walls of the moat formed the ramparts of the town.

In the center of the east wall of the town was located the Town Gate over which was a tower containing sentry boxes. Leading from this tower was the bridge over the moat which gave entrance to the Town of Frederica. This entrance on the east was known as the "Landport," while the western entrance located near the river was called the "Waterport."

Oglethorpe sometimes used the moat for target practice. In 1743 when he was preparing to invade Florida, the soldiers who were to make the invasion ". . . marched out of the Town, and each Platoon fir'd at a Mark, before His Excellency for the Prize of a Hat and Machet, to the Man who made the best Shot at an hundred yards Distance, in the Fosse round the Fortifications. He afterwards gave Beer to the Soldiers . . ."

During the centuries which have passed the moat was abandoned, great trees of pine and live oak have grown up on its banks. Today, their moss-draped forms present a peaceful scene which is very different from that contemplated when the threat of the Spanish Invasion brought about the construction of the moat.

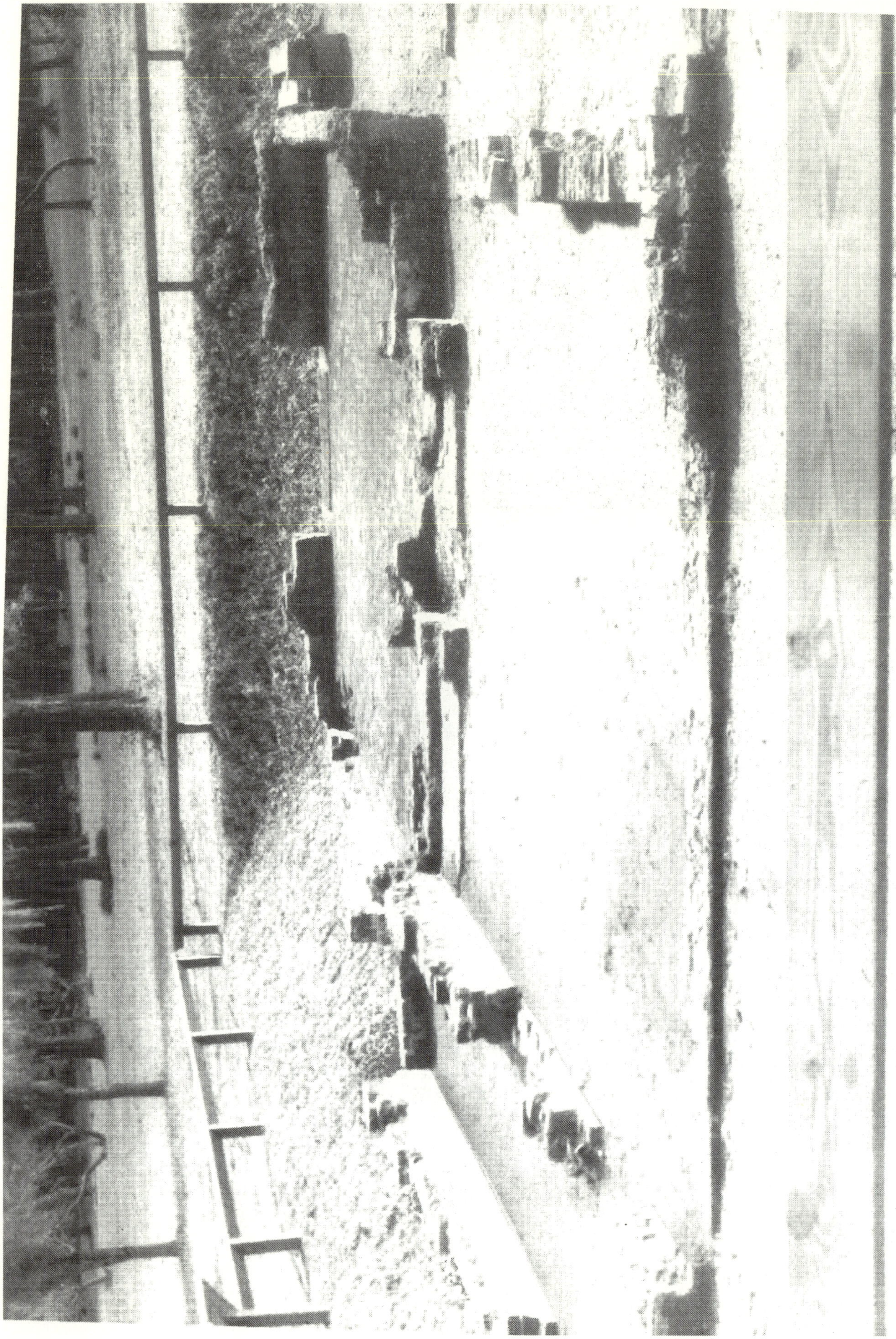

Foundations of Frederica's Old Houses

During the Military Era the old Town of Frederica was a thriving settlement. Its streets were lined with houses built of tabby, of brick, and of wood. Some were substantial dwellings, two were log cabins, and some were described as "huts."

Here the settlers lived and conducted their businesses, which included taverns, an apothecary shop, and several stores, in one of which iron goods were sold. Among the trades and professions represented were those of shoemaker, cordwainer, brazier, husbandman, dyer, tallow candler, baker, tanner, coachmaker, carpenter, bricklayer, woodcutter, blacksmith, millwright, miller, pilot, accountant, surveyor, recorded, magistrate, tithingman, constable, doctor, and officers of Oglethorpe's Regiment.

After the Regiment was disbanded, Frederica became a 'dead town." The shopkeepers and professional men who had depended on the soldiers for their livelihood had no customers. Abandoned by their owners, the houses fell into decay, the brick walls tumbled, and the brick and tabby were hauled away to be used in buildings erected on other parts of St. Simons and by a new generation of settlers. New families came to live on the site of the old Town and every trace of its buildings and streets was lost. Gone, also, were the beautiful orange trees that had lined Broad Street. It was only in musty records that this old town lived.

Through old maps and the letters and records of these first settlers it has been possible to locate the town lots and streets, and through archeological excavations to prove that these homes had existed. In 1952 this program was inaugurated under the direction of Charles H. Fairbanks, Archeologist of the National Park Service, who excavated lots #1 and #2 of the South Ward.

The rooms in the foreground of this picture were in the house on lot #1 which was the home of Dr. Thomas Hawkins, the medical doctor for the Frederica community; later, the surgeon of Oglethorpe's Regiment. To the left can be seen the walls of the stairwell for the outside stairs which led to the Hawkins' front door on the main floor. In the background can be seen the brick of the floor in the Davison house located at lot #2.

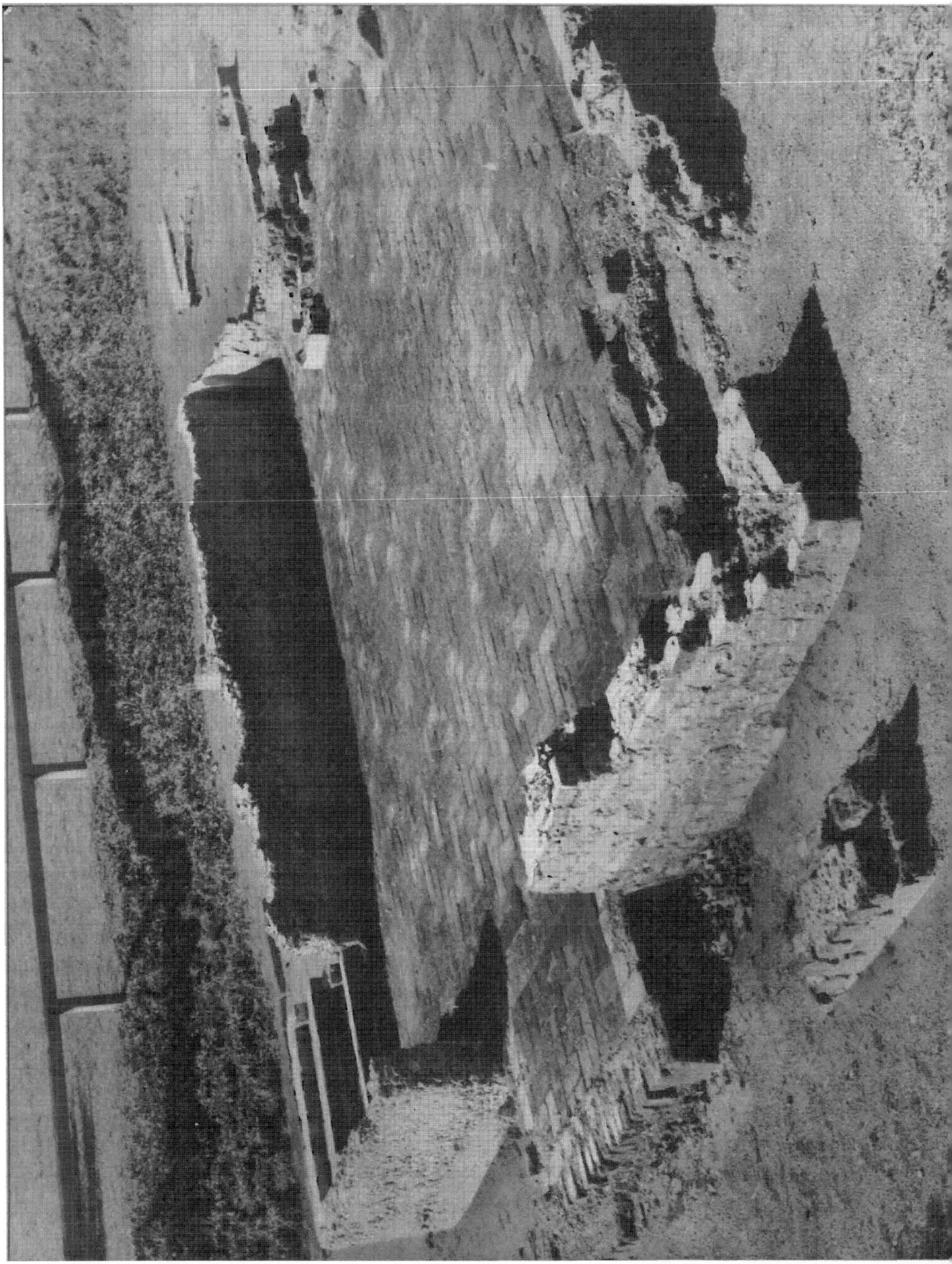

Hawkins-Davison Houses

With all the lots in Frederica available, it was decided to excavate these two houses first because they were built with a common wall which lay along the line between the lots. By locating this wall it would be possible to fix the location of all the lots in the old town. These houses, built of brick and three stories high, were among the best of the Frederica houses. Lot #1 had been granted to Dr. Thomas Hawkins, who, with his wife, Beata, accompanied the first settlers to Frederica.

Lot #2 was granted to Samuel Davison, who with his wife, Susannah, and their year-old daughter, Susannah, was also among the first settlers. Later, the Davisons had two more children born here. Davison was a "chairman" and was brought over at this time because, in addition to making carriages, he "had been bred to making stocks for guns." Although Davison was a Presbyterian, John Wesley said he was one of the best of his parishioners. He was a "good Samaritan" to Charles Wesley, nursing him during a severe illness. Davison kept a tavern in his house but said he never suffered "any disorderly meeting or late hours." The floor shown in this picture was in his kitchen; and, as it had been set in tabby mortar, the bricks are still in place.

During the excavation of these buildings many interesting artifacts were found that told of the way of life of these people. In the Davison house were hundreds of pieces of dishes, clay pipes, bottles, and other items to be expected in a tavern. The excavations also showed that Davison had a well-built house. The inside of this room was finished with a "studding" on which were nailed laths to which plaster was applied.

The Hawkins house, however, was of cheaper construction, the plaster being applied directly to the brick walls. Also, the brick of the floor, set in sand, has been carried off along with the brick of the walls. In this house were found some fine pieces of porcelain with the gold decoration still intact; also, bottles of many sorts — a snuff bottle, an ink bottle, medicine bottles, ointment jars, and an enema tube made of ivory. Just what you would expect to find in a doctors house.

As these houses and furnishings were in sharp contrast, so were the families. Everyone spoke well of the Davisons, but the Doctor's wife was known as a mean woman; in fact, it was she who made life so miserable for John and Charles Wesley.

[23]

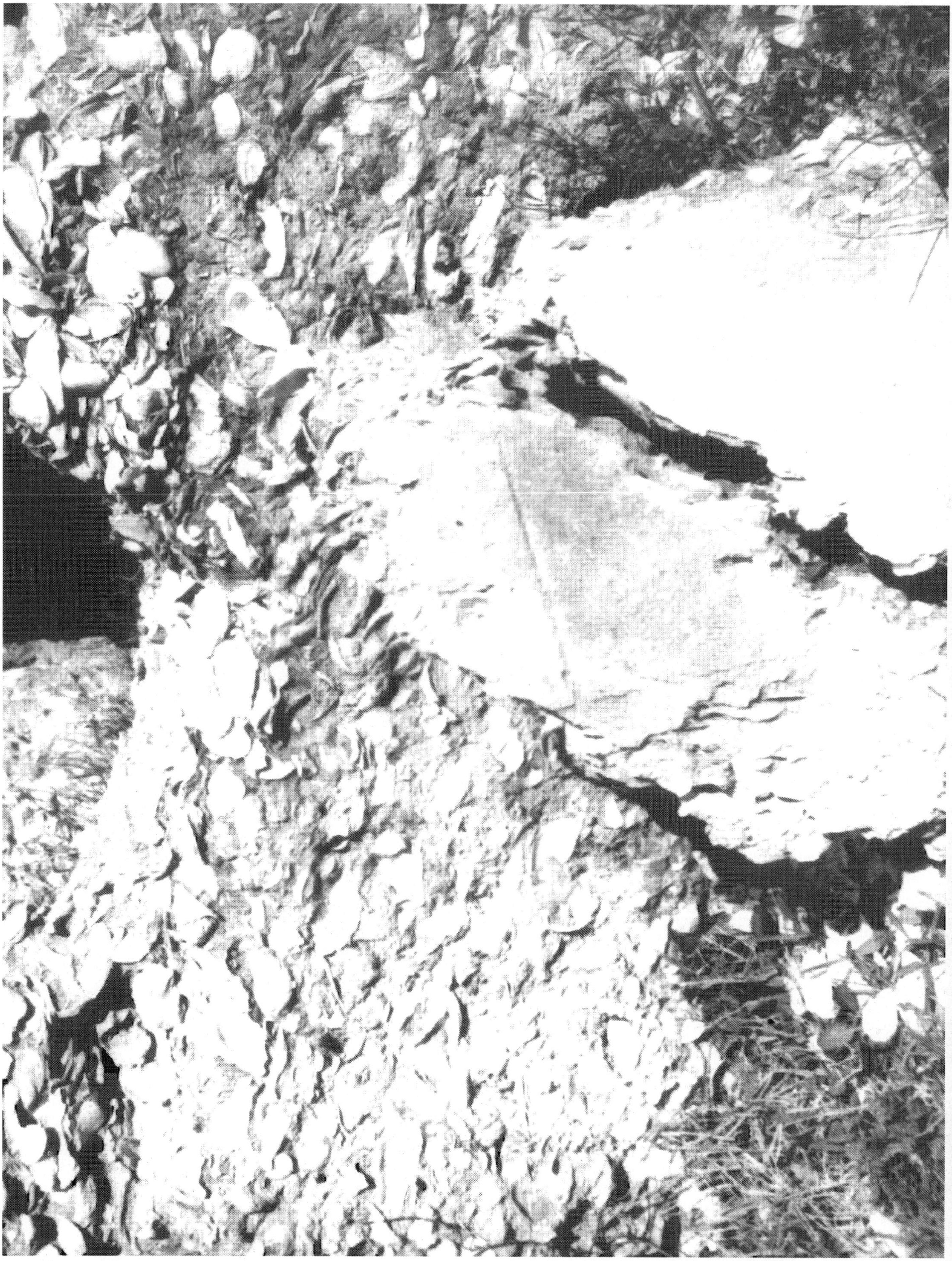

Tabby

Tabby was the building material for walls, floors, and roofs widely used throughout this section during the Military Era and the Plantation Era. It was composed of equal parts of sand, lime, oyster shell and water, mixed into a mortar and poured into forms. Those forms were set up just one board high and for the entire outline of the building, being held firmly in place and the proper distance apart by wooden pins.

The mortar was poured into the forms, firmly packed, and allowed to harden. The wooden pins and forms were then removed and placed in position for the next layer, and so on until the walls reached their full height. The pouring of two layers a week was considered good work.

After the tabby walls were completed, they were given a stucco finish of mortar made of lime and sand. This was considered necessary in order to make the buildings water-proof since tabby was very porous and absorbed water readily; this coat of stucco also covered the streaks which showed the width of the boards used as forms, and the round holes made by the wooden pins.

The lime used in tabby was made by burning oyster shell taken from Indian Shell mounds or "Kitchen Middens," the trash piles of the Indians. Into the lime kilns were piled wood and oyster shell, layer on layer, into a great mound, with as much as two hundred to three hundred bushels of shell at each burning. When it was time to start the fire, musicians would appear and food and drink were brought forth. Indeed the affair was a festive occasion that, as a social community gathering, ranked with cock fights and wrestling matches or celebrations of the King's Birthday and of St. Andrew's Day. Some of the men watched the fire throughout the night and the resulting pile of powdered shell was lime. The Lime Kiln on St. Simons was south of the German Village and about four miles from Frederica.

The word *tabby* is African in origin, with an Arabic background, and means a wall made of earth or masonry. This method of building was brought to America by the Spaniards. However, when the coquina (shell-rock) quarries near St. Augustine were opened, hewn stone superseded tabby for wall construction there. Coastal Georgia has no coquina, so tabby continued to be used here even as late as the 1890's.

[25]

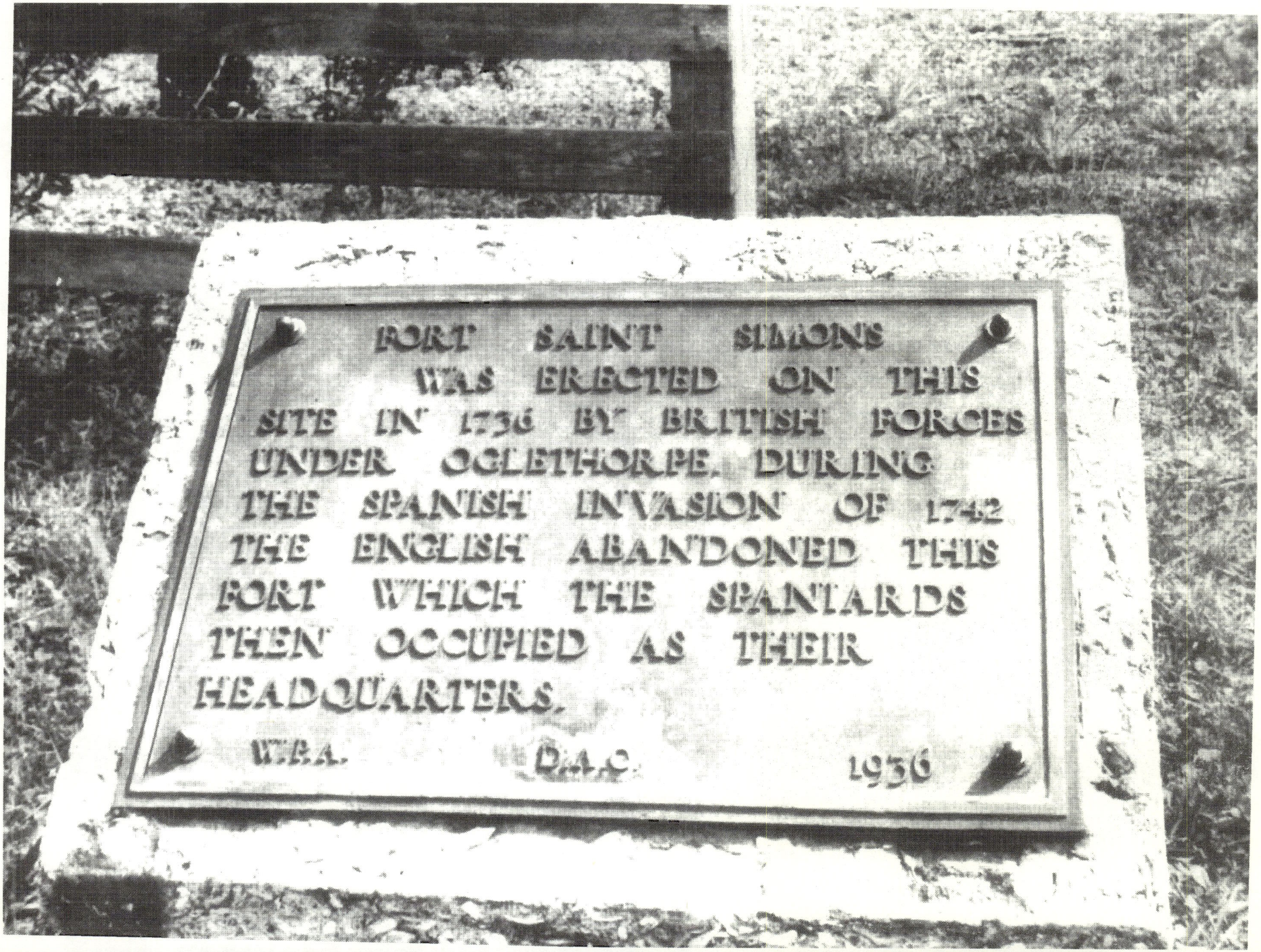
FORT SAINT SIMONS
WAS ERECTED ON THIS
SITE IN 1736 BY BRITISH FORCES
UNDER OGLETHORPE. DURING
THE SPANISH INVASION OF 1742
THE ENGLISH ABANDONED THIS
FORT WHICH THE SPANIARDS
THEN OCCUPIED AS THEIR
HEADQUARTERS.
W.P.A.
D.A.C.
1936

Fort St. Simons

A few weeks after the Frederica settlers reached St. Simons and established themselves in their new home, a group of thirty soldiers arrived here. These were part of the Independent Company who had been stationed at Port Royal, S. C., under the command of Lieut. Philip Delegal.

Oglethorpe posted them on the southeast point of St. Simons at a place which projected into the sea so that the position commanded the entrance to the harbor. He chose this site because all ships that came in must pass "within shot" of this place, "the channel lying under it by reason of a shoal that runs off from Jekyll Island."

This was known as Delegal's Fort at Sea Point and was fortified "with gabions filled with sandy earth," between which were mounted thirteen cannon: in a short time the garrison numbered one hundred men.

Oglethorpe then went back to England to obtain the necessary men and equipment to fortify Georgia adequately, returning in 1738 with a regiment of 650 British soldiers. Oglethorpe was named Colonel of this regiment and General and Commander-in-Chief of the military forces of South Carolina and Georgia.

A larger and stronger fortification, known as Fort St. Simons and sometimes called the Soldiers' Fort, was now built here and the soldiers of the Independent Company stationed at Delegal's Fort were taken into the regiment. At this time British regiments were not numbered, the only designation used being Oglethorpe's Regiment.

The area around Fort St. Simons presented the appearance of a neat village, with streets regularly laid off, and with more than one hundred clapboard houses occupied by the soldiers and their families.

The land occupied by Delegal's Fort and Fort St. Simons has been washed away, leaving no trace of either.

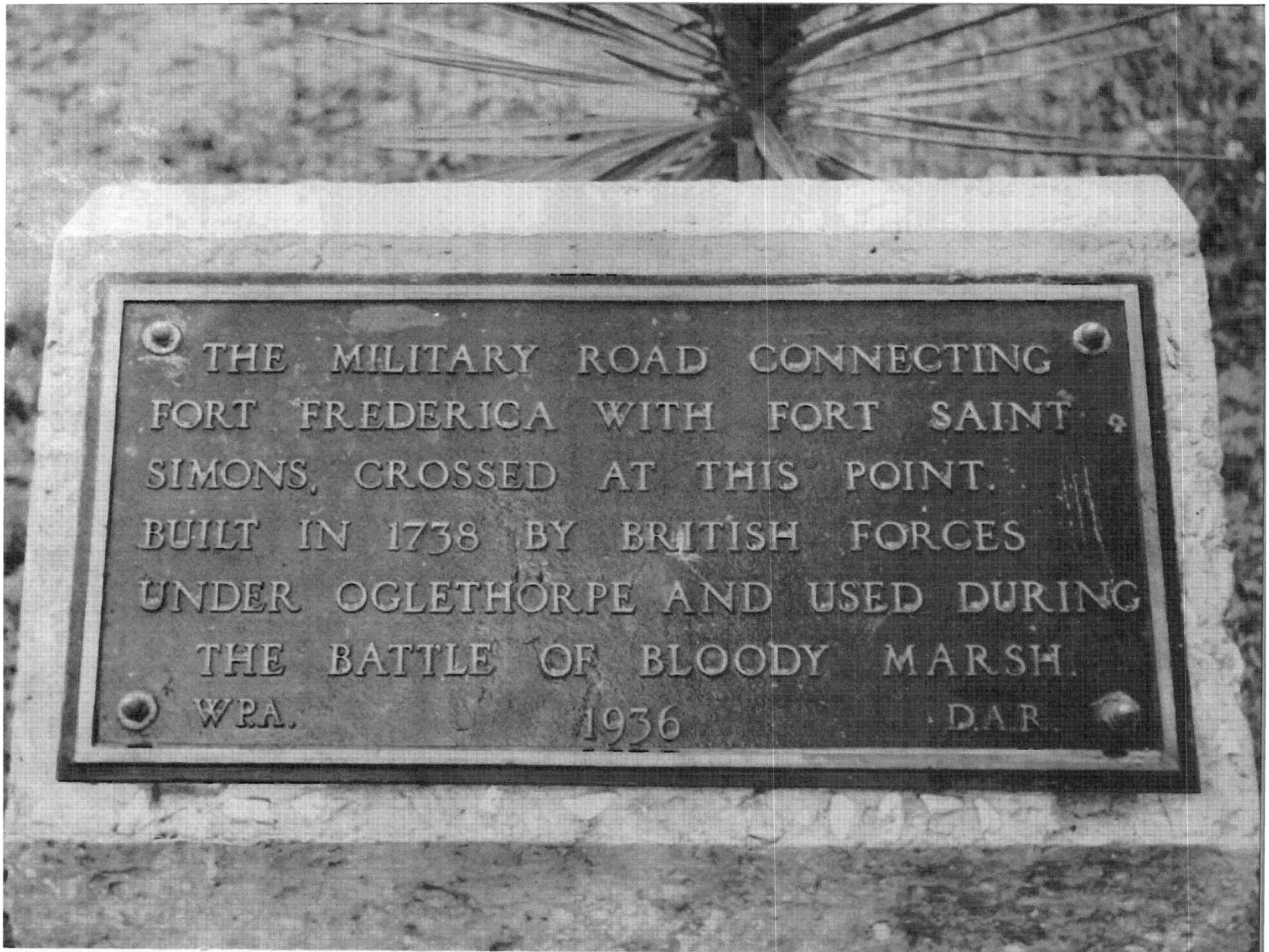
THE MILITARY ROAD CONNECTING
FORT FREDERICA WITH FORT SAINT
SIMONS, CROSSED AT THIS POINT.
BUILT IN 1738 BY BRITISH FORCES
UNDER OGLETHORPE AND USED DURING
THE BATTLE OF BLOODY MARSH.
W.P.A.
1936
D.A.R.

Marker on Military Road

As soon as the Independent Company was stationed at Delegal's Fort at Sea Point, Oglethorpe arranged that "a communication was opened with Frederica," a distance of about nine miles. No doubt this path followed an Indian trail and was sufficient for the needs of that time, but it could not have been very well marked. On his third visit to Frederica, John Wesley and his friend, Mark Hird, walked from Frederica to Delegal's Fort and on the return trip in the late afternoon were lost and had to spend the night in the woods, sleeping on the ground.

When Oglethorpe's Regiment reached St. Simon's, a better means of communication was necessary; so Oglethorpe laid out a road which led from the Town Gate of Frederica due east by the old Burying Ground and across the marsh and Gully Hole Creek. Here it turned in a southeasterly direction for about two miles, passing Oglethorpe's cottage, continuing in this southeasterly direction through the present Negro settlement known as Harrington, and touching the eastern marsh of St. Simons, a short distance north of Black Banks. From this point the road followed the edge of the marsh to a place which was to become famous as the site of the Battle of Bloody Marsh. From Bloody Marsh the road again followed high land and led in a direct line to Fort St. Simons.

At the point where this Military Road crossed the present Frederica Road, this marker was erected in 1936 by the Brunswick Chapter, Daughters of the American Revolution as a part of the community program to celebrate the founding of Fort Frederica.

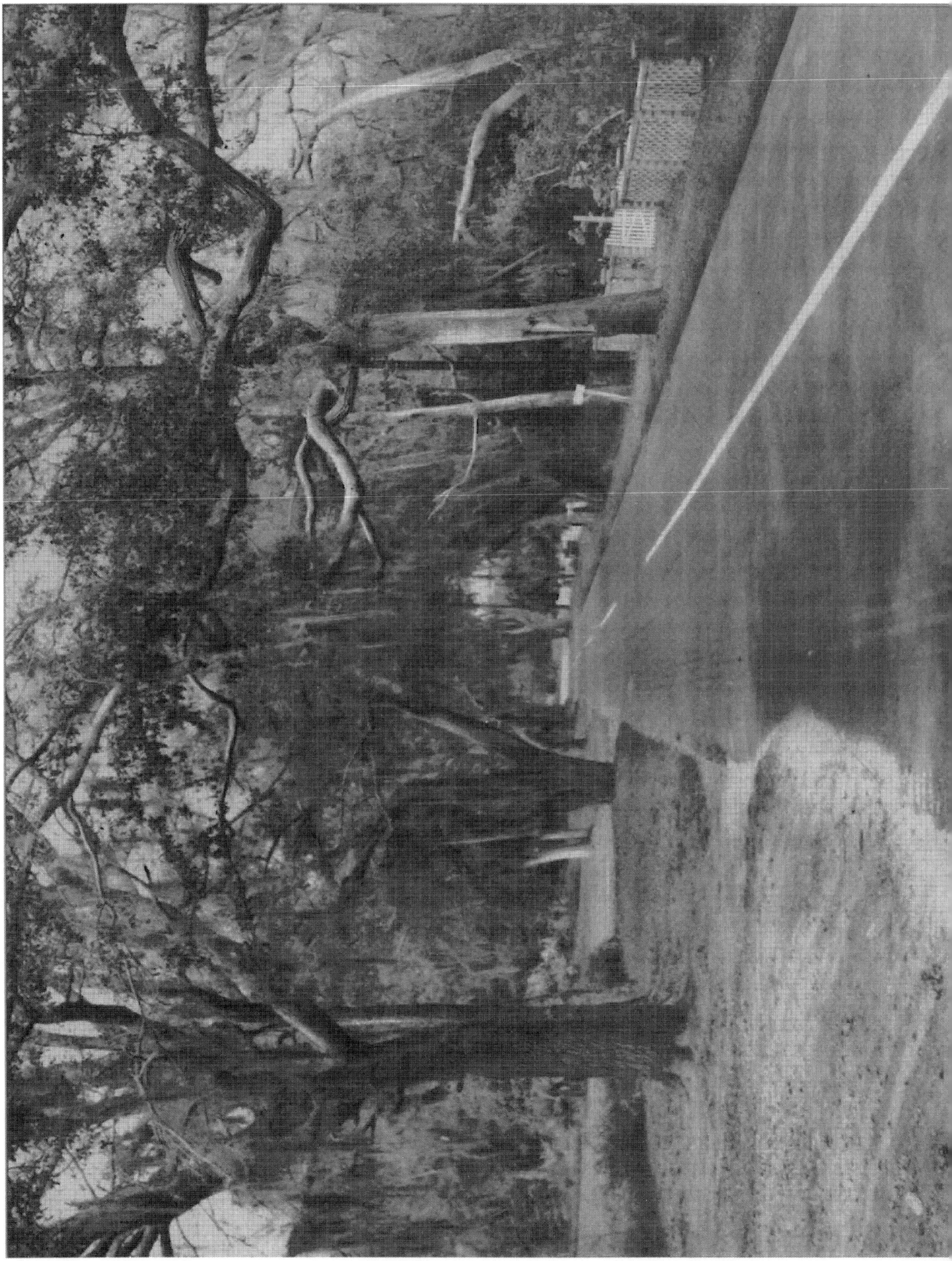

Military Road Near Bloody Marsh

In laying out this Military Road to connect Fort Frederica and Fort St. Simons, Oglethorpe planned that ". . . two men only can march up abreast . . ." and it was laid out so as to be "very convenient for ambuscades all the way."

Oglethorpe engaged the Frederica settlers to cut the road. They went out on September 25, 1738, "with the General at their head," and in three days had completed the task. They did this work without pay but Oglethorpe rewarded them with drinks at the Frederica tavern to the extent of a shilling apiece! Thus this military highway, the location of which played such an important part in making possible a British victory in the Spanish Invasion of 1742, was built at a cost of seventeen shillings!

Through the woods the path had to be cut and "through the marshes rais'd upon a Causeway." Near Frederica the road crossed the marsh and Gully Hole Creek where Oglethorpe found "it was necessary to build a clapper or wooden foot bridge across a watery savanna near half a mile across and till it was done the people going to the Fort [Frederica] were . . . obliged to wade up to their knees." This "clapper" was constructed by Samuel Davison, one of the Frederica settlers, who was paid six pounds for his work.

Communication between these two settlements, an important contribution toward the happiness of the people, was further heightened when Oglethorpe established mail service. William Forrester, the postman, made daily trips between Fort Frederica and Fort St. Simons, his pay being twelve pence per day. Another mail messenger carried mail from Frederica to Savannah and on up to Augusta, so that St. Simons had direct mail service to all parts of the Colony of Georgia and the other American Colonies, as well as with Europe.

A small part of the original Military Road is still in use, being that part of Demere Road from the Bloody Marsh monument to its intersection with Ocean Boulevard. Today, mail is carried over this part of the old Military Road as it was in the 1740's, making it one of the oldest mail routes in Georgia.

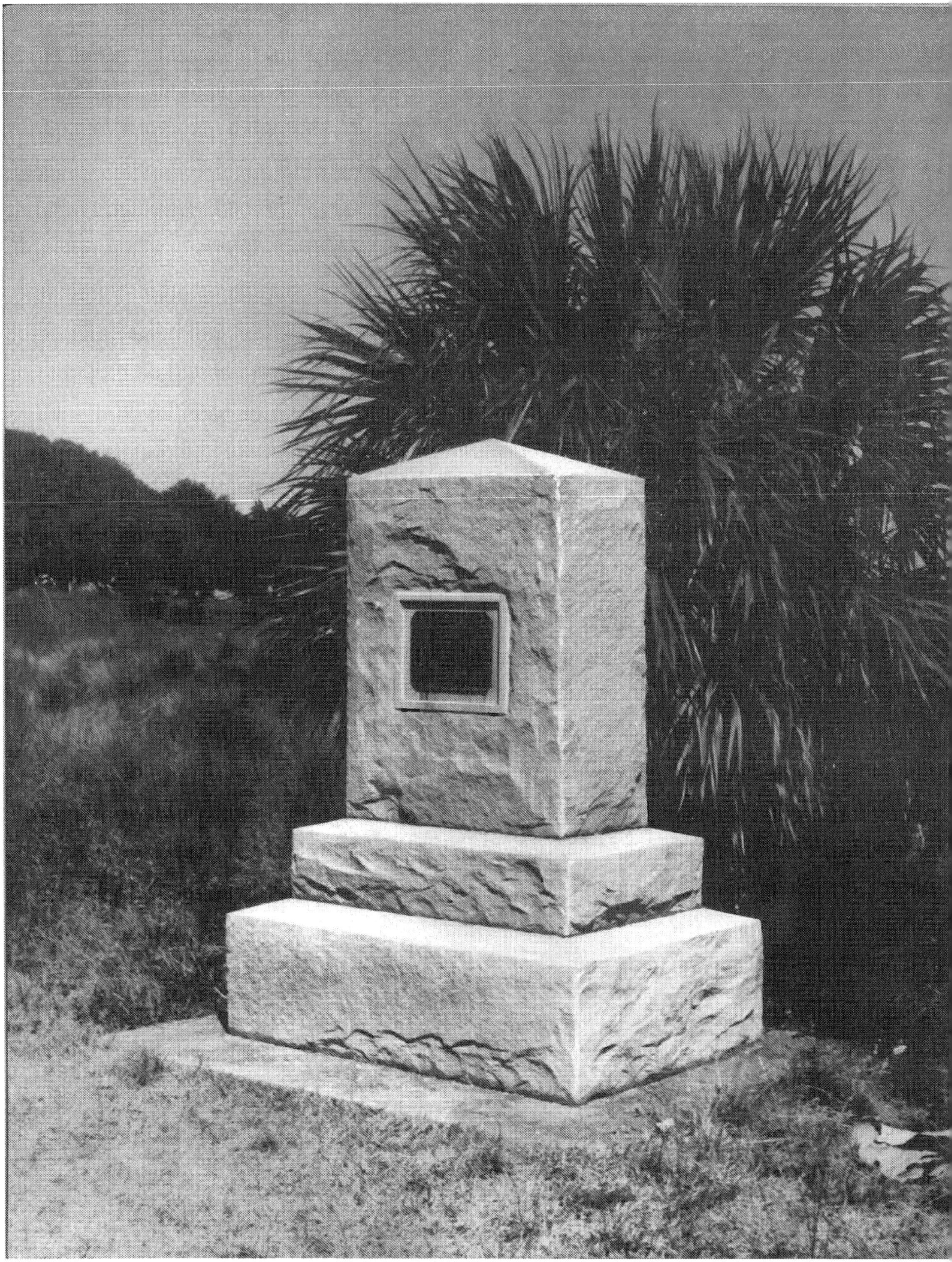

Bloody Marsh Monument

In June, 1742, Oglethorpe learned that the Spaniards were assembling a fleet at St. Augustine. Knowing this meant an attack against Georgia, he sent messengers asking for assistance. From Savannah came Noble Jones and the Rangers; from Darien, the Highlanders; and from Carr's Fields, the present site of Brunswick and the Hermitage, Capt. Mark Carr and his Marine Company of Boatmen. These, added to the soldiers of the Regiment, gave Oglethorpe about nine hundred men with which to oppose a Spanish Invasion of fifty-one vessels and three thousand men.

Oglethorpe hoped that the guns of Ft. St. Simons would be sufficient to prevent the enemy from entering the harbor. However, the Spaniards succeeded in passing the Fort and sailed up to Gascoigne Bluff where they landed. Oglethorpe then abandoned Fort St. Simons and concentrated his entire army at Fort Frederica, while the Spaniards took possession of Fort St. Simons.

On the morning of July 7th an enemy force of about two hundred men, sent out as a reconnoitering party, proceeded up the Military Road to within a mile or so of Frederica. Here an engagement took place; the enemy retreated with Oglethorpe in pursuit. About a mile from the Spanish camp Oglethorpe halted and stationed his forces in a good location while he returned to Frederica to check on conditions there. The Spaniards then sent out three hundred Grenadiers to attack the British force. The British retreated; but, later, fifty of their number formed an ambuscade where they destroyed the entire Spanish force.

Though the small number lost in this Battle of Bloody Marsh could not have crippled the enemy force, it did create in their minds some doubt as to the possibility of victory. By the clever use of a letter which he wrote to a soldier who had deserted to the enemy, Oglethorpe succeeded in making the Spaniards believe that he had superior forces and that assistance would shortly arrive from Virginia. Thereupon the Spanish commander hastily withdrew his forces. This was the turning point in the struggle which made this southeastern section of our country safe for Britain.

In 1913 this monument was erected on the edge of the battlefield by The Georgia Society of the Colonial Dames of America and The Society of Colonial Wars in the State of Georgia.

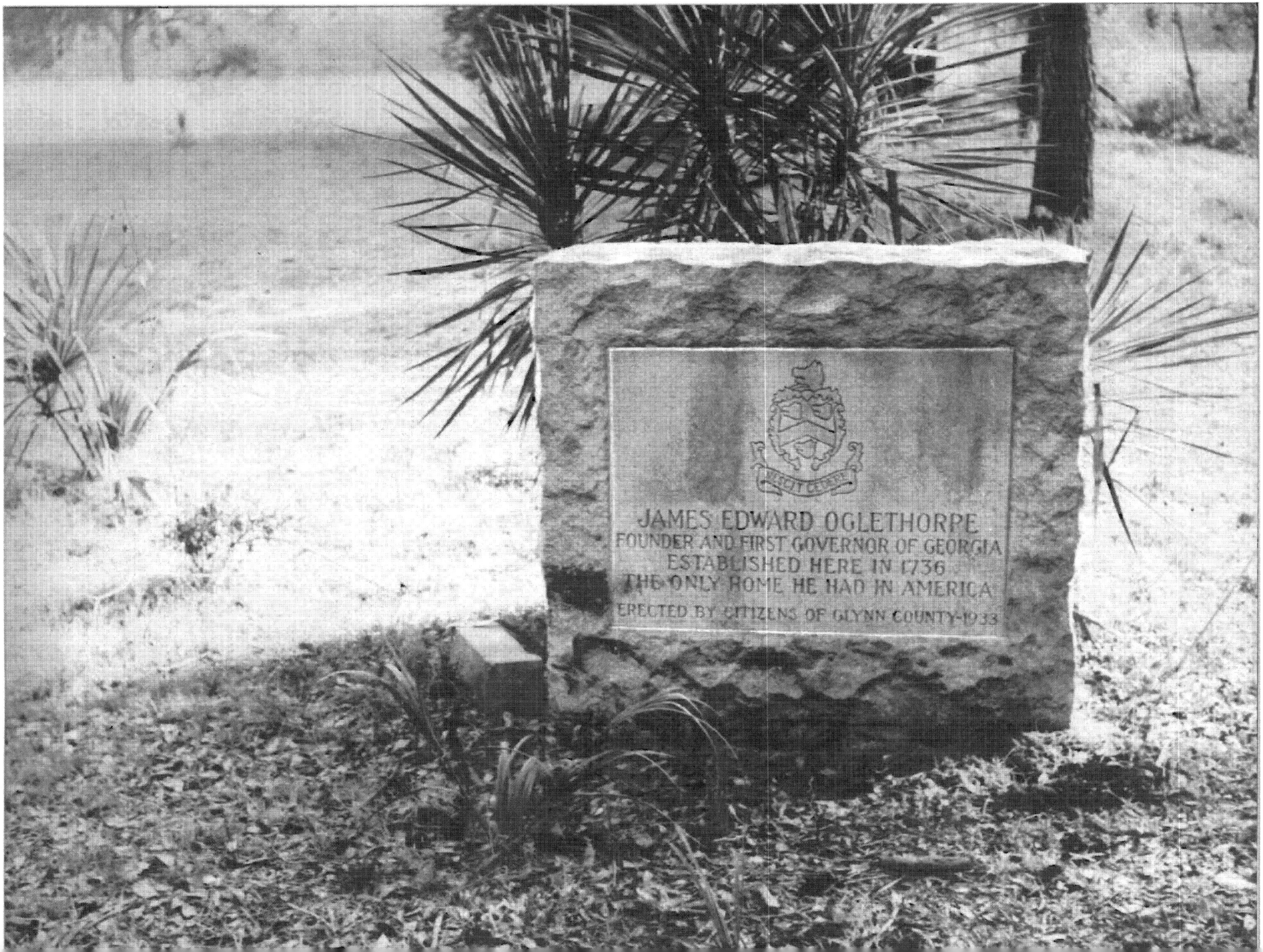
JAMES EDWARD OGLETHORPE
FOUNDER AND FIRST GOVERNOR OF GEORGIA
ESTABLISHED HERE IN 1736
THE ONLY HOME HE HAD IN AMERICA
ERECTED BY CITIZENS OF GLYNN COUNTY-1933

Oglethorpe's Home

This monument, erected in 1933 by the citizens of Glynn County to commemorate the Bicentennial of the founding of the Colony of Georgia, marks the site of the only home Georgia's founder had in America.

Oglethorpe's home, a modest tabby cottage, was located on a three-hundred-acre tract known as "the farm," sometimes "the General's farm." Though it was called a cottage, it is thought to have been a story and a half with bedrooms in the half-story. In 1740 Stephens wrote that Oglethorpe was suffering from ". . . a lurking Fever that hanged on him for a long Time past had worn away his Strength very much; so that he indulged himself pretty much on his Bed, and seldom came down Stairs . . . "

A visitor to St. Simons in 1743 stated that the settlement ". . . at Distance, looks like a neat country Village, where the Consequences of all the various Industries of an European Farm are seen. The Master of it has shewn what Application and unabated Diligence may effect in this Country." The best description, however, is from the pen of Thomas Spalding of Sapelo who was born in this house and stated, "I am only describing a scene traveled over by infant footsteps and stamped upon my earliest recollections." He wrote that, located on the Military Road "just where the road entered the wood, Gen. Oglethorpe established his own humble homestead. It consisted of a cottage, a garden, and an orchard for oranges, figs, and grapes. The house was overshadowed by oaks of every variety. It looked to the westward across the prairie . . . upon the entrenched town and fort, and upon the beautiful white houses . . ."

After Oglethorpe's return to England this cottage was perhaps occupied by Major William Horton, who succeeded as commander of the military forces stationed here and whose home was on Jekyll Island.

In 1771 this home and fifty acres of land on which it stood were granted to James Spalding, father of Thomas Spalding. In 1786 Spalding sold the tract to Thomas Clubb, whose father had been a soldier in Oglethorpe's Regiment; later, it was owned by one Mazoe who, too, was descended from one of Oglethorpe's soldiers.

[35]

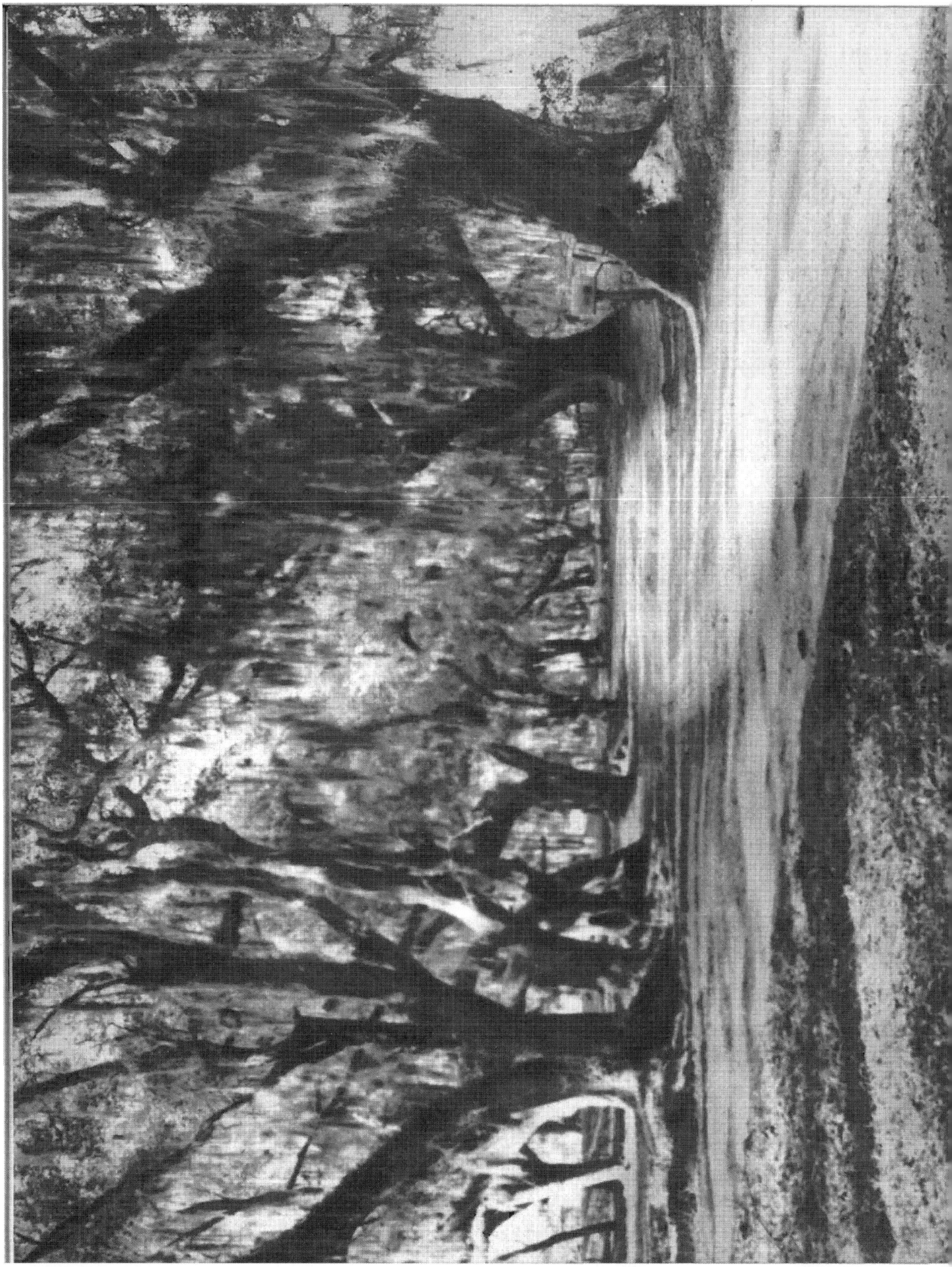

Frederica's Oaks

When Oglethorpe first landed at the bluff which he called Frederica, he gave orders that the giant live oaks there should be left standing because of their welcome shade. Though the live oaks which Oglethorpe spared no longer stand at Frederica, there are others, younger trees, which still give welcome shade. Indeed, one cannot think of Frederica without thinking of live oaks, for they are beautiful and numerous.

Those pictured here have grown up on either side of this winding road near the southeast bastion of the Old Town of Frederica and they continue in an almost unbroken grove over the area surrounding Frederica.

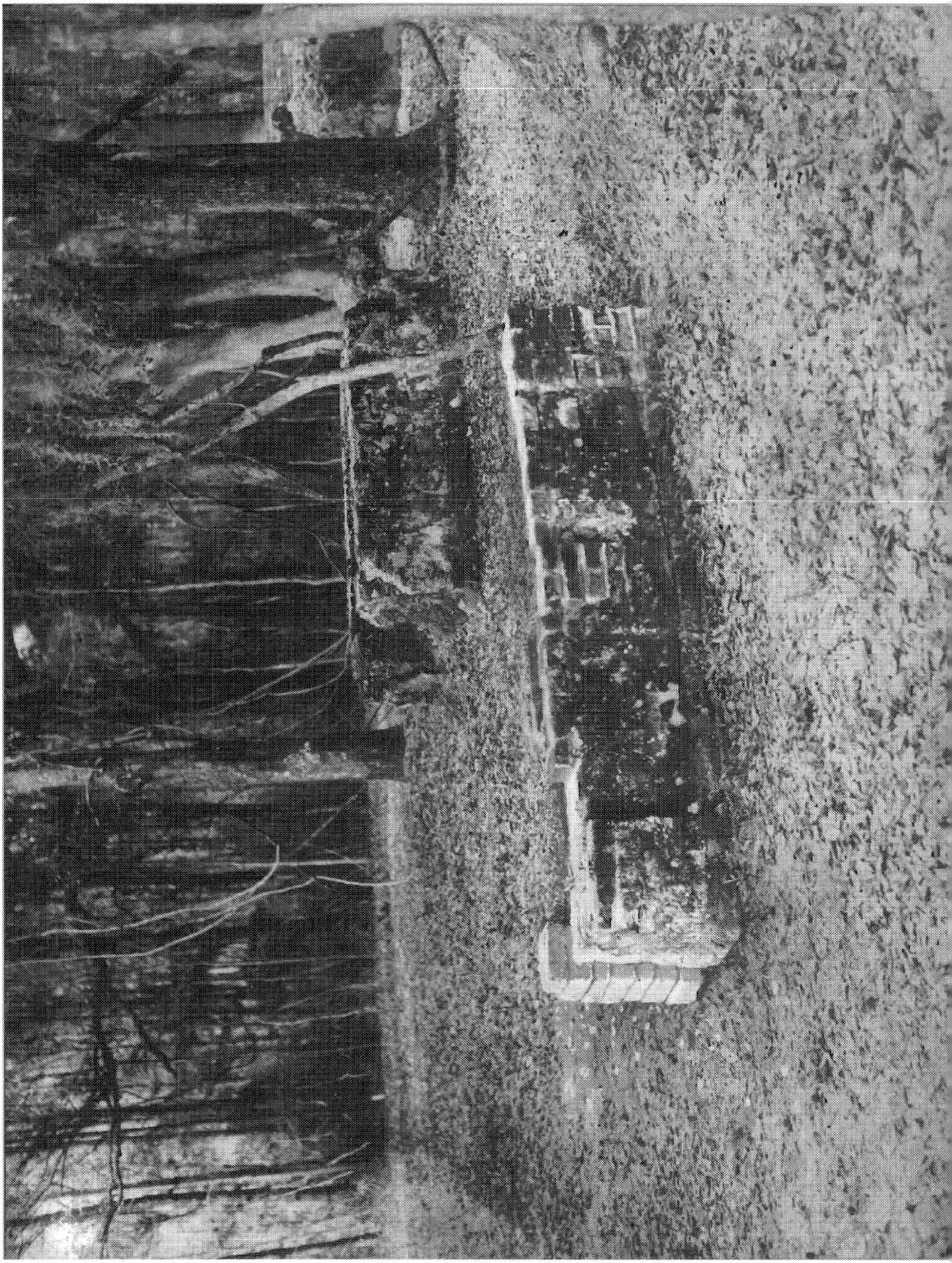

Frederica's Old Burying Ground

In this grove of live oaks is located the old burying ground where lie the bodies of many of those first settlers who came to Frederica with Oglethorpe. Here was preached the first funeral at Frederica, which was also the first funeral of Charles Wesley's great ministerial career.

The first death among the British settlers here was that of a young boatman who had been firing the swivel gun in the bow of the boat as a signal. He overloaded the gun and the explosion caused a piece of metal to pierce his brain. Charles Wesley sat up with him that night, ministered to him in his last moments, and preached his funeral.

John Wesley preached many funerals here. On his second visit to Frederica he noted in his diary that he buried Mr. Germain in the evening. A few days later he was with the surgeon, Dr. Henry Lascelles, in his last illness, made his will, and several days later buried him in the evening. A year after, the son, Henry Lascelles, the only other member of the family in Georgia, ". . . was unfortunately Drown'd being in the River with many Other Boys . . . and Buried by his Father. . ."

Some of these vaults of brick or of tabby are to be seen in Frederica's old burying ground, but there are no markers to tell whose body lies in any of the graves.

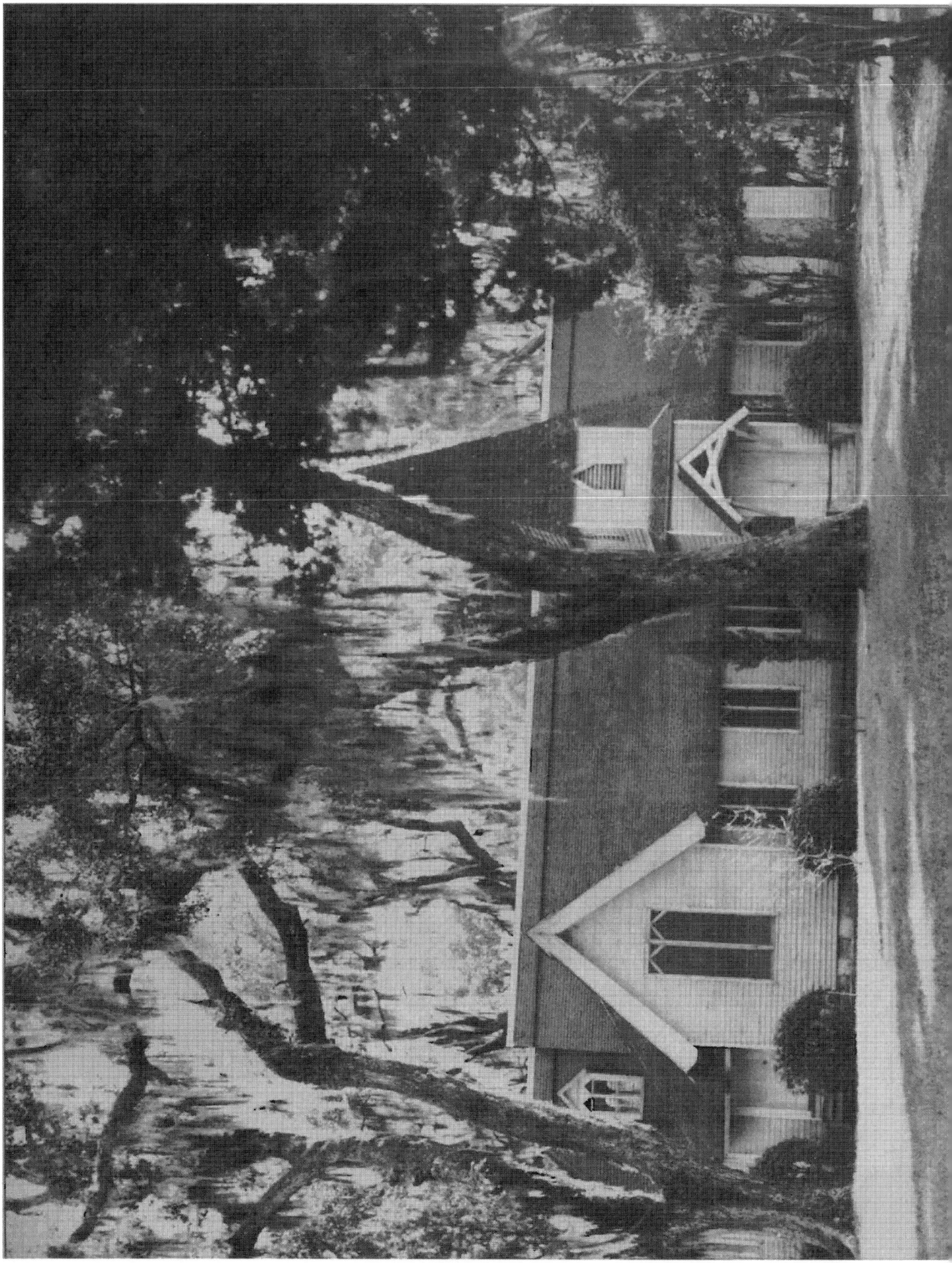

Christis Church, Frederica

In the group which accompanied Oglethorpe on his 1736 voyage to Georgia, bringing the Frederica settlers, were John and Charles Wesley, founders of Methodism.

These Wesley brothers came as missionaries of the Church of England, their salaries being paid by the Society for Propagating the Gospel in Foreign Parts. John Wesley had charge of the religious affairs of the Colony and was stationed primarily at Savannah. Charles Wesley, who had received holy orders just before sailing from England, came to Frederica as Oglethorpe's secretary and as Secretary for Indian Affairs, in addition to his duties as minister for the Frederica settlers.

Charles Wesley was at Frederica little more than two months and John Wesley made five trips here. While at Frederica the Wesleys preached in the storehouse within the confines of Fort Frederica and in the open under the great oaks. After the Wesleys returned to England, others took their place.

In 1808, lands which had formerly been garden lots of the old Town of Frederica were granted to Christ Church and a building was erected here by the plantation owners of St. Simons. During the Civil War St. Simons was occupied by Federal forces and Negro troops desecrated the church, destroying the altar, burning the pews, and breaking the windows. After the war, though there was no house of worship, the parishoners kept their church alive by meeting in their homes with the services of lay readers and occasional visiting ministers from Brunswick or Savannah.

This building was erected in 1884 by Anson Green Phelps Dodge, Jr., in memory of his bride, Ellen Ada Phelps Dodge, who had died in India. Returning to St. Simons where his family had business interests, Mr. Dodge decided that the rebuilding of this ruined church would be a fitting memorial for his wife whose body was placed in a brick vault under the chancel. Mr. Dodge then took holy orders and became the rector of this church which he had built, serving it until his death in 1898.

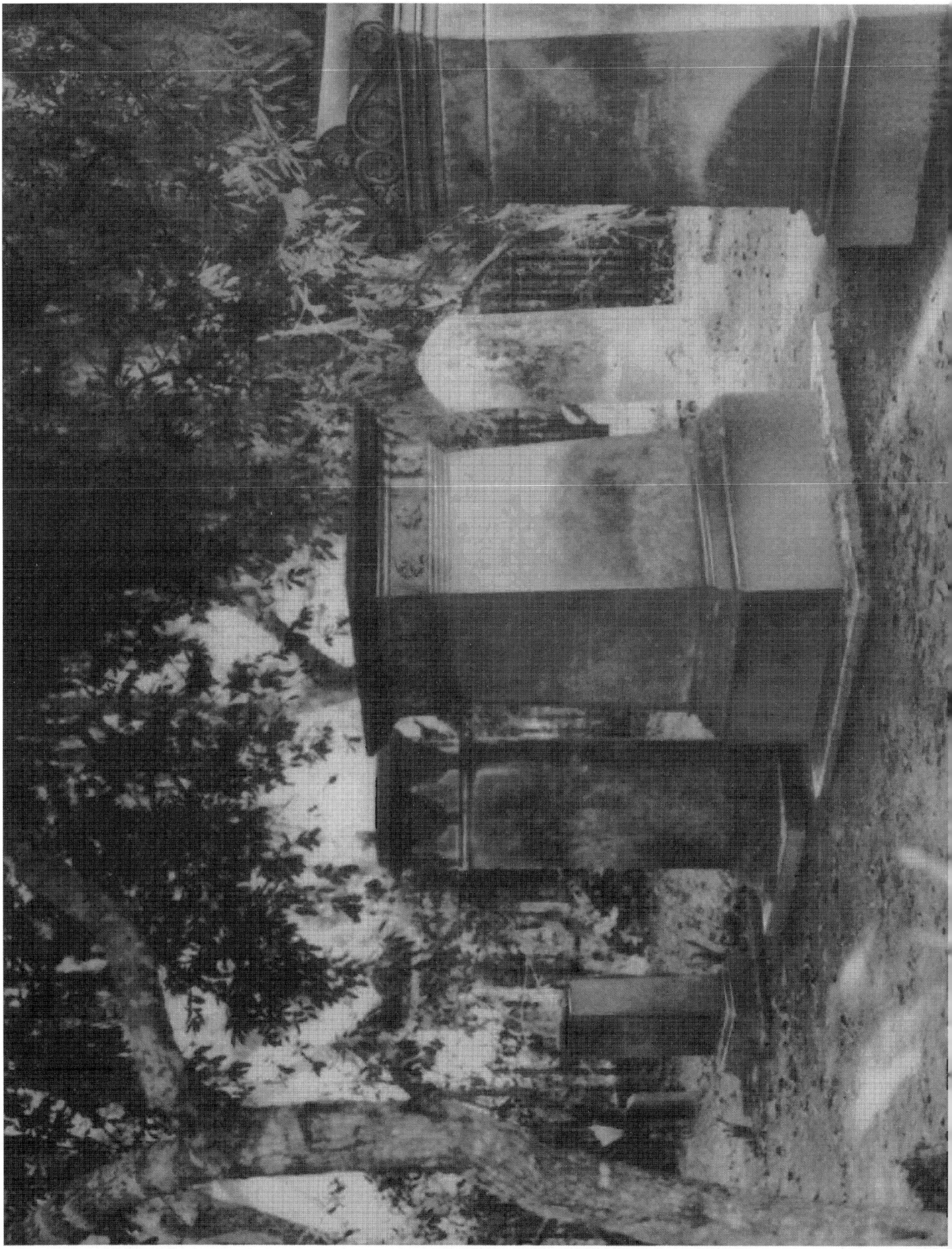

Couper Tombstones, Christ Church Cemetery

There are many interesting and impressive tombstones in Christ Church Cemetery, but none is more beautiful than these of Italian marble which mark the graves of John Couper; his wife, Rebecca (Maxwell) Couper, and their daughter, Isabella Hamilton (Couper) Bartow.

Mr. Couper, a native of Scotland, came to America in 1775, living in Savannah and in Liberty County before coming to St. Simons in 1796. Here, he located at the North End of the Island at a place known as Cannon's Point, which had been granted more than half a century earlier to one of the first settlers of the Town of Frederica, Daniel Cannon. Cannon and his two sons, Joseph and Daniel, were the carpenters who built some of the first houses at Frederica. The Cannons left St. Simons in 1741 and moved to Charleston, where they continued to build good houses.

At Cannon's Point John Couper developed one of the finest plantations in the South. Though Sea Island cotton was his staple crop, he was interested in the diversification of his crops; and, among other things, he brought in dates from Persia and olives from France. Thomas Jefferson interested him in olives and a quarter of a century after their importation there were 250 bearing trees in the Cannon's Point olive grove. These trees were killed in a freeze in 1886 and, today, the only reminder of this grove is the landing on Jones Creek, which is still known as "Olive Grove Landing."

In the lower left-hand corner of this picture we see the dead stump of one of Mr. Couper's old olive trees. From this stump came the tree which stands at the left. Today, that, too, is gone, but from its root came another — the third generation of Mr. Couper's olive trees to grow over his grave. A proper monument to a great planter!

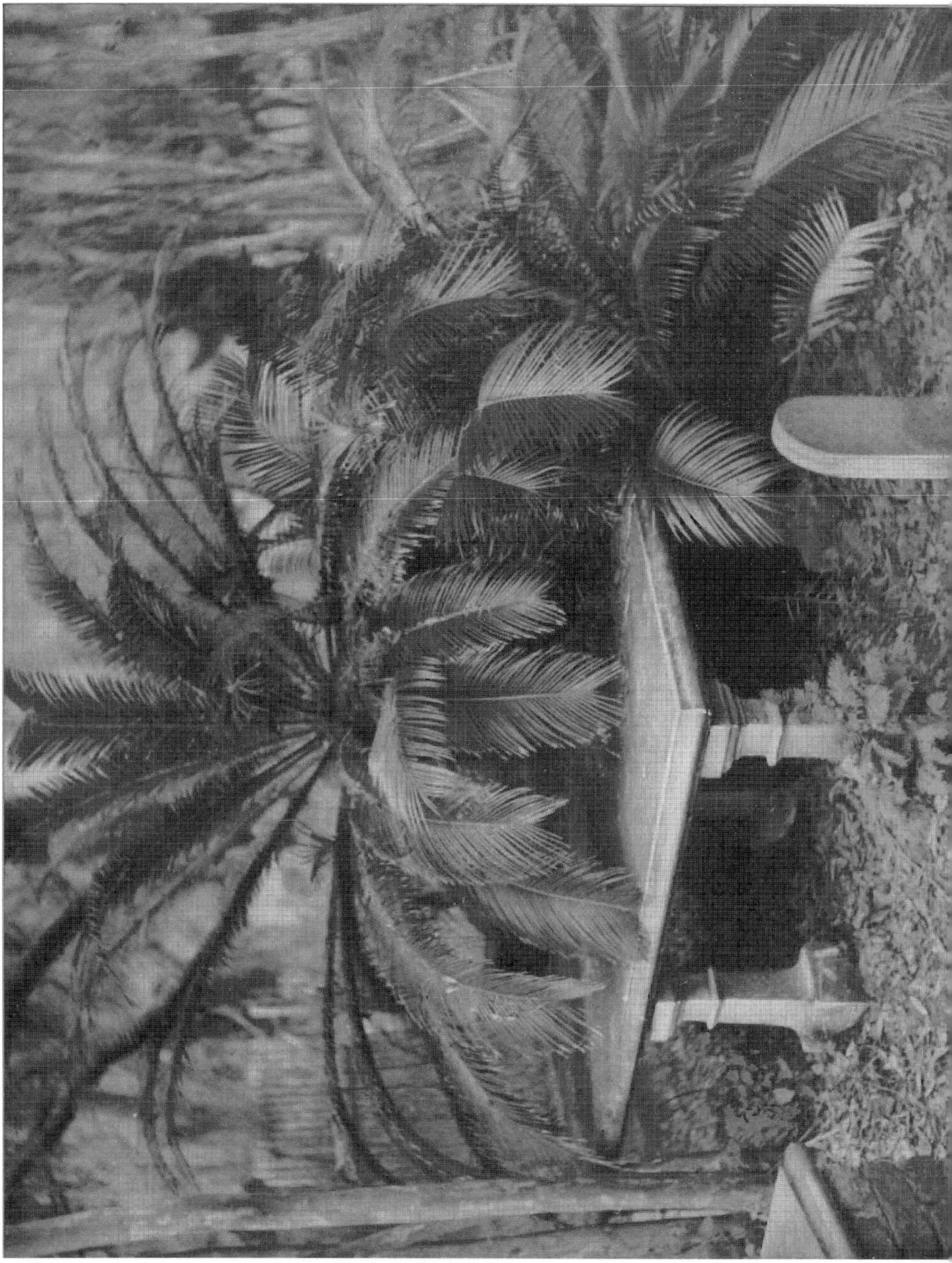

Armstrong Tomb, Christ Church Cemetery

The Armstrong family had lived in the American Colonies before the Revolutionary War, but during that struggle they remained loyal to the Mother Country and refugeed in the Bahama Islands. While living there, William Armstrong died and his widow Mrs. Ann Armstrong, whose tombstone is pictured here, returned to this land and settled on St. Simons Island.

It is said that she brought from the Bahamas to St. Simons the sago palm *Cycas revoluta* which, in time, was planted in every local plantation garden. Indeed, if one should try to find just one plant which would typify such a garden, it could well be the sago palm. Mrs. Armstrong died in 1816 and a sago palm has been planted at her grave.

The Armstrongs married into the other plantation families here. The oldest son of Mrs. Ann Armstrong, William, had married in the Bahamas. His daughter, Ann, married Benjamin Franklin Cater of Kelvin Grove Plantation and their only child, Ann Armstrong Cater, married James Postell.

Mrs. Armstrong's youngest child, Margaret, married Alexander Campbell Wylly, who lived at The Village, and whose children married into the families of the Spaldings of Sapelo Island, the Coupers of Cannon's Point, and the Frasers of Darien.

Perhaps there is no one person who lived on St. Simons Island during the Plantation Era who was connected with as many families as was Mrs. Ann Armstrong, whose beautiful marble tombstone, with its lovely sago palm, is pictured here.

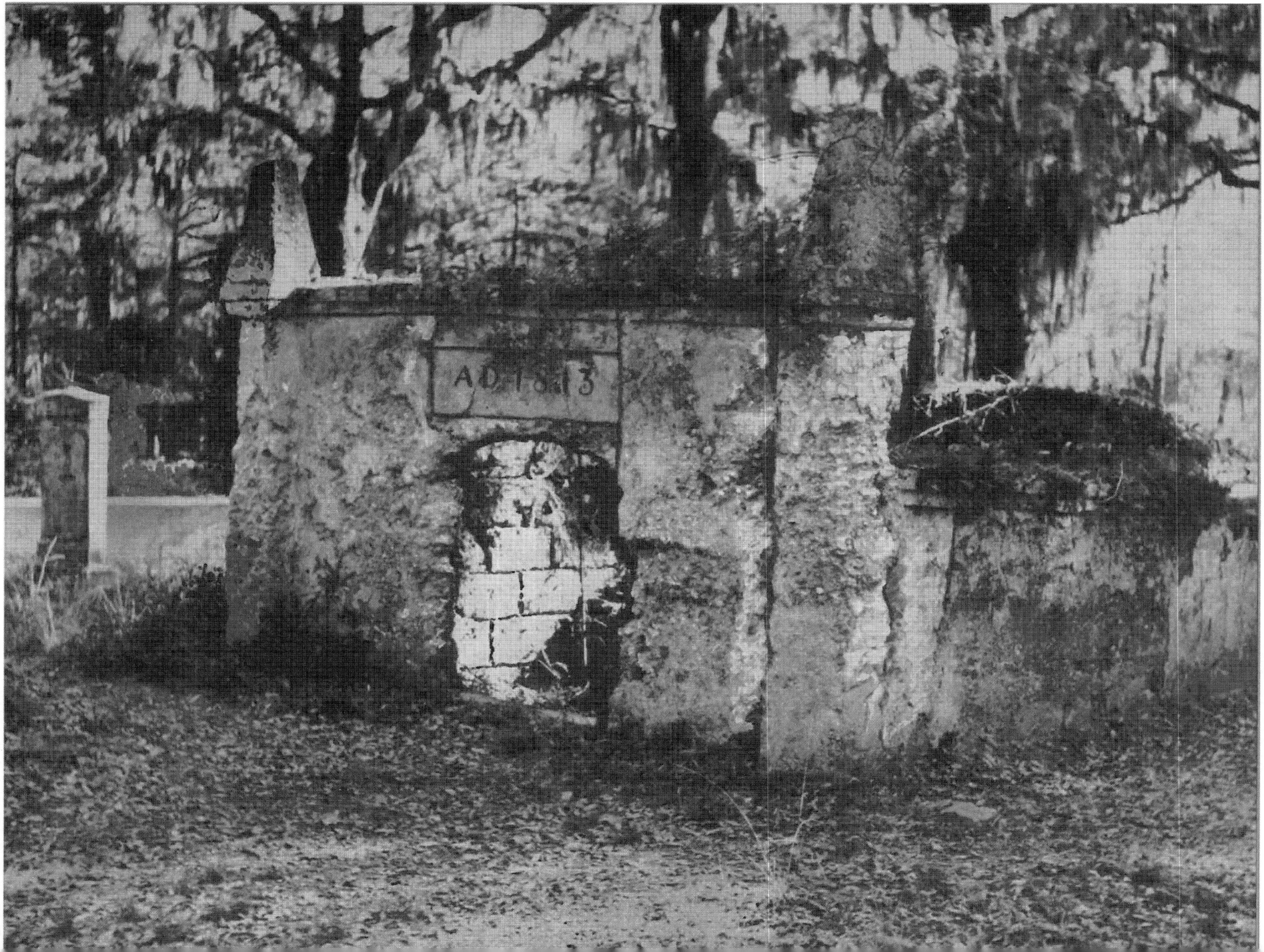
AD 1813

Hazzard Vault, Christ Church Cemetery

Built in 1813, this Hazzard family vault has been in ruins since the Civil War, when it was desecrated by Negro troops of the United States Army stationed on St. Simons Island at that time.

Even though St. Simons Island and the waters surrounding it were occupied by Federal forces, Capt. William Miles Hazzard of the Confederate States Army led a group of nine soldiers in a successful raid against Federal installations on St. Simons, burning the coaling wharf at Gascoigne Bluff and causing other damage. In addition to Capt. Hazzard who was the son of Col. William Wigg Hazzard of West Point Plantation, several members of this small group of Confederates lived on St. Simons and they knew how to move around the island without being detected. So successful were they in accomplishing their objectives in spite of overwhelming odds, that they were cited for bravery.

While on this raid Capt. Hazzard saw the damage which had been done to his family vault at Christ Church and addressed a communication to the officer in command of the Federal forces:

> I have more than once been informed . . . that the graves of our family and a friend had been desecrated by your forces . . . This rumor I could not believe, as the custom, even of the savage, has been to respect the home of the dead. But the sight which I now behold convinces me of the truth of the report I shuddered to think of . . . let me tell you, sir, that beside these graves I swear by heaven to avenge their desecration. If it is honorable to disturb the dead, I shall consider it an honor, and will make it my ambition to disturb your living. I fancy, sir, the voice of the departed issues from their desecrated homes exclaiming that such a nation may truly say to corruption, thou art my father; to dishonor, thou art my mother; to vandalism, thou art my ambition.
>
> William Miles Hazzard

The commander of the Federal forces, finding this note attached to a stick and placed in a prominent position in the road, sent it to his commanding officer with the acknowledgment that "the complaint of the writer is but too true" and that the Negro troops "committed grave outrages, firing upon the church, pulpit, gravestones, etc."

[47]

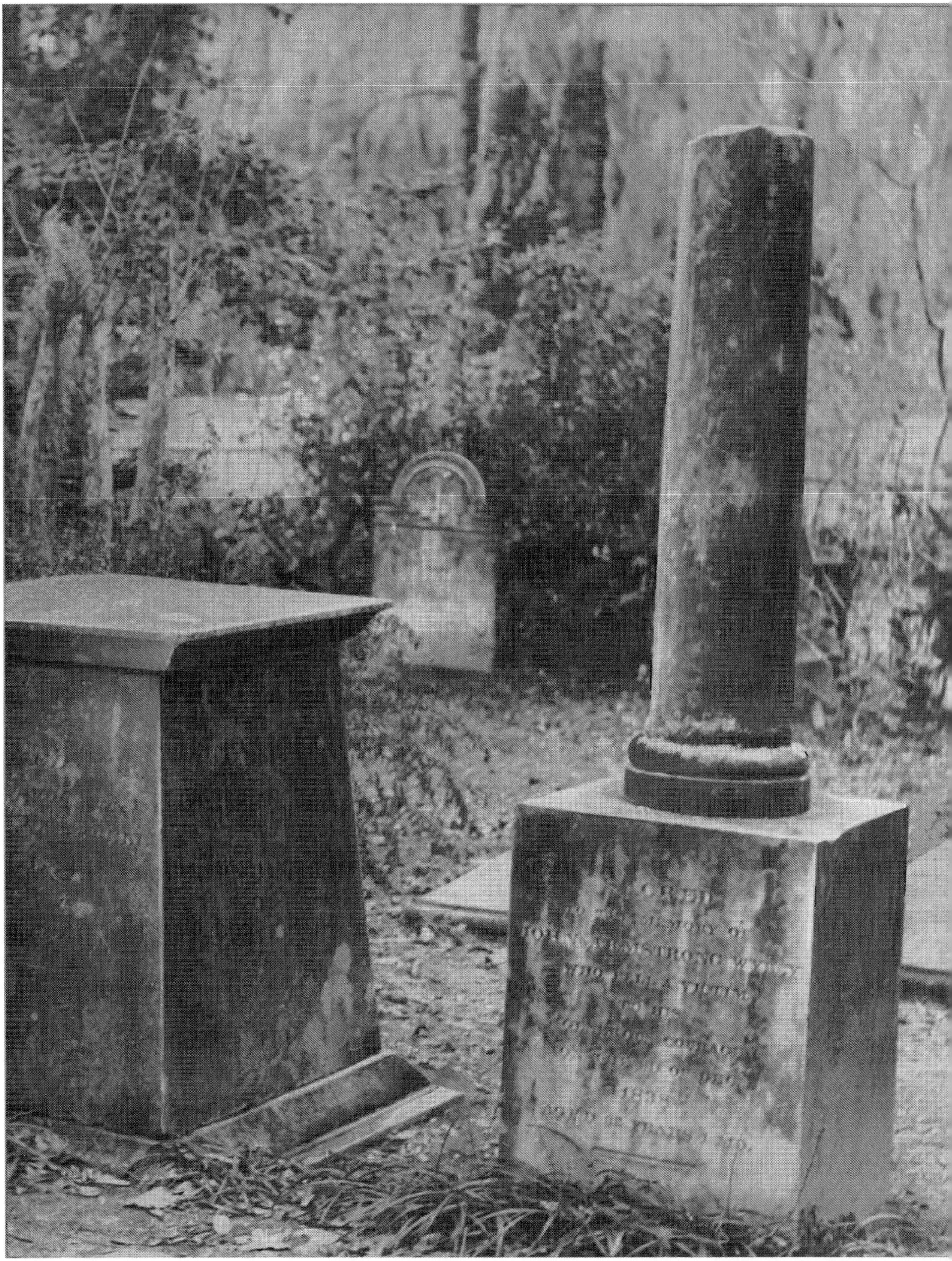

John Wylly's Tombstone

This broken shaft, emblematic of early death, marks the grave of John Armstrong Wylly, who was killed Dec. 3, 1838, by Dr. Thomas Fuller Hazzard. Bad feeling had existed for some time between these men and, of course, there are many tales about the cause. It is known that they did have differences about the boundary line between their property. The Wylly family owned the German Village tract, generally called "The Village," on the eastern shore of St. Simons, while the Hazzards lived on the western shore of the Island, with their lands joining in a north-south line.

In those days plantation owners used dams of earth to mark the boundaries of their property. Erected by slave labor these earthen dams, several feet high and as many feet wide, are to be found all over St. Simons. The Wyllys built their earthen dam on the line they claimed, while the Hazzards constructed a dam on what they claimed was the correct line. Today, these Hazzard and Wylly dams still stand, in some places being only a few feet apart.

Several months before the fatal encounter, Dr. Hazzard challenged Mr. Wylly to a duel; Mr. Wylly refused to fight, whereupon Dr. Hazzard "posted him" by attaching a notice to a tree telling of Mr. Wylly's refusal to accept the challenge. A letter describing this stated this notice was posted on a pine tree "as the road turns in to Frederica . . . Poor tree . . . at the rising of the sun the next morning it was found prostrate with the ground and cut up into billets and this work of noble revenge was done by some fairy friend of Mr. W's — for no human creature knows anything about it . . ."

The death of Mr. Wylly took place in Brunswick where these men happened to meet on the steps of the Oglethorpe House. After exchanging a few words, Mr. Wylly struck Dr. Hazzard with a cane. Friends intervened and separated them. However, a short time afterward they chanced to meet in the entry of the Oglethorpe House, when Mr. Wylly spat in Dr. Hazzard's face; whereupon Dr. Hazzard pulled a pistol and shot Mr. Wylly, the bullet passing directly through the heart. Dr. Hazzard was arrested and charged with manslaughter, but the jury failed to convict him.

The inscription on the tomb shown in this picture states that John Wylly "fell a victim to his generous courage."

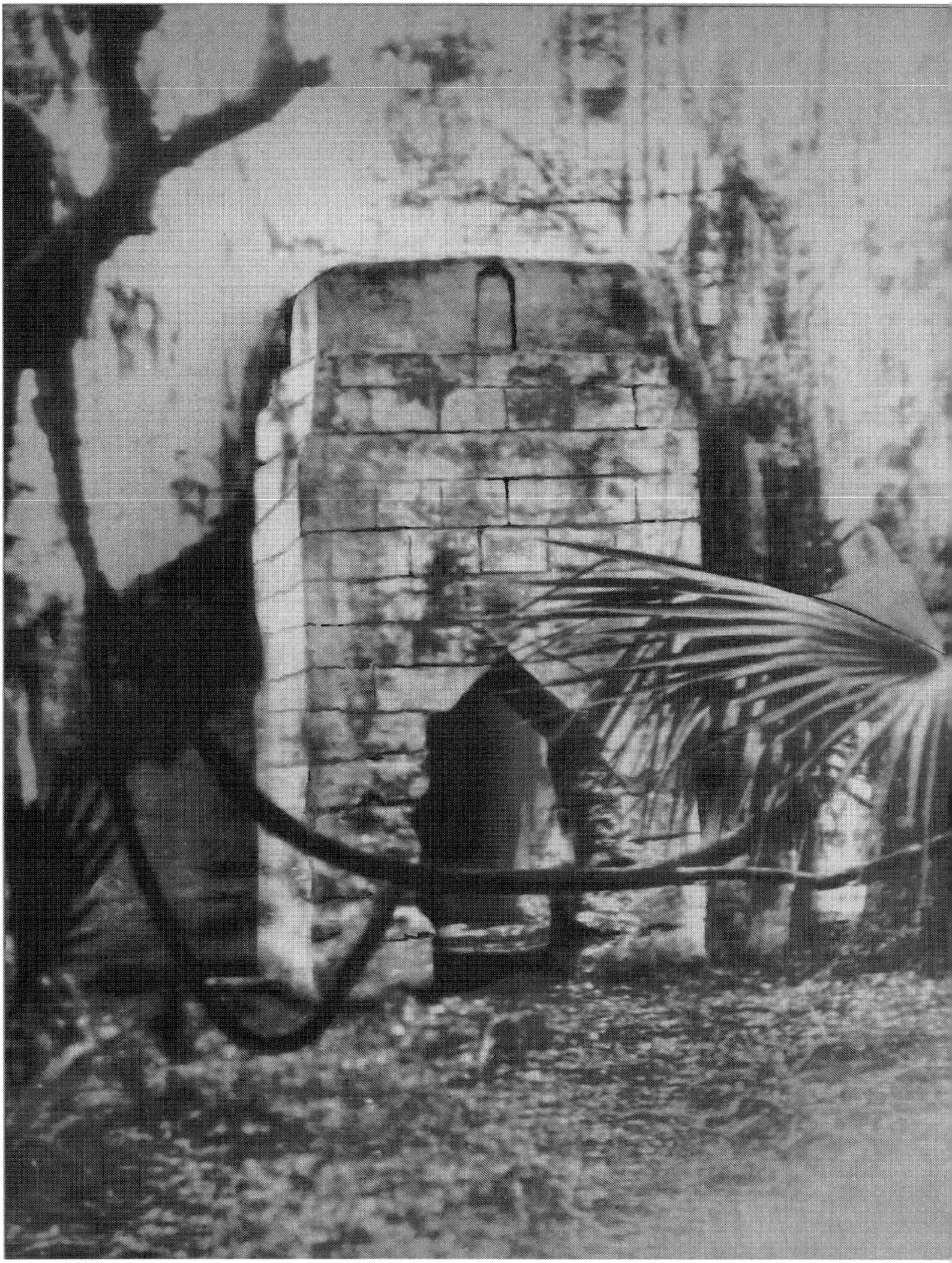

Pink Chapel, West Point Plantation

Following the death of John Armstrong Wylly, the two Hazzard families, those of Dr. Thomas Fuller Hazzard of Pike's Bluff Plantation and his brother, Col. William Wigg Hazzard of West Point Plantation, found themselves cut off from all the other plantation families of St. Simons Island.

The Wyllys were one of the old families of the Island and were connected by blood or marriage, with almost every other plantation family in the area. John Armstrong Wylly's older brother had married the daughter of Thomas Spalding of Sapelo Island, while his younger sister had married James Hamilton Couper of Cannon's Point. Another of his sisters had married into the Fraser family and the Frasers had married into the Couper and Demere families; in addition, Wylly's first cousin had married Benjamin F. Cater of Kelvin Grove Plantation. With this solid wall of relatives and family connections to take the part of the dead man, the Hazzard families were practically ostracized.

Rather than attend and worship at Christ Church, Frederica, in the hostile atmosphere of their critical neighbors, the Hazzards erected their own family chapel at West Point Plantation. Built of tabby and only large enough for the use of the people of their own plantations, it still stands, though in ruins.

A beautiful pink lichen, *Chiodecton sanguineum,* which grows only in dense shade on old walls and trees, now colors the old tabby ruins of the Hazzard Chapel, giving it the name Pink Chapel.

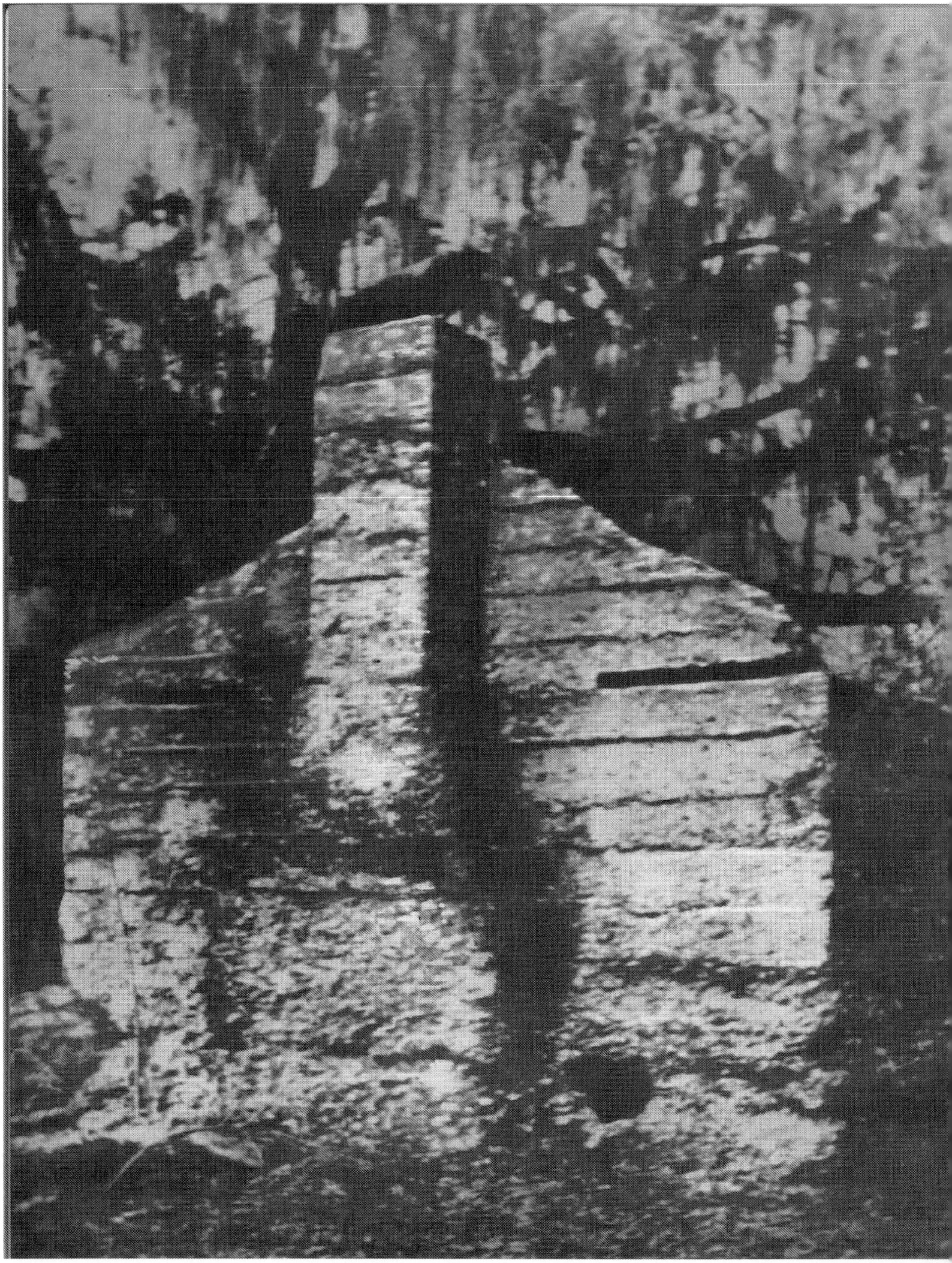

Slave Cabin, West Point Plantation

The tabby ruin shown here was one of the slave cabins of West Point Plantation, the home of Col. William Wigg Hazzard.

These Hazzards were from South Carolina and the first to move to St. Simons Island was Major William Hazzard of the Revolutionary War. Major Hazzard died in 1819, but his two sons continued to live here and made their homes on adjoining plantations. Col. William Wigg Hazzard of the War of 1812 and of the Mexican War, with his wife Mary Blake (Miles) Hazzard, made his home at West Point, while his brother, Dr. Thomas Fuller Hazzard, and his wife Sarah Turner (Richardson) Hazzard, lived at Pike's Bluff. Both of these men died about the time of the Civil War; but Col. Hazzard's son, Capt. William Miles Hazzard of the Confederate States Army, continued to live at West Point until "after the War."

This picture, taken in 1936, has preserved for the record a tabby cabin with a tabby chimney. Generally, these tabby houses had brick chimneys since it was easier to build a chimney of brick than to change the shape and size of the forms for the chimney with the pouring of each layer of tabby.

This cabin would have been the sort used to house a small Negro family. Larger cabins had the chimney in the middle of the house with a fireplace on either side. Soon after this picture was made, the tree in the background was blown over, finishing the ruin of the cabin.

[53]

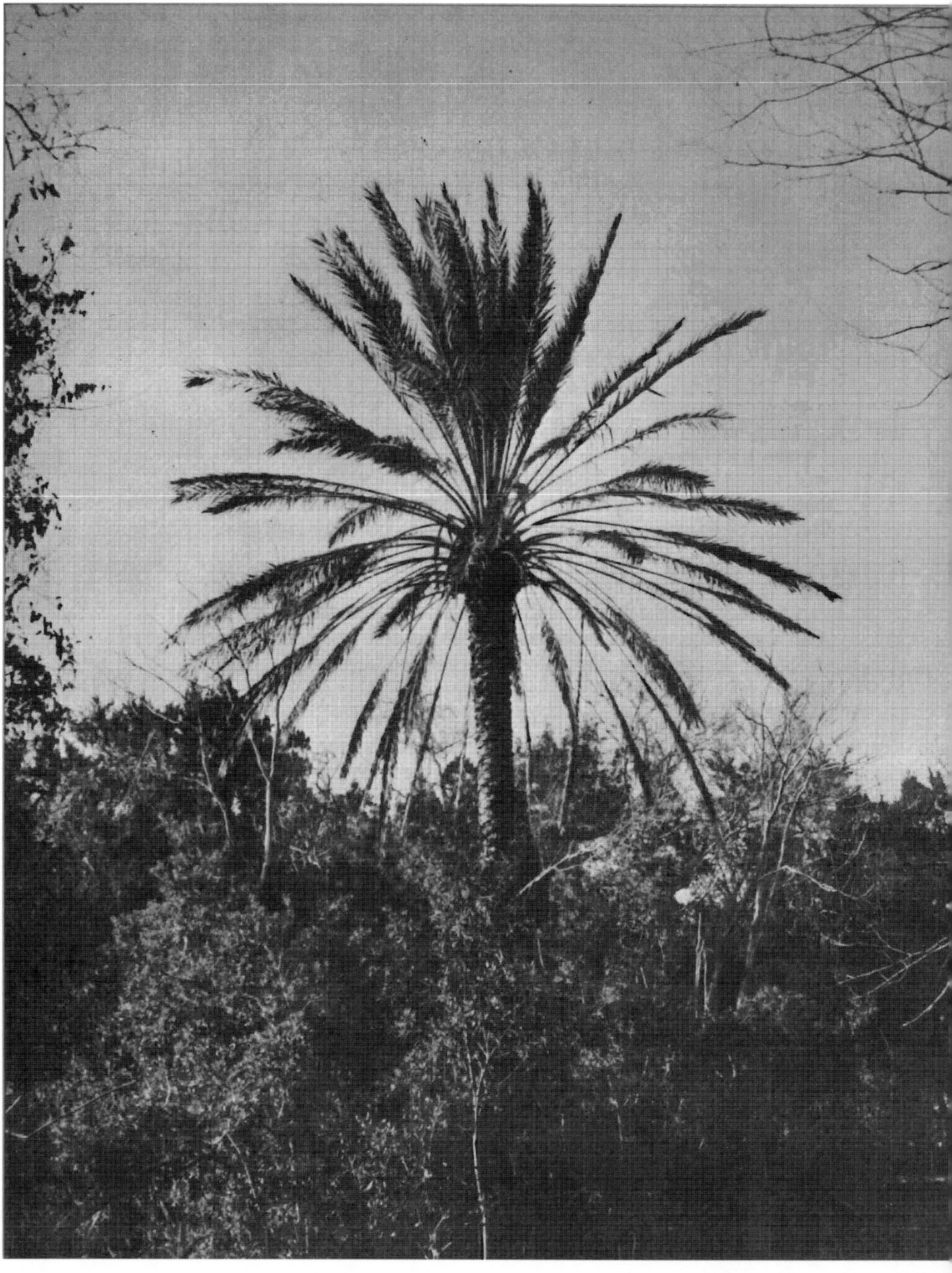

Date Palm at Cannon's Point

Date palms were among the plants imported by John Couper for his Cannon's Point Plantation. They were brought from Bussora, Persia, and for many years produced ripe fruit. This palm now growing at Cannon's Point is not the original. The old tree died in 1885 and from its root came a shoot which grew into this palm. Standing near the eastern entrance to the Couper residence, it is a silent reminder of days gone by.

When John Couper mover to St. Simons in 1796 to make his home, he occupied the modest story-and-a-half house which had been built by Daniel Cannon in 1738. Later, Mr. Couper built a large two-and-a-half story house, the handsomest plantation house on St. Simons, and here the Coupers dispensed lavish hospitality. Their guests came from every part of this country and from Europe.

Aaron Burr, vice-president of the United States, came to St. Simons in 1804 after the duel which resulted in the death of Alexander Hamilton. During his five-week stay at Butler Point, he went over to visit the Coupers. In his letters to his daughter Burr described life "in the benevolent home of Mr. Couper." In 1828, Capt. Basil Hall of the British Navy, with his wife and daughter, spent some days here. Capt. Hall's *Travels in North America* describes the operation of the plantation, while Mrs. Hall's letters (edited by Una Pope Hennessy and published under the title, *The Aristocratic Journey*) give a picture of the social life. Fanny Kemble, noted English actress and wife of Pierce Butler of Butler Point Plantation, had nothing but kind words for the Coupers, though little else that she saw in Georgia met with her approval! Sir Charles Lyell, president of the Geological Society of London, with Lady Lyell, was here in 1846. In *A Second Visit to the United States of North America,* Lyell gives a vivid picture of life at the Couper home.

Frederika Bremer, Swedish novelist and abolitionist, made a pleasant visit here in 1851 and records that fact in *Homes of the New World.*

After the Civil War the Cannon's Point property passed into the possession of the Shadman family and in 1890 the house was struck by lightning and burned.

[55]

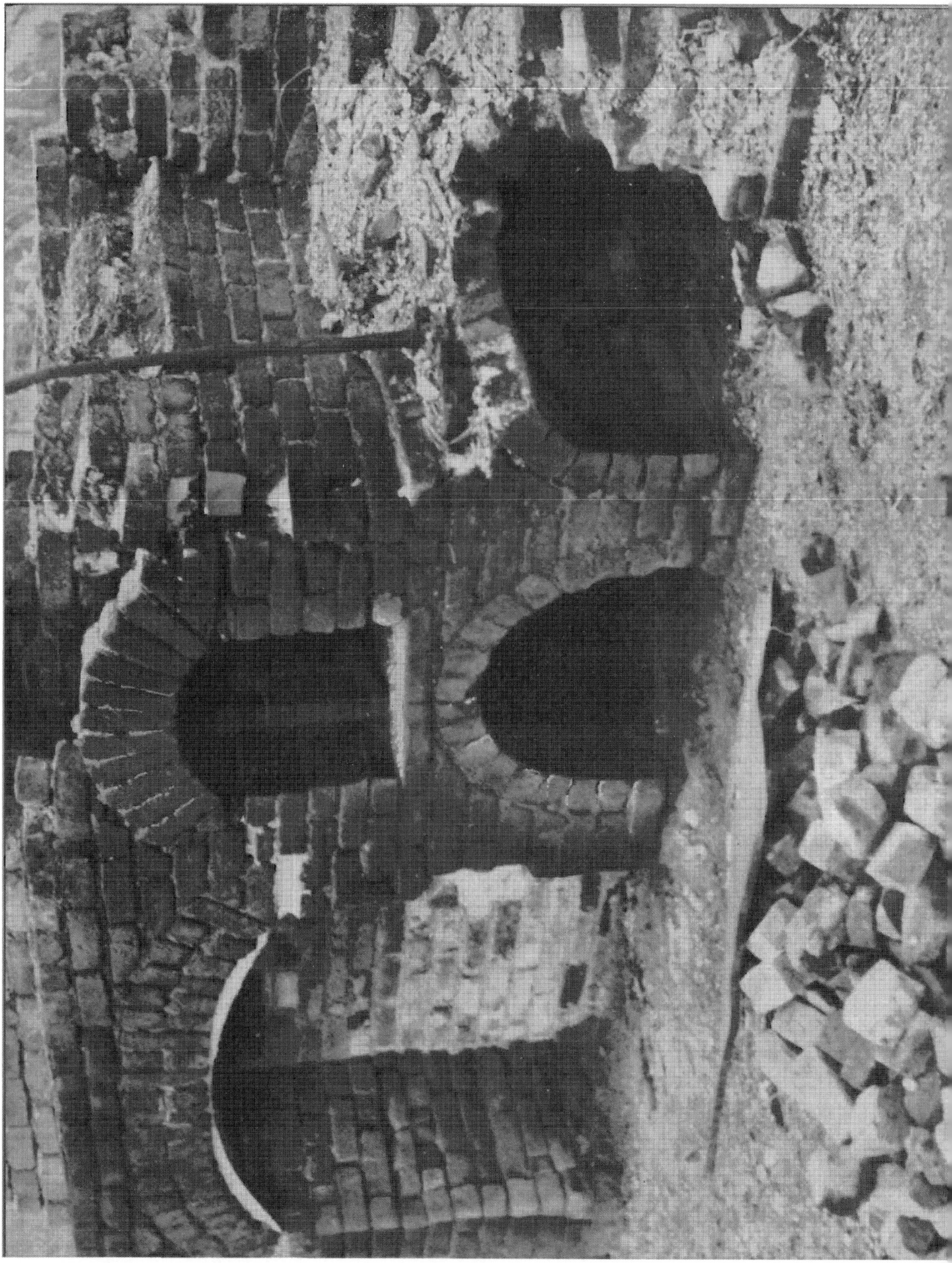

Ruins of the Kitchen,
Cannon's Point Plantation

In this fireplace and in these ovens of the old kitchen at Cannon's Point, was prepared the food served to the members of the Couper family and their guests. As was customary on Southern plantations, this kitchen was in a separate building and a short distance from the plantation residence, an arrangement which removed from the residence the noise and confusion of preparing the meals and, in addition, lessened the danger of fire.

From this kitchen the food was carried to the "Big House," where a door at ground level gave entrance to a small room with stairs leading up to the butler's pantry, adjacent to the dining room on the main floor.

One of the famous cooks who presided over the Cannon's Point kitchen was Cupidon. Cupidon had been the slave of the Marquis de Montalet, a refugee from San Domingo, residing at the North End of Sapelo Island at the former home of de Chapedelaine, which he called "La Chalet" — a name which the Negroes corrupted to "Chocolate."

Montalet spent his days at La Chalet immersed in his dreams and his memories. He and his friend, Chevalier de la Horne, early in the morning and late in the afternoon, walked through the live oak forests of Sapelo with a pig on a leash hunting truffles! Oh, that one day they might find them!

When the Marquis died, his will decreed that Cupidon should be freed, along with his wife, Venus, and their son, Hercules. When old Venus heard the news, she was worried: "Nobody ter look atter us; no house ter lib in; what we gwine do?"

Cupidon said: "Don' you worry; we gwine ter St. Simons ter lib wid Mr. John Couper!" And so they came to Cannon's Point and adopted Mr. Couper as their master. Cupidon presided over the kitchen and trained many others in the culinary arts of which he was master.

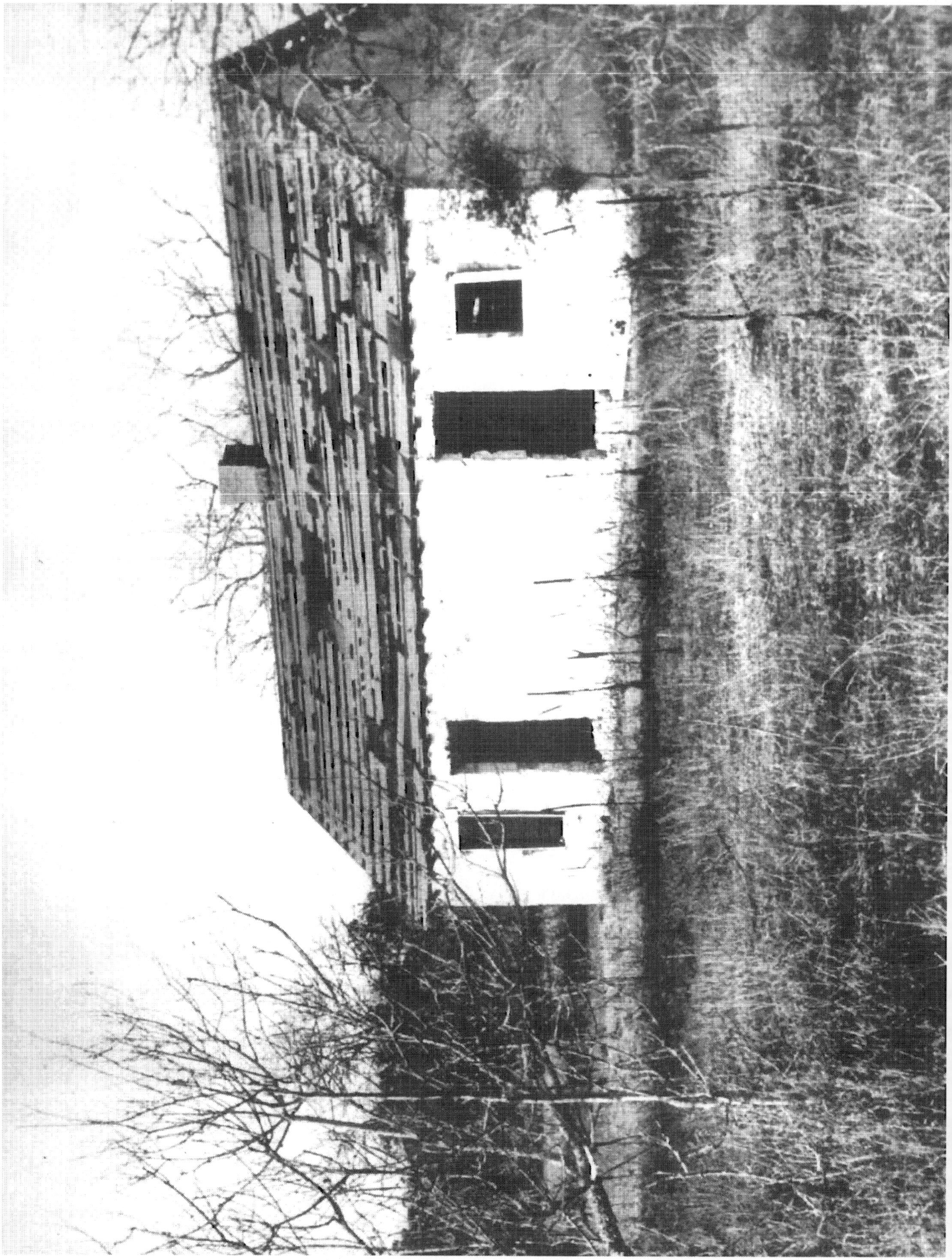

Slave Cabin, Butler Point

This slave cabin was one of a row of cabins standing at Hampton, or Butler Point, when Fanny Kemble was here during the winter of 1838-39.

In December, 1838, Pierce Butler came to Georgia to take over the management of these estates from Roswell King, who was moving to North Georgia, where he founded the town of Roswell. On this trip he was accompanied by his wife, Fanny Kemble, and their two children, Sarah, aged three years, and Fanny, aged seven months.

Arriving at the close of the year 1838, they went first to the rice plantation in the delta of the Altamaha River, Butler Island, where they stayed about two months after which they moved to Butler Point. Here, on St. Simons, they remained until the middle of April before returning to Philadelphia. This four-month stay was the only trip Fanny Kemble ever made to Georgia.

While here she kept a journal of the daily happenings on the plantation. Published in 1863 as *Journal of a Residence on a Georgian Plantation 1838-39,* it throbs and burns with a fine hatred of slavery, and is said to have caused more criticism of the South than any book that was ever written except *Uncle Tom's Cabin.*

Though Fanny Kemble was extremely critical of all she saw that man had done, she reveled in the beauties of Nature. From the house at Butler Point she looked out "on these green woods, this unfettered river, and sunny sky" and was fascinated by the beauty of the scene.

While walking in the woods she stood still to admire the beauty of the shrubbery and felt that "the wood paths . . . were really more beautiful than the most perfect arrangement of artificial planting in an English park." The beauty of the sky brought forth high praise and she decided that "Italy and Claud Lorraine may go hang themselves together!" "The moonlight slept on the broad river," she wrote, and, all in all, "It was lovely."

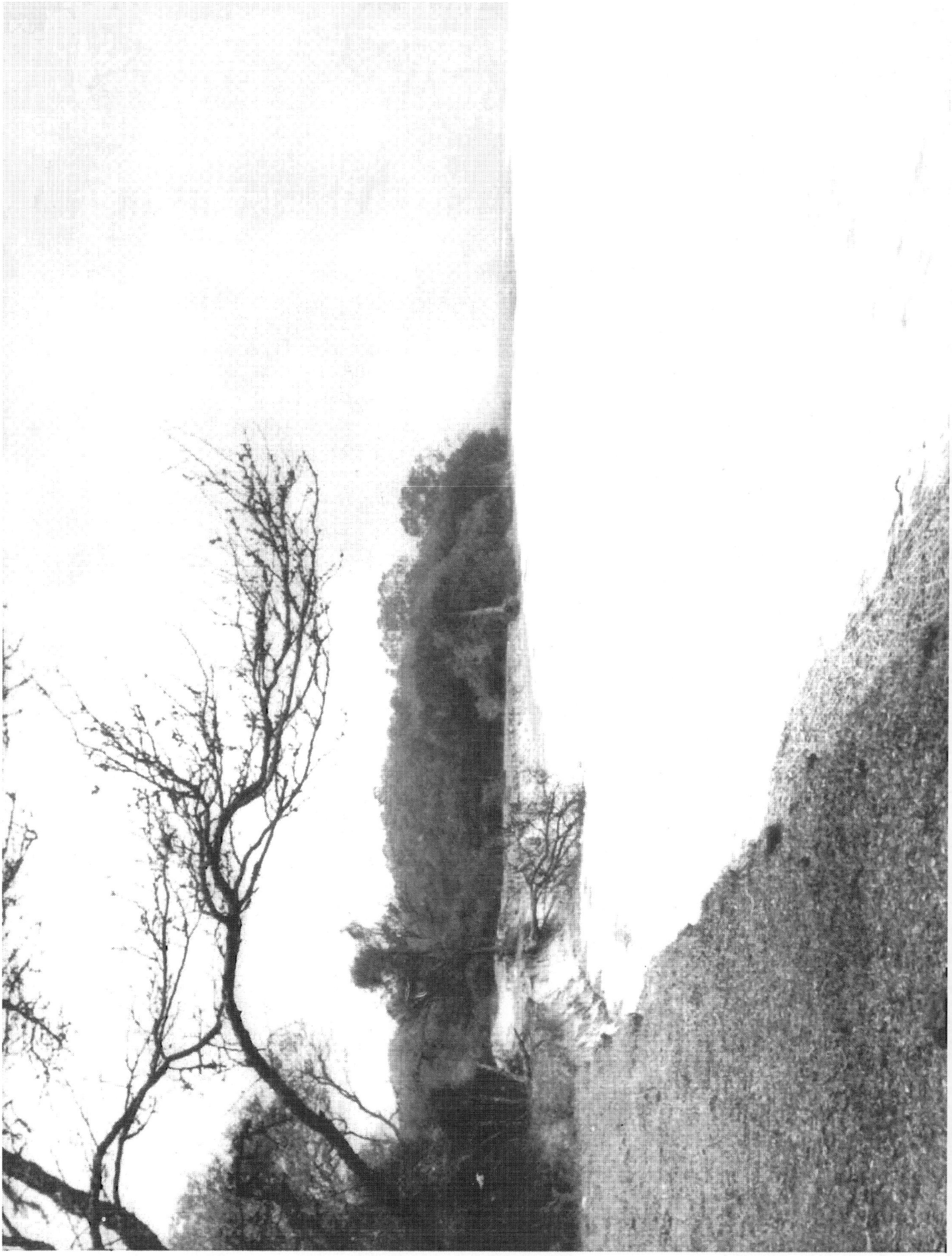

Hampton River at Butler Point

When Oglethorpe fortified St. Simons Island he stationed soldiers of his regiment at various bluffs so that they might give the alarm if the enemy attempted to land at any of these places. Nineteen soldiers received grants of fifty acres each at the northwest point of the island and here they lived with their families. They called the place Newhampton, but soon it was shortened to Hampton; even that name is lost today, though the river which flows past is still know as Hampton River.

The invention of the cotton gin brought about the development of great cotton plantations throughout this section and this tract of land was acquired by Major Pierce Butler. Major Butler was the younger son of Sir William Butler and was descended from the Dukes of Ormond. He came to America in 1766 as the Major of the 29th British Regiment and was stationed in the New England Colonies. After his marriage in 1771 to Mary ("Polly") Middleton, daughter of Col. Thomas Middleton of South Carolina, he resigned his commission in the British Army and took up life as a South Carolina planter.

During the Revolutionary War he became an officer in the American Army and later was prominent in South Carolina politics, being a member from that State to the Convention which framed the Constitution of the United States and a signer of that document. Major Butler was then elected Senator from South Carolina and sat in that first Senate of the United States, which met in New York City. When the Capital was moved to Philadelphia, he moved with it; and from then on, Philadelphia was home.

In his will, Major Butler stipulated that his Georgia estates should become the property of his two grandsons, provided they would take the name Butler. These grandsons, John Mease and Pierce Butler Mease, were the sons of his daughter Sarah, who had married Dr. James Mease of Philadelphia. This grandson, Pierce Butler Mease, now Pierce Butler, married the noted English actress and violent abolitionist, Fanny Kemble.

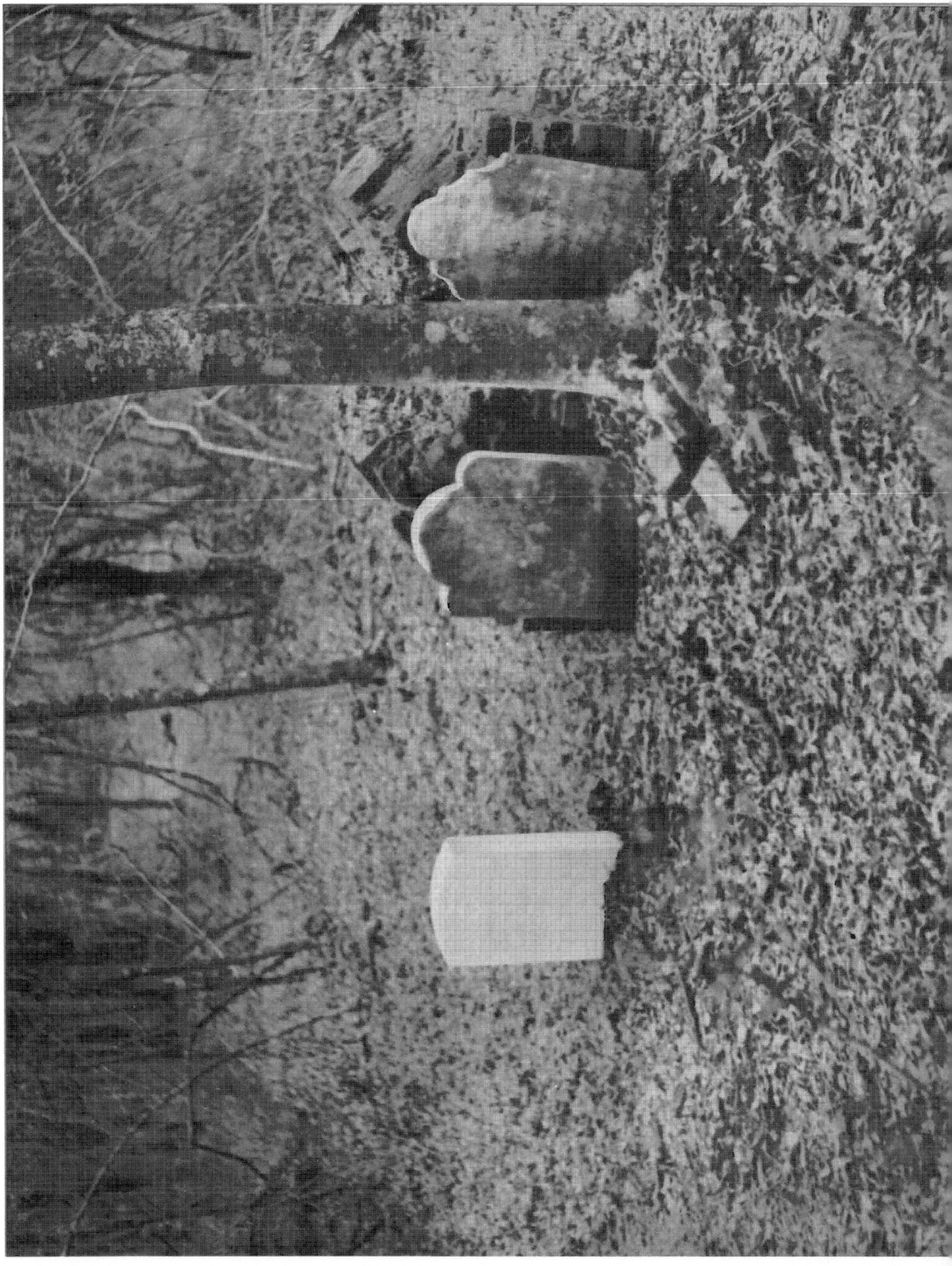

Mackintosh Vaults

Here, in the deep forest of Sinclair Plantation, are two brick vaults which entombed the bodies of John Lachlan and Sarah, the only children of Major William Mackintosh of the Revolutionary War.

This tract of land was first granted to Archibald Sinclair, tithingman of the South Ward of the Town of Frederica. Sinclair built here a tabby house which became his plantation home. After the disbanding of Oglethorpe's Regiment, St. Simons Island was practically deserted and Sinclair abandoned his plantation, which in 1765 was granted to Donald Forbes as bounty land for his services in Oglethorpe's Regiment. Forbes sold these lands to Gen. Lachlan McIntosh of Revolutionary fame, whose son, Major William Mackintosh, lived and died in the old tabby house. Major Mackintosh's body lies near those of his children whose vaults are pictured here. The marker for his grave was erected in 1940 by the Brunswick Chapter, Daughters of the American Revolution. Later, this tract became the property of Major Pierce Butler of Butler Point Plantation.

In 1832, the plantation masters of St. Simons formed an organization, known as The Agricultural and Sporting Club of St. Simons Island, who used Sinclair's old tabby home as their Club House. This Club held regular meetings and, in addition, celebrated special anniversaries, such as the Centennial of the Founding of Fort Frederica. For this event they invited the members of the Camden Hunt Club "and their ladies" to be special guests.

At meetings of The Agricultural and Sporting Club, papers were read by the members which were published later in the agricultural periodicals of the day, and included John Couper's talk on *The Culture of the Olive Tree;* Thomas Spalding's papers on *The Mode of Constructing Tabby Buildings* and *The Origin of Sea Island Cotton,* and Dr. Thomas Fuller Hazzard's paper on *The Culture of Flowers as Conducive to Health, Pleasure and Rational Amusement.* The Club House had a well-stocked library, as well as facilities for quoits and billiards, and also was used as an informal meeting place where deer drives and fishing excursions were arranged.

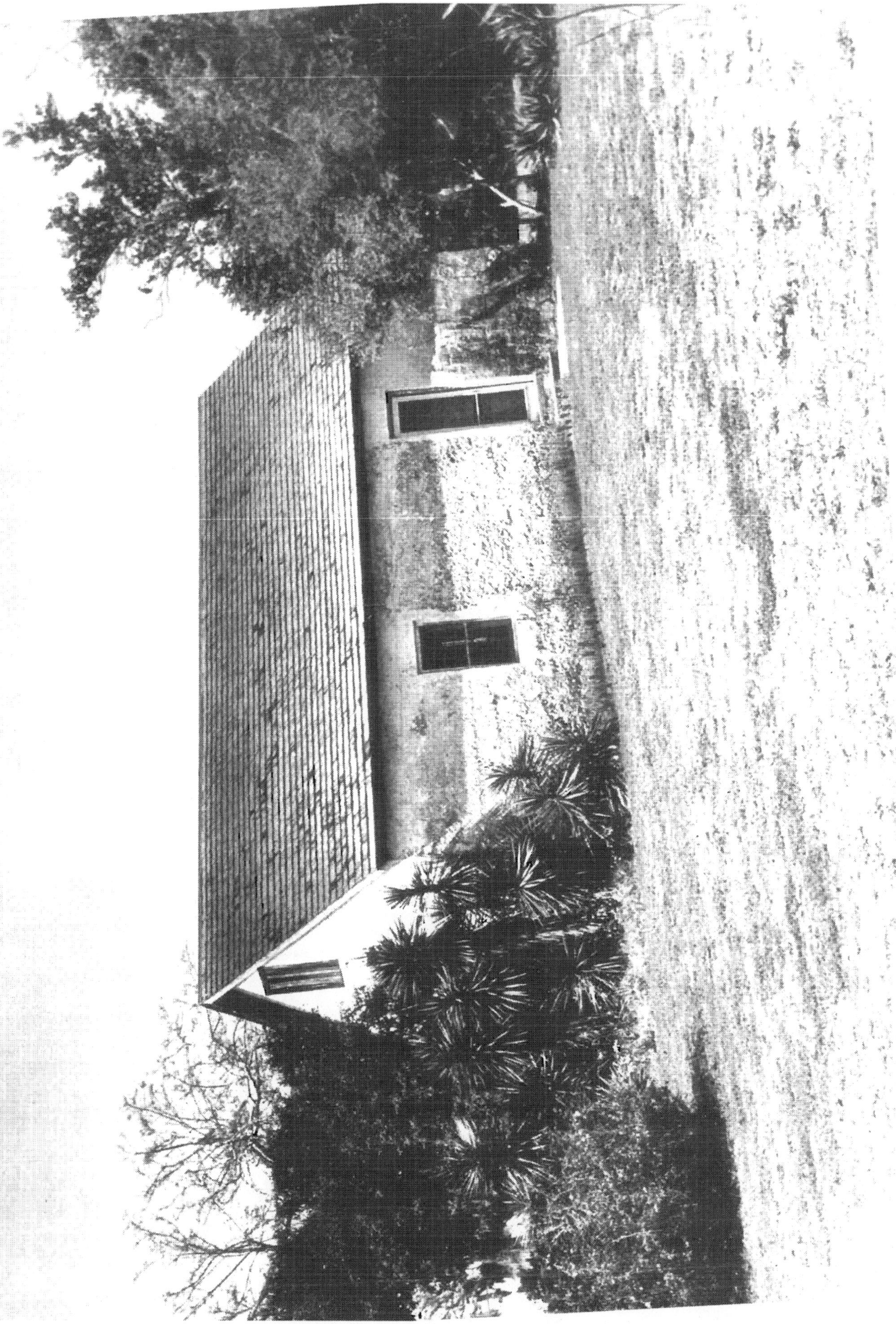

Slave Cabins of Hamilton Plantation

This plantation, located at Gascoigne Bluff, was the property of James Hamilton of Scotland who came to America with his friend John Couper about the time of the Revolutionary War. Here he made his home in a two-story tabby house, later removing to Philadelphia where he died in 1829.

This property then came into the Corbin family through the marriage of Agnes Rebecca Hamilton to Francis P. Corbin. The Corbins lived in Paris where the daughters married into the French nobility. However, they considered themselves citizens of the State of Georgia. When their State cast her lot with the Confederate States of America, the son, Richard W. Corbin, was not content "in these stern times, with a horizon bounded by the Bois de Boulogne and the Jockey Club"; but felt that he must "act as it becomes a man who wishes to earn the respect of his countrymen" and offered his services to his country. He slipped into the port of Wilmington, N. C., on a blockade runner, made his way to Virginia and became an Aide on Gen. Field's staff of Gen. Longstreet's Corps, and gave devoted service to the cause of the Confederacy. With Lee's surrender, he returned to France, secure in the knowledge he had not been found wanting when duty called.

In 1874 a lumber mill operated by Urbanus Dart of Brunswick and his sons was erected at the lower end of Gascoigne Bluff. In 1876 the Dodge, Meigs Co., later the Hilton, Dodge Lumber Co., operated a mill at the upper end of the Bluff, occupying the site of Hamilton Plantation and utilizing the plantation buildings, including the tabby barn, the slave cabins and the tabby house which had been the Hamilton residence. Vessels from every part of the world lined the wharves to load cargoes of long-leaf yellow pine and cypress lumber until the mills ceased to operate and were dismantled in 1903.

Hamilton Plantation was purchased in 1927 by Mr. and Mrs. Eugene W. Lewis of Detroit, Michigan, who made it their winter home. In 1949 the South Georgia Conference of the Methodist Church established here the Methodist Center, Epworth-By-The-Sea.

These old slave cabins are now the home of the Cassena Garden Club. Its members have carefully preserved the original lines and character of the cabins and are developing an old plantation garden.

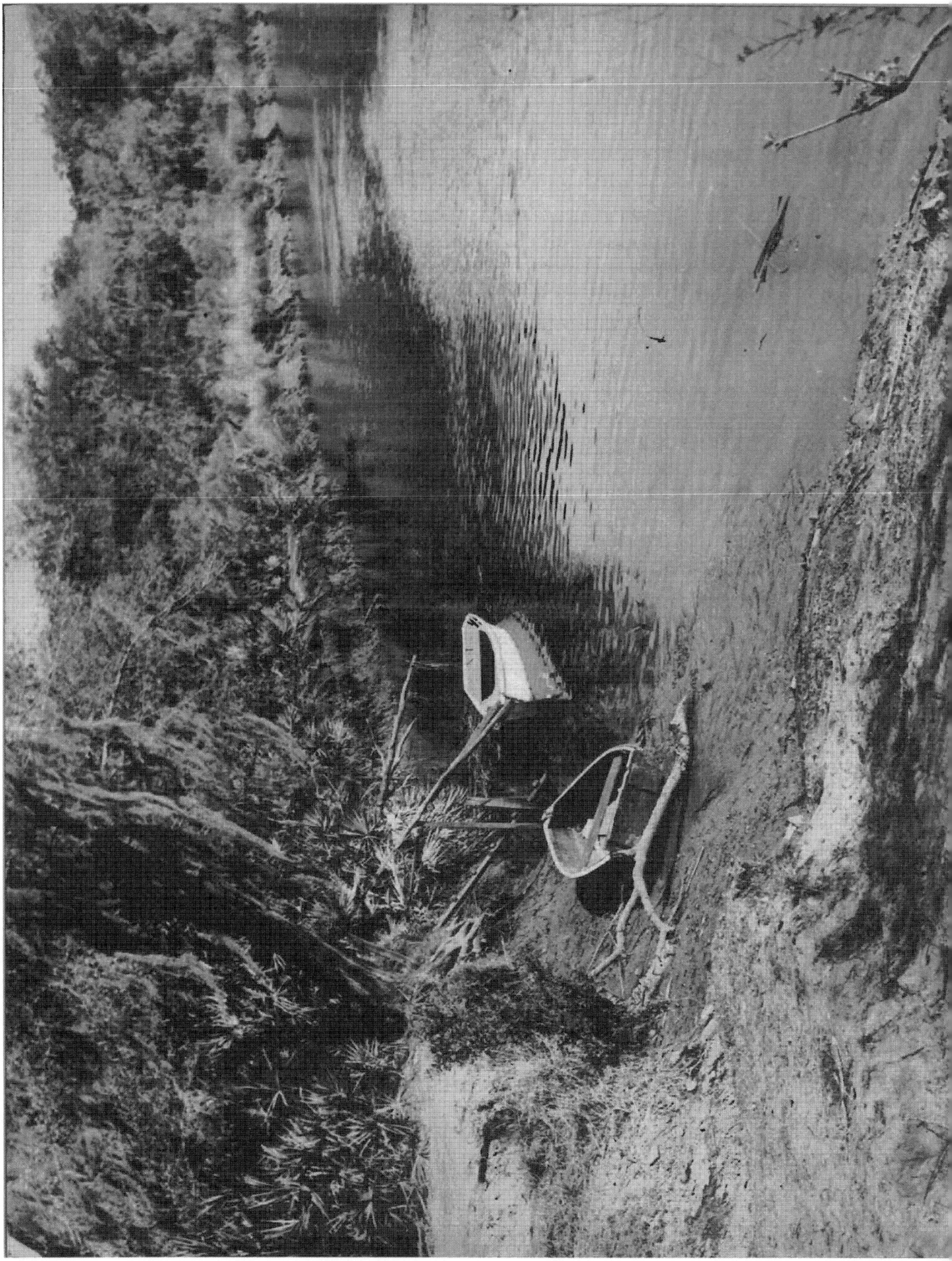

Ebo Landing

The importation of Negro slaves into the English Colonies began in 1619 when they were brought into Virginia. Founded as a military colony, Georgia prohibited Negro slavery since it was desired that all men brought into the Colony should bear arms and no Negro slave was ever allowed a gun. This was the only one of Britain's Colonies in North America to prohibit slavery and for the first twenty years of the life of the Colony there were no Negroes in Georgia.

In 1798, Georgia prohibited the importation of Negroes direct from Africa and about a decade later the United States passed similar laws. From that time all Negroes from Africa were smuggled into the country and kept in hiding until they could be disposed of to plantation owners.

The winding creeks and waterways of Coastal Georgia afforded ideal landing places for such cargoes, just as in a previous century they had harbored pirates, and a century later they were to provide safety for bootleggers. Ebo Landing on Dunbar Creek was one of the best of these. Sheltered from view of traffic in Frederica River by the dense growth on Hawkins Island, Ebo offered these slave traders a haven for their illicit merchandise. Tradition says that a group of Ebo Negroes who were being held here walked into the water and drowned themselves rather than be slaves, saying "The water brought us here; the water will take us away."

The Eboes were described as having "a sickly yellow tinge in their complexion, jaundiced eyes, and prognathous faces like baboons." The women were said "to be diligent but the men lazy, despondent and prone to suicide." Slave traders avoided cargoes of these Ebo Negroes and freighted them only when no others were available.

So, be it fact or fiction, the story of Ebo Landing fits into the known characteristics of this tribe and the name Ebo has been attached to this site for a century and a half. In the olden days no Negro would drop a hook to fish at Ebo. It was "ha'nted"!

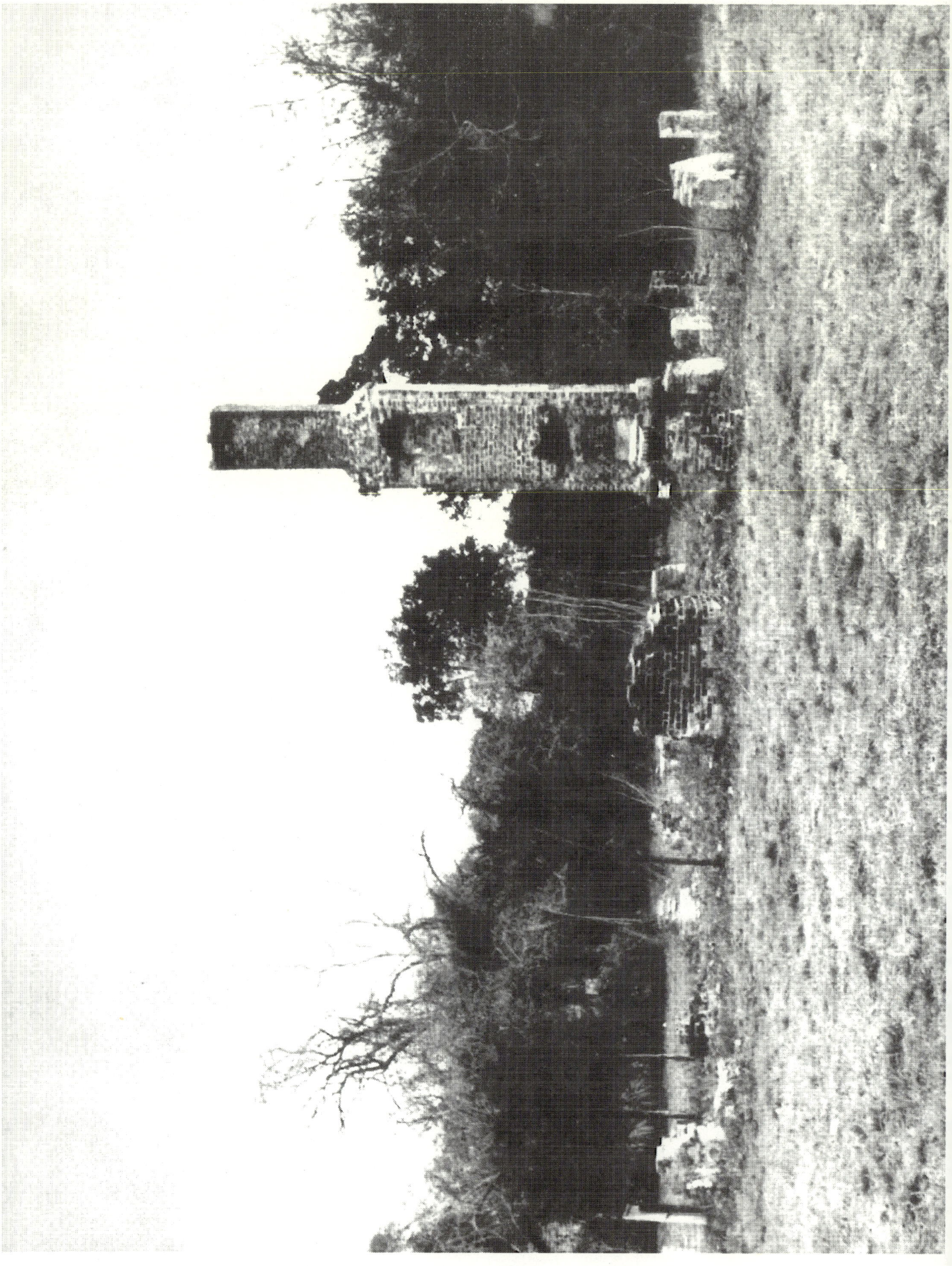

Ruins of Retreat Plantation House

The first occupation of the lands which became Retreat Plantation was in 1736 when Oglethorpe stationed John Humble here and appointed him the first pilot for this harbor. Humble's home stood about where the Sea Island Golf Club house now stands.

Later, these lands were granted to John Clubb as bounty for his service in Oglethorpe's Regiment. Clubb made his home here and in 1786 sold the property to Thomas Spalding, son of James Spalding, of Ashantilly, Perthshire, Scotland. The Spaldings lived at Retreat for some years and then Thomas Spalding, having purchased Sapelo Island, sold Retreat to Major William Page, who with his wife, Hannah Timmons, had come to St. Simons to visit their friend, Major Pierce Butler of Butler Point. On this visit which lasted a year, their only living child, all the others having died young, grew healthy and strong, so they decided to make St. Simons their home. This last child, Anna Matilda Page, grew to womanhood at Retreat and was married to Thomas Butler King of Massachusetts.

As Mr. King was prominent in public life, he was away from home much of the time, so that the management of the plantation was in Mrs. King's hands. The account books in her handwriting record the receipts from the sale of the cotton, the expenses of the family, and many interesting items connected with the management of the plantation. In addition to running the plantation, Mrs. King reared a family of nine children — five boys and four girls. As the family grew, a four-room, two-story addition was built on to the residence and used for the boys and their tutor. These houses were destroyed by fire about 1905 and nothing remains today except a brick chimney and some of the foundation of the residence.

Retreat remained in the possession of the King family until 1926, when it was purchased by the Sea Island Company for a Golf Course.

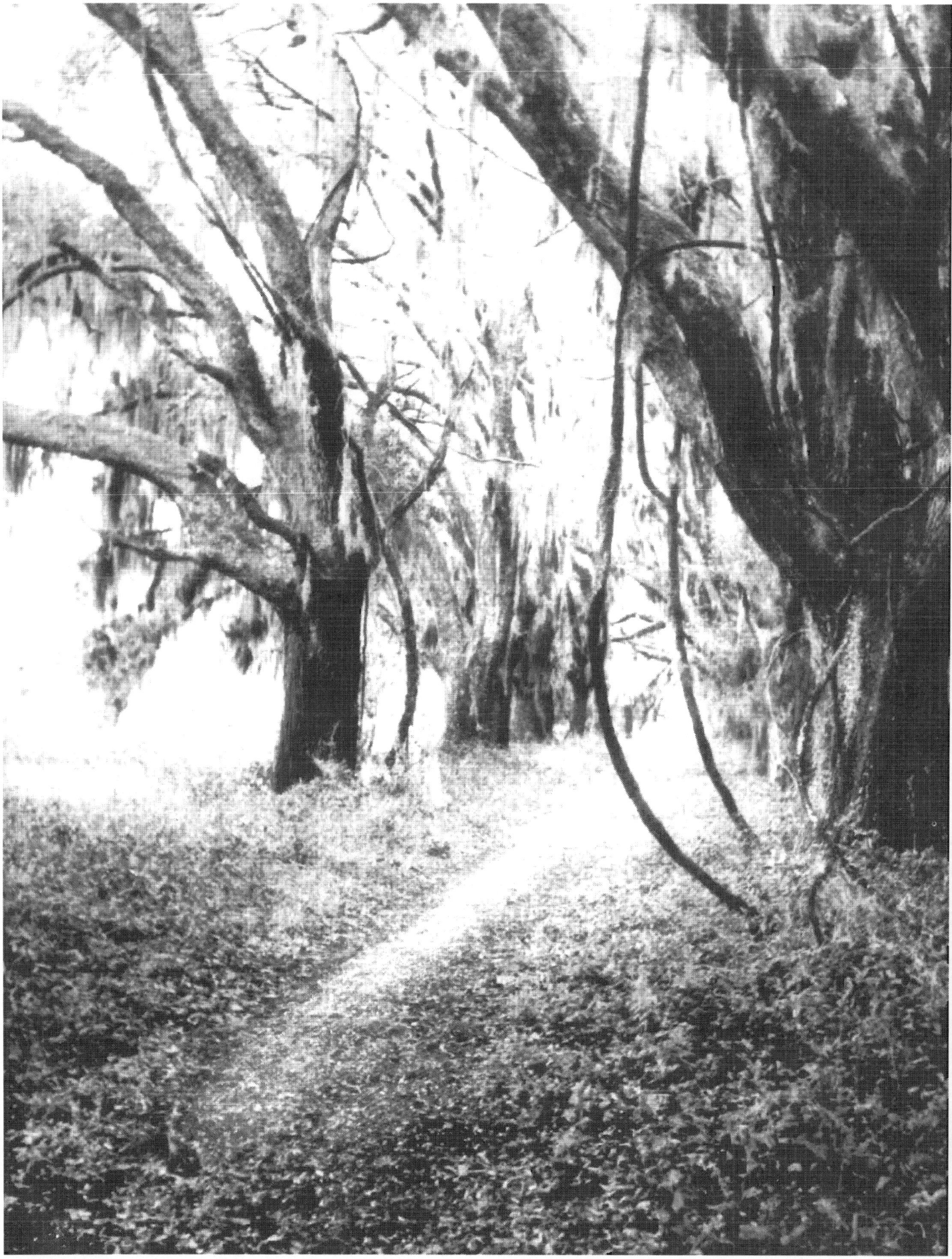

Retreat Avenue

This beautiful avenue of live oak trees *Quercus virens* formed the entrance to Retreat Plantation. In Plantation Days the road was wide enough for carriages; but, for its use today, a paved road on either side of the avenue leaves the trees, with the old plantation road, just as they were "before the War."

Among the King family letters now in the Southern Historical Collection at the University of North Carolina Library at Chapel Hill, there is one written by Anna Matilda (Page) King, mistress of Retreat Plantation, to her teen-age son, Henry Lord Page King, who was away at school, in which she tells of the building of this road and the planting of these trees.

Work such as the building of roads was planned for the seasons when the crops had been gathered and the slaves could be spared from work in the fields.

In Georgia, men were required to do road work in the militia district in which they resided in order to keep the public roads in good condition. Mr. King obtained permission to use The Retreat slaves in building this new road and let it suffice for the road work required of them.

Writing on December 1, 1848, Mrs. King announced that a new road to New Field was being made and that all the field hands had been at work on it. She said, "It goes in a direct line from Sukey's house and shortens the distance by a quarter of a mile."

Her letter continued: "The labor is great for there were several low places to be filled up and one continuous mass of palmetto roots to cut through." She added that trees were being set out "all along the road and it will take 500 trees to go the distance."

Time, and the relentless hand of man, have spared only this short stretch of the century-old oaks of Retreat Avenue.

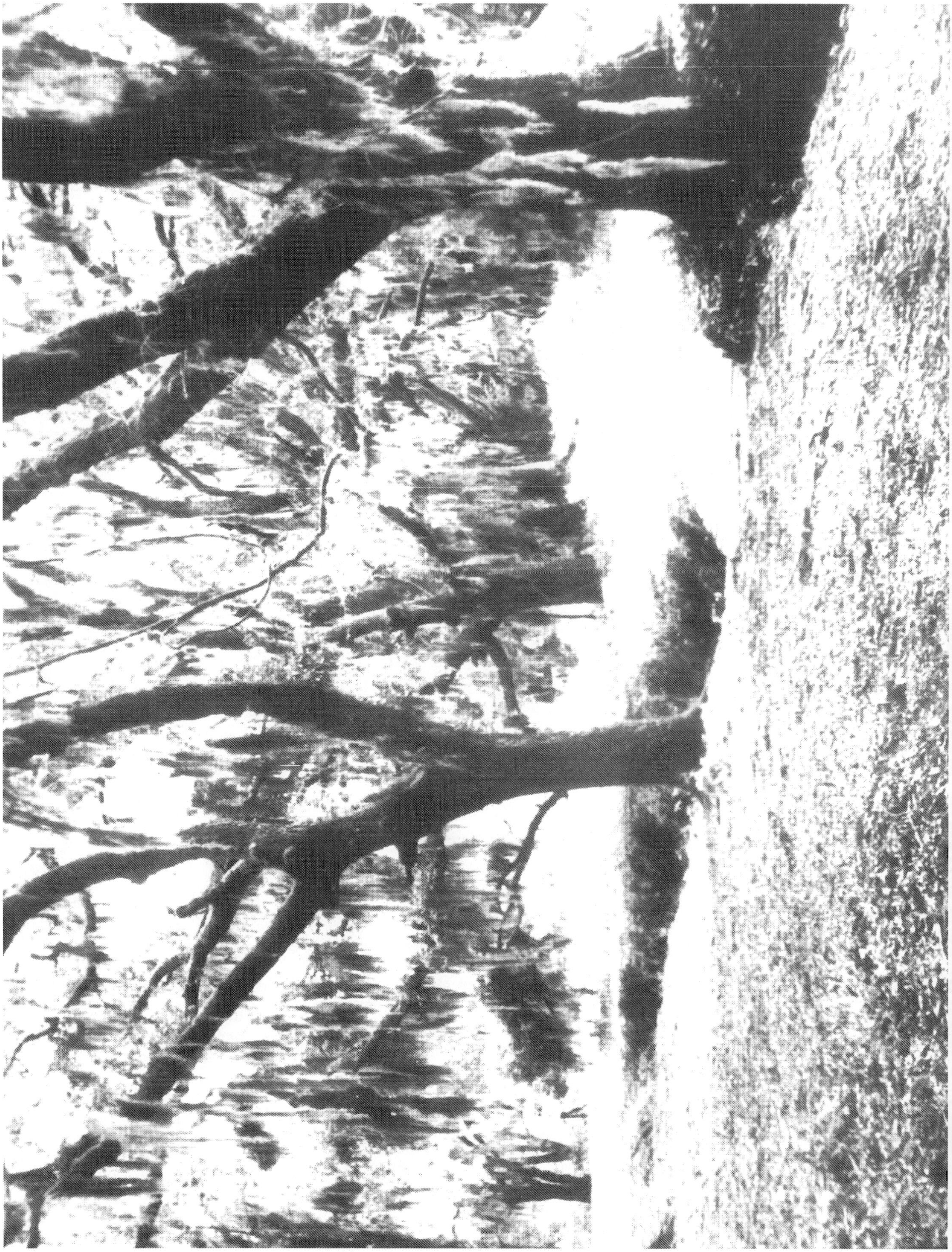

Retreat Avenue and Baldwin's Ditch

This view of Retreat Avenue, beautiful and serene, arouses no thought of the busy outside world; yet, there is something here which tells another story.

Thomas Butler King of Retreat was a national figure. After a term in the Georgia Legislature, he was elected to the United States Congress, where he was chairman of the Committee on Naval Affairs. While serving in this capacity, he instituted a program for modernizing the Navy. He advocated setting up bureaus so as to develop specialists in every branch — naval architecture, armaments, etc. — and, under his plan, in 1842 the Navy was reorganized practically as it is today. His progressive measures were acclaimed by business men over the country and by the Navy.

In 1849 he was sent to California as the personal agent of President Zachary Taylor to report on the advisability of admitting California to the Union. A year later President Fillmore named him Collector of the Port of San Francisco. This appointment brought about his second trip to California when he was accompanied by his eldest son, Thomas Butler King, Jr., who served as a clerk in the Customs House.

Mr. King's work was along the line of internal improvements, one of his projects being the building of a railroad from Brunswick to the Gulf of Mexico. As a part of this project there was to be a canal from the Altamaha River to the Port of Brunswick. Boston interests bought stock in the railroad and canal and the engineer sent down to make the survey was Loammi Baldwin, a Yale graduate and son of a Revolutionary General, also an engineer, but remembered best as the man who propagated the Baldwin apple.

Loammi Baldwin had worked on the Bunker Hill monument, had designed and built the dry docks at Charlestown, Mass., and Norfolk, Va., and came to be known as "The Father of Civil Engineering in America." While Baldwin was here to make the survey for the railroad and the canal, Mr. King utilized his services in surveying the drainage ditch for Retreat, which is shown in the foreground of this picture. Dug in 1836 by slave labor, this ditch still serves its purpose as do Baldwin's famous works elsewhere.

[73]

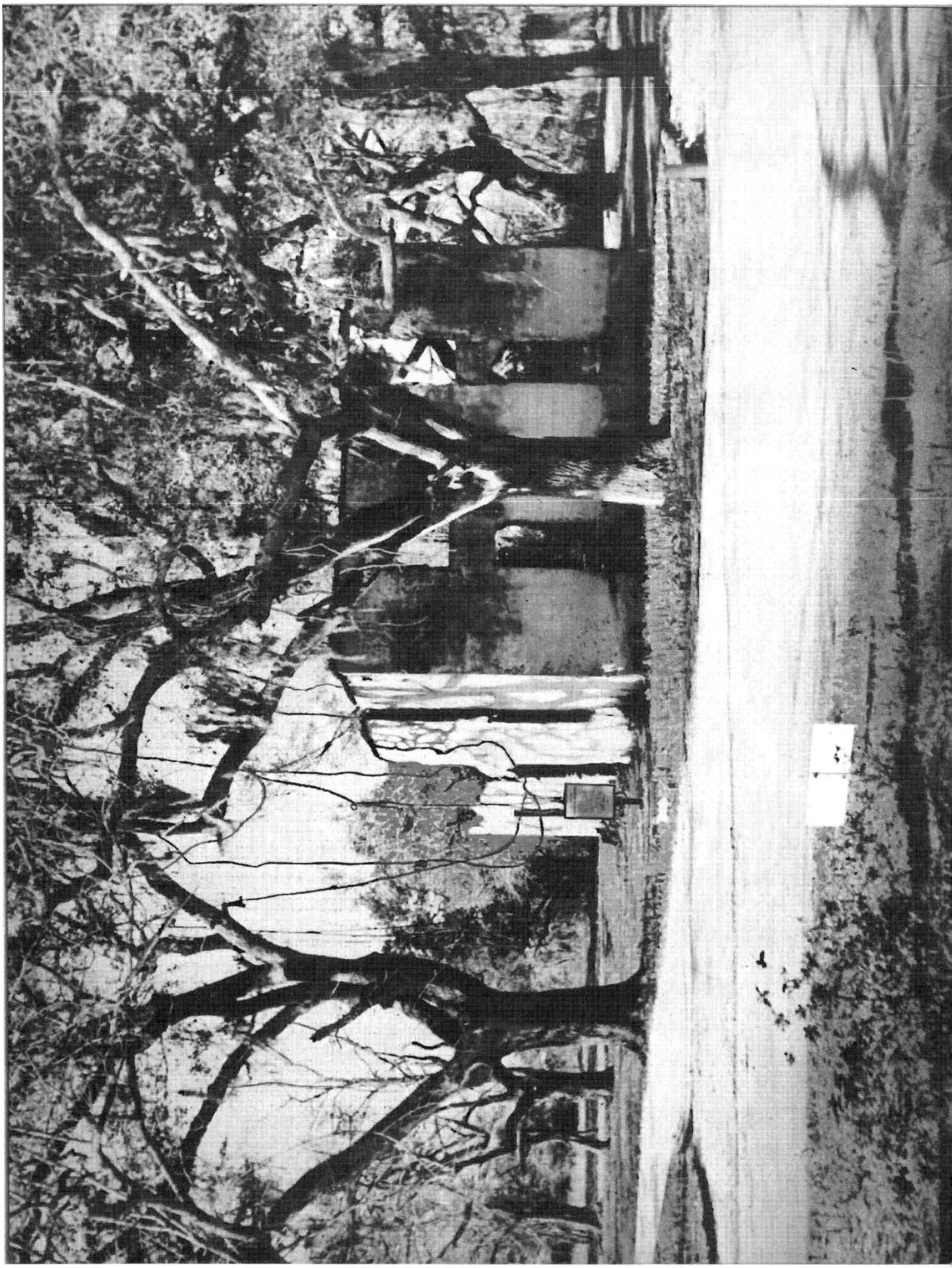

Retreat Hospital

This ten-room, tabby building was the slave hospital of Retreat Plantation. The rooms on the ground floor were used for the women, the second floor for the men, while the attic rooms were occupied by the two nurses, who lived here. The rooms were twelve by fifteen feet, each room having a fireplace and two windows. The staircase was in the wide hall in the middle of the house.

It was customary on all plantations in the South for the slave hospital to be built near the residence of the plantation owner. Of all the plantation buildings at Retreat the hospital was nearest to the master's home, the sick Negroes being the special interest of the mistress of the plantation, who made frequent trips to the hospital to supervise their care.

In Mrs. King's plantation record book she itemized the births and deaths of the slaves, as well as causes of illness. A list of twenty-eight children and two adults had measles in 1856. A notation at the bottom of the page gave the names of five who were "infants and did not take it."

In recording the deaths of her servants Mrs. King paid tribute to them. The record of Hannah's death is a fine example: "My good and faithful servant Hannah after years of suffering expired on the night of 3d August, 1854. For honesty, moral character, unselfishness and perfect devotion to her owners she had not her equal. She died resigned, with firm trust in her Redeemer."

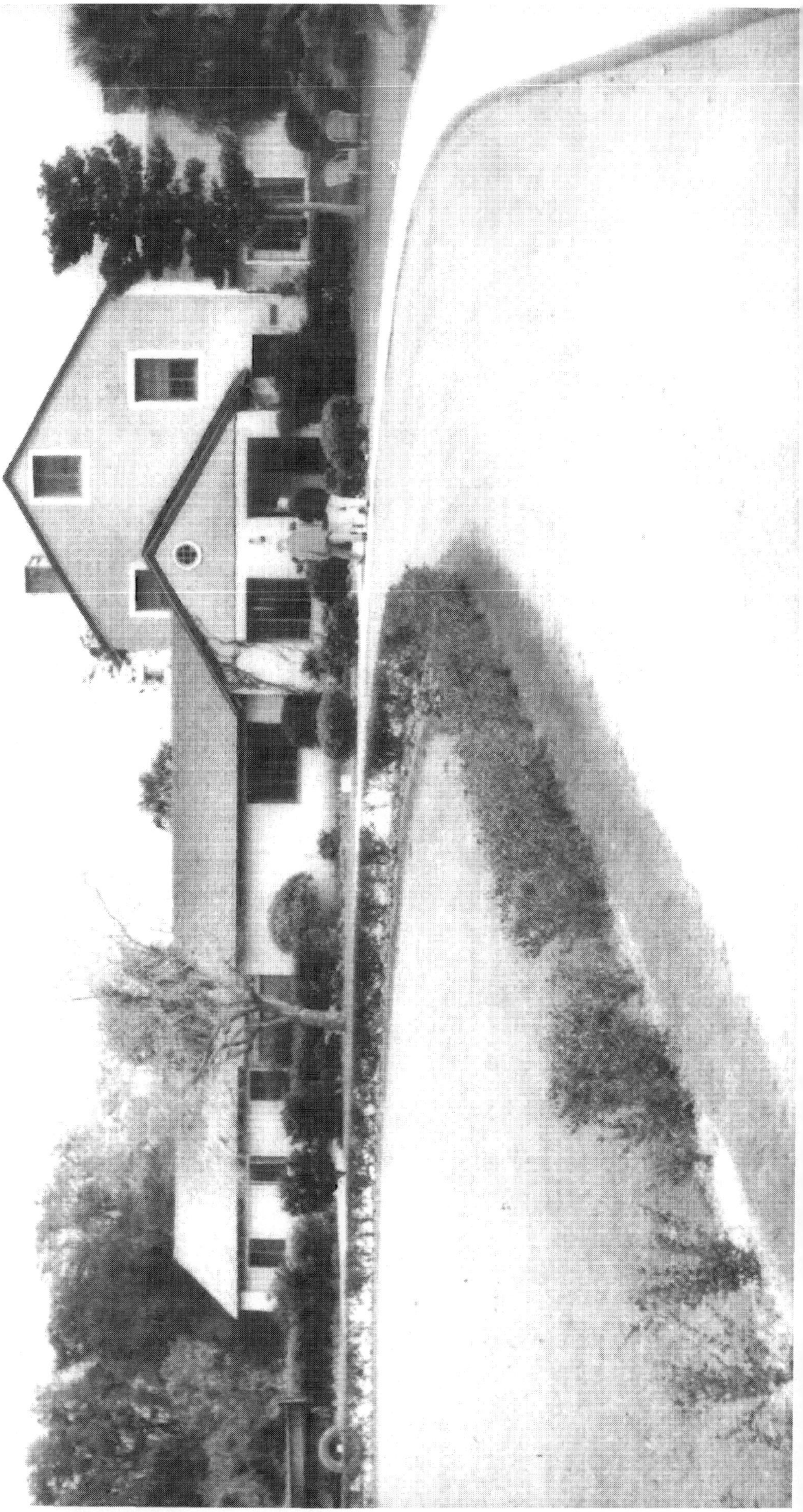

Sea Island Golf Club House

The Sea Island Golf Club House was formerly the corn barn of Retreat Plantation. Built of tabby and constructed by slave labor, the original walls of the old barn form the two-story part of the building, the one story wings being new construction. During plantation days the horses were stabled on the ground floor, with the corn and fodder stored above.

Nearby stood the four-story wooden cotton barn, shown on old maps as "King's Cotton House." Built in 1842, it was equipped with the most modern gins of the day, where the Sea Island cotton for which this plantation was famous was prepared for market.

In the preparation of cotton for market the staple was first dried, whipped for the removal of trash and dirt and carefully sorted into grades according to color and quality. It was then sent to the gins, after which it was spread on tables for "moting" — picking out the small seed which clung to the lint and which the gin failed to remove. After being packed into bags, averaging about three hundred pounds, it was ready for shipment. Cotton from Retreat was considered a superior product and brought top prices in the markets of England, being of the variety known as Anguilla cotton and, later, as Sea Island cotton.

In 1786 the seed of this variety of cotton had been sent to James Spalding of Retreat Plantation by his friend, Col. Roger Kelsal, a Loyalist who had refugeed in the Bahamas during the Revolutionary War. Developed on the Island of Anguilla, this cotton for many years after its introduction into Georgia was known as Anguilla cotton. (A plantation on the mainland a few miles from Brunswick, where the cotton was successfully grown, is still known as Anguilla.) Later, Anguilla cotton became known as Sea Island cotton and was the staple crop for all the plantations of these coastal islands as well as for those of the mainland.

[77]

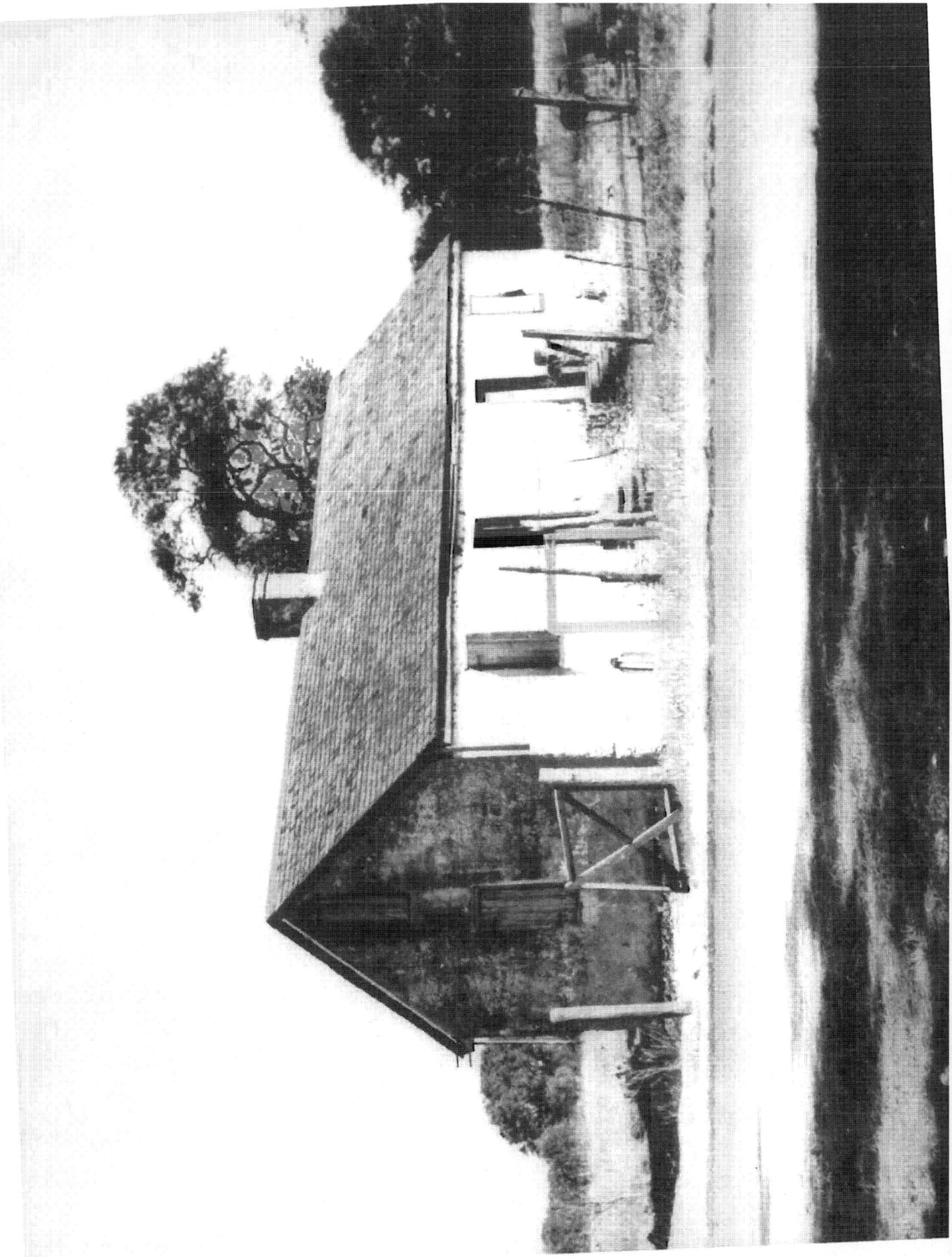

Slave Cabin of Retreat Plantation

This old tabby house is one of eight slave cabins which stood in a row. There was one across the road to the north and six others were south of this building. Today, only this one survives.

The building contained four rooms on the main floor and an attic, which was used for sleeping quarters. With the chimney in the middle of the house and a large fireplace on either side, such a building could have been used for two small families or one large family. The attic was divided into two rooms, reached by steep stairs on either side of the chimney.

This picture shows the original doors and shutters; in fact, the only part of the cabin as here pictured which is not the original is the roof — and that is made of cypress shingles which duplicated those formerly used. Even the floor of the cabin is the original, being hand-worked, tongue and groove pine boards — as good a floor as would have been found in homes of many of the plantation masters.

A correspondent for the *New York Daily Tribune,* writing from St. Simons on July 16, 1862, described these cabins as "far surpassing, for neatness and comfort, anything I have yet seen in the South. The houses are 18 feet by 48 feet, with a wall partition and chimney in the center, making two apartments. . . . The 'loft' makes a very comfortable room. The floors are good and the apertures for light and air large. There are eight of these double houses, each about four rods distant from the others. . . . Around all, and between them, is a row of beautiful shade trees of live oak."

The settlement formed by these eight cabins was known as "New Field" and the slaves who lived here tilled the Sea Island cotton fields nearby, which are now covered by the runways of Malcolm McKinnon Airport.

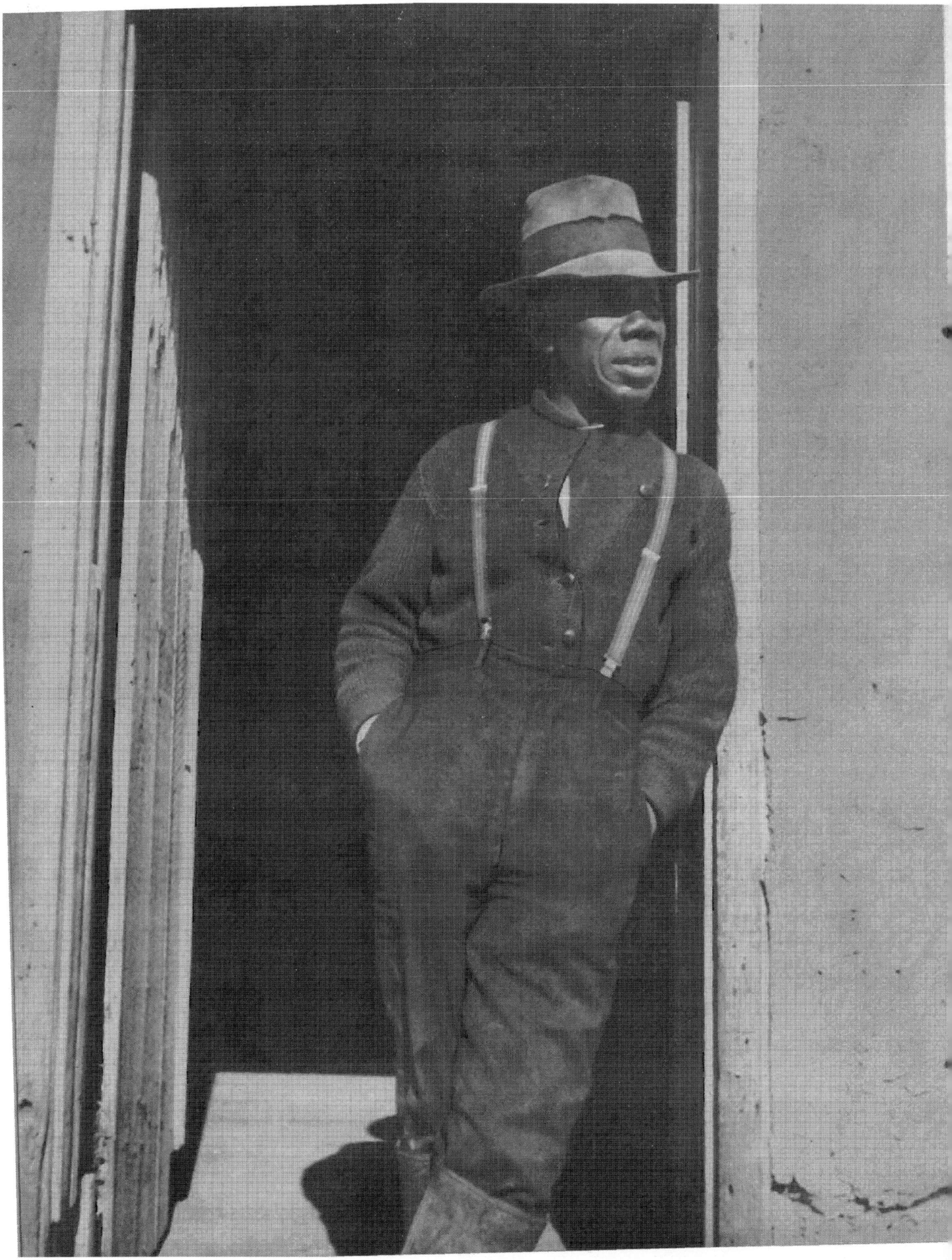

Floyd White

Standing in the doorway of the old slave cabin of Retreat Plantation is Floyd White who was born in this house and was the last Negro to live here. His Mother, Victoria, was a slave of Retreat, but his father, Jupiter, belonged to the Postells of Kelvin Grove Plantation. Plantation masters encouraged their Negroes to get their wives on the "home" plantation but, when a man found a wife on a neighboring plantation, it was sometimes allowed; in those cases he was said to have "a broad wife," meaning he went abroad to see his wife.

Negro slaves were rated according to their age and ability as "full hands," "three-quarter hands," "half hands," or "quarter hands" and were given work in proportion, a "full hand" having a full task while a "three-quarter hand" was expected to do only three-quarters of a task. This "task" was a definite measurement of land marked off in the fields with stakes set up at the four corners 105 feet apart, making a quarter of an acre.

Each slave cabin had a plot of ground where the Negro had his garden and where he could raise such vegetables as he wished for his own table; in addition he often raised cotton for sale. Floyd's garden was a part of that which had been tilled by his parents; but he explained that he did not plant all of the garden — only "about two tasks."

Floyd's name, "White" — which perhaps was the product of wishful thinking — was typical of the way the Negroes of St. Simons found surnames for themselves after the War. In other parts of the South, the former slaves took the name of the master, but here the Negroes found other names, apparently feeling that the name of the white man belonged to him alone.

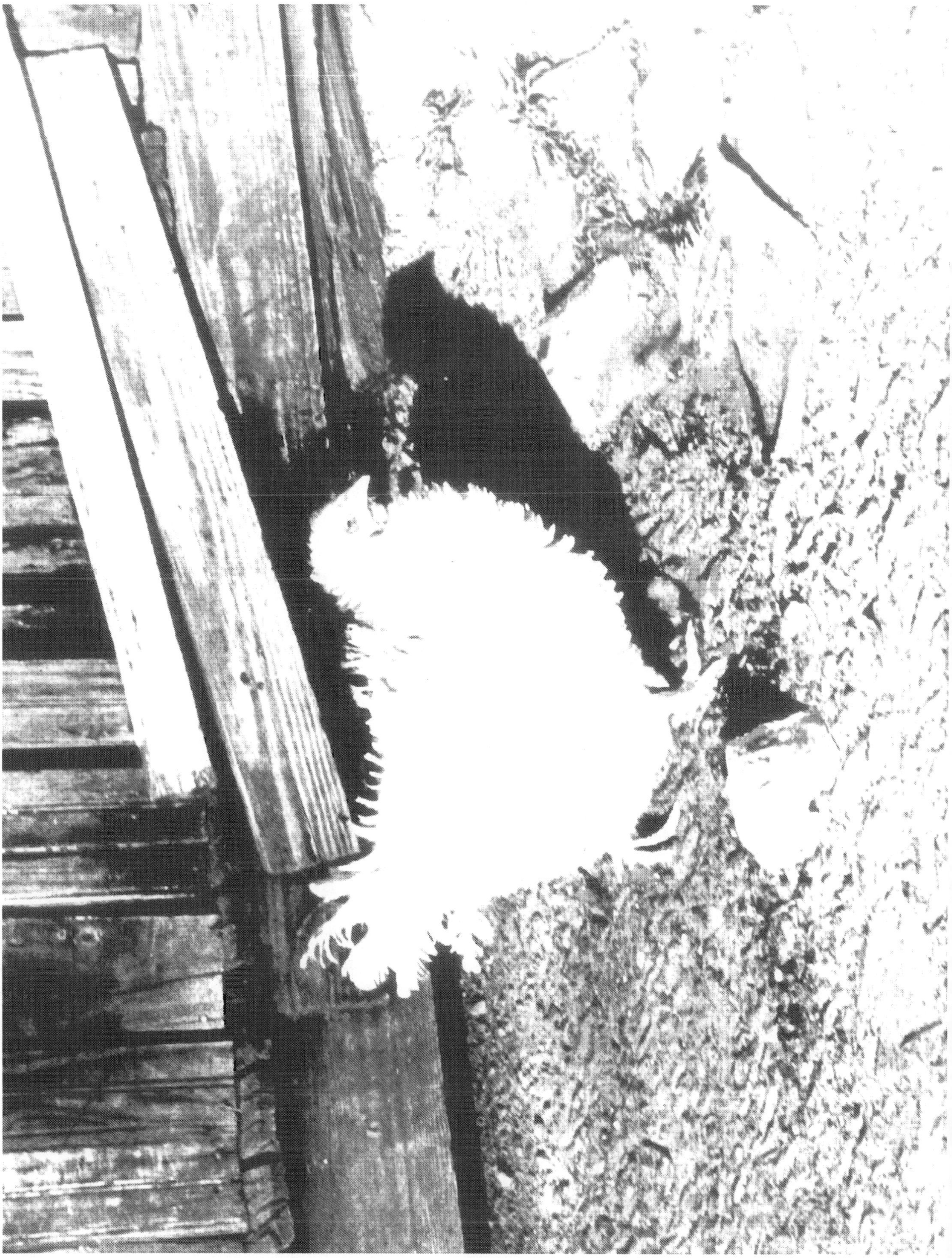

Frizzle Chicken

This is a variety of chicken whose feathers curl up and give the impression that they are pointing the wrong way. Negroes kept them in their yards in the belief that a frizzle chicken would protect its owner by scratching up any "voodoo" or "conjur" that might be placed there by some enemy.

This enemy was supposed to go to the witch doctor, or "voodoo man," and get a charm to use against you. Anything — hair off a black cat, dirt from a Negro burying ground, or any other thing — would do the work, provided it was properly conjured by the witch doctor. This article was then buried in the ground near the home of the intended victim, who was supposed to get sick and die — or so they believed. However, if this person had a frizzle chicken around to protect him, the chicken would dig up the "conjur" and expose it to the sunlight, and thus destroy the efficacy of the charm.

The Negroes had all sorts of explanations for these great powers of the frizzle chicken. By some it was supposed to have feathers pointing the wrong way because it came out of the eggshell backwards! Others thought that a person eating a frizzle would in some way become immune to the power of any "conjur"; while a third group thought this chicken belonged to the devil and refused to kill one of them. It was also believed that the lining of the gizzard of a frizzle chicken made into a tea would cure certain forms of "conjur."

A visitor who had heard the story of the frizzle chicken, but who wanted to hear what the Negro himself would say on the subject, asked Floyd about his chicken, saying: "I wouldn't have an ugly chicken like that around my house. What do you keep him for?"

Floyd indignantly replied: "Dat a good chicken. Dat a sma't chicken. Dat chicken allers scratchin,' alers lookin' fer sumpin."

A local resident who knew Floyd and the reason for his having the frizzle chicken then said: "Now, Floyd, do you really mean that that chicken scratches more than any other chicken?" To this Floyd replied: "Mor'n any udder chicken ob any udder nationality!"

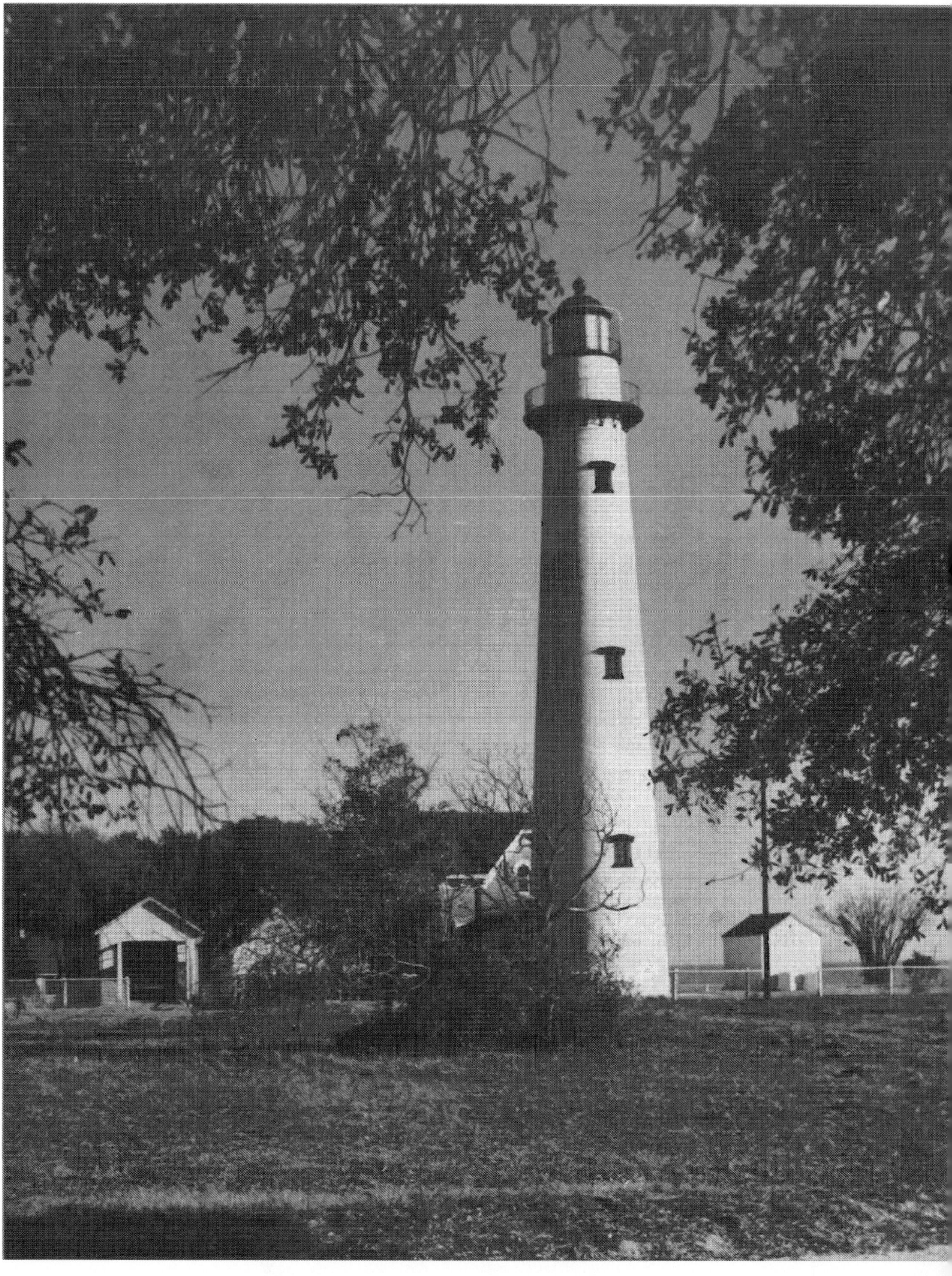

St. Simons Lighthouse

Soon after the founding of our new Nation, plans were made for the erection of a lighthouse at the South End of St. Simons Island. In 1808 a contract was made with James Gould of Massachusetts for the erection of a lighthouse, as well as a dwelling and kitchen which would be used by the lighthouse keeper. The lighthouse was in the form of an octagonal tower seventy-five feet high and built of tabby salvaged from the parapets of Fort Frederica and from the abandoned houses of the old fort and town. This light was commissioned in 1811 and James Gould, the builder, became its first keeper.

During the Civil War, a Confederate battery was located near the lighthouse. Built by the Jackson Artillery of Macon, Ga., who were sent here for the purpose in January, 1861, the fortification was named Fort Brown in honor of Georgia's War Governor, the Hon. Joseph E. Brown. The battery was a strong earth-work; the magazine and other parts of the fort were well supported and braced with massive timbers, being roofed over with railroad iron and timbers and covered with "a dozen feet of sand" to make them bomb-proof. Mounted on top were an eight-inch and a ten-inch columbiad as well as five thirty-two pound and two forty-two pound cannon.

Fort Brown and a similar work at the north end of Jekyll were situated so as to command the entrance to St. Simons Sound.

In February, 1862, the lighthouse was destroyed by the Confederates, the forts on St. Simons and Jekyll were abandoned, the guns being sent to Savannah. The troops who had been stationed at these forts were sent to Brunswick to protect and command the Brunswick & Florida Railroad.

The Lighthouse pictured here was built in 1871, a few feet from the old tower. It was constructed of brick, as was the home of the keeper, erected at the same time. These were the only brick buildings in Glynn County, although there had been several such structures at Frederica in 1736 and Mark Carr had a two-story brick residence on Blythe Island in 1752.

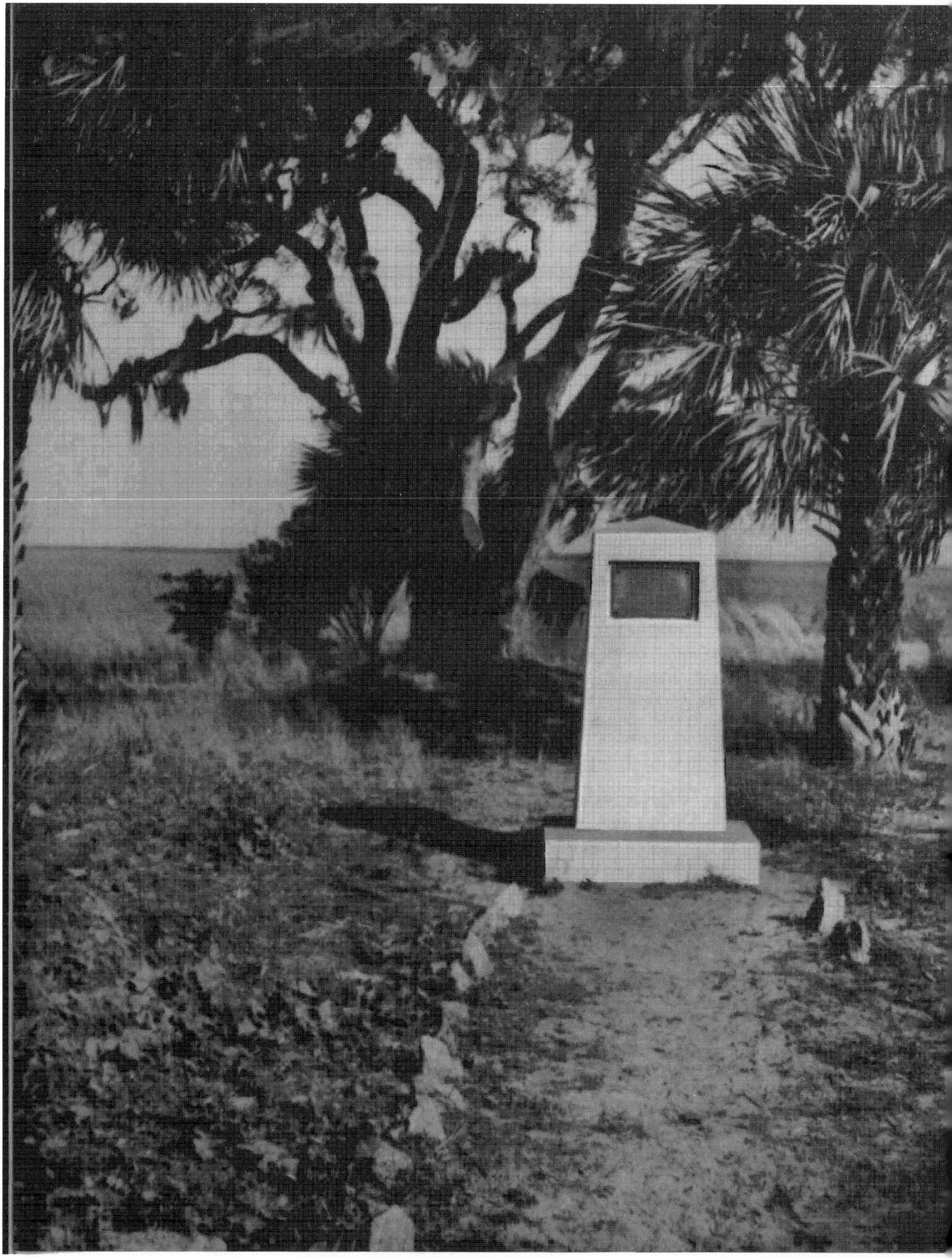

Lanier's Oak

Sidney Lanier, Georgia's greatest poet, found rest and inspiration here under this live oak tree, known as Lanier's Oak, which stands near the marsh on the eastern shores of Brunswick, Georgia. It was here that he received the impressions to which his great genius was to give expression in his marsh poems.

Lanier, a native of Macon, was graduated from old Oglethorpe College near Milledgeville. With the outbreak of the Civil War, all the professors and students having joined the Confederate Army, the college closed and never opened again.

Lanier gave four years of service to the cause of the Confederacy, serving in Virginia with the Macon Volunteers and at Fort Fisher near Wilmington, N. C. While serving as a signal officer on a vessel which ran the blockade at Wilmington, he was captured and imprisoned at Point Lookout. It was here that tuberculosis laid its hold on him. Released from prison he made his way back to Macon, where he lay dangerously ill for weeks.

With improved health Lanier faced the necessity of earning a living. It was a bleak situation. As he himself expressed it, ". . . pretty much the whole of life has been merely not dying." He taught school, clerked in a family hotel, and studied law in his father's office, all the while yearning for the life of which he had dreamed — one of music or of poetry.

Breaking away, he went north, and finally became the first flute in the Peabody Symphony Orchestra and a lecturer in English Literature at Johns Hopkins University. So, in Baltimore, Lanier found the life of which he had dreamed.

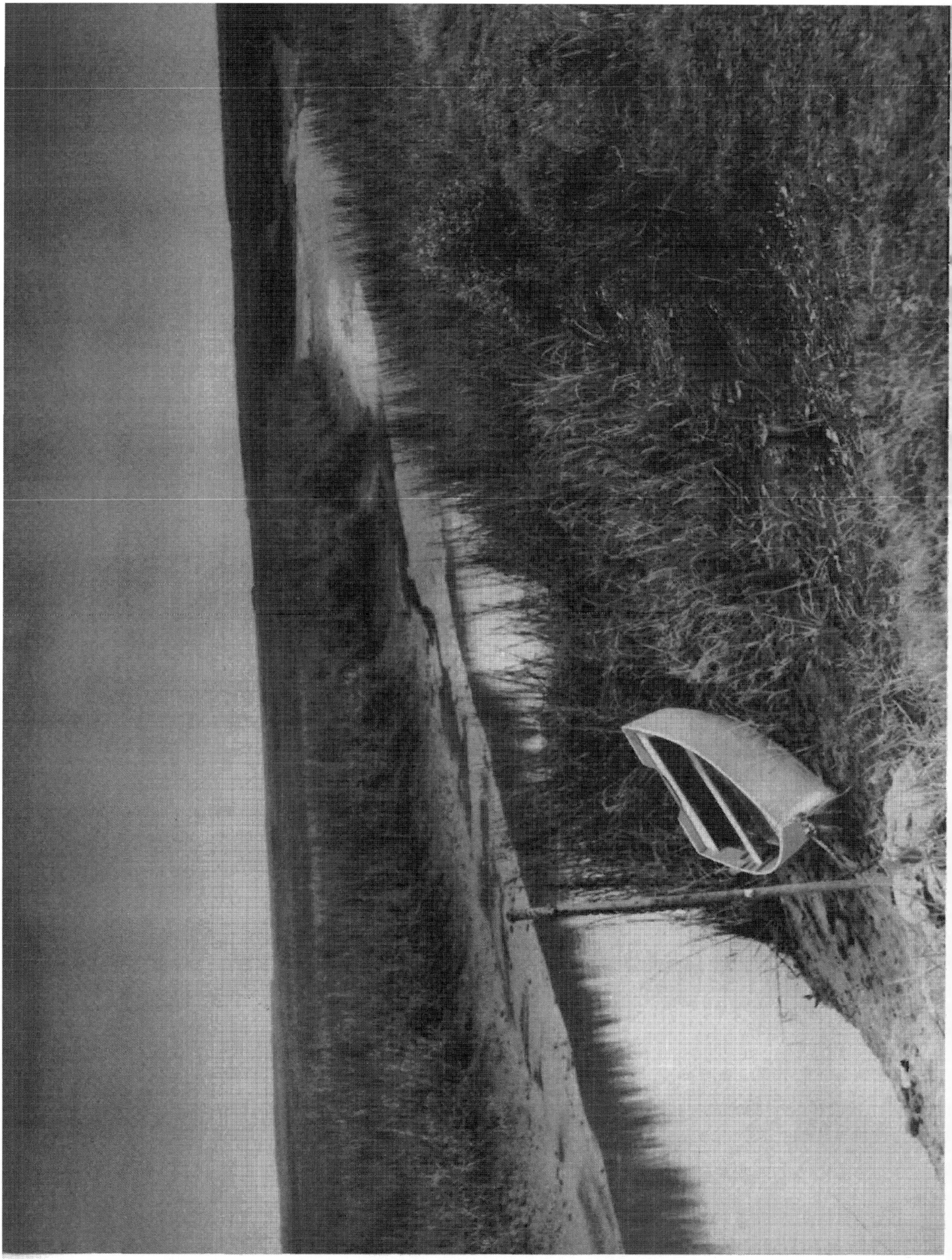

The Marshes of Glynn

Lanier visited many places in search of health and in each found something beautiful of which he wrote. "Tampa Robins," "The Song of the Chattahoochee" and other poems tell of the charm of these places for Lanier, but it was these marshes of Glynn County, Georgia, that gave him his greatest inspiration.

While in Brunswick, Lanier and his family visited at the home of his wife's brother, Henry C. Day. When his health improved and he was strong enough, he delighted in daily rides in a basket phaeton. Driving through the "glooms of the forest" formed by a thick grove of live oaks, he reached the "leagues of marsh grass" which border the eastern shore of the peninsula on which Brunswick is located.

Beneath a live oak tree near the marsh he would sit for hours, musing and drinking in the beauty of the scene before him. His note-books received copious entries of his impressions, which he expected to incorporate later into a series of *Hymns of the Marshes*.

The first step in the realization of this ambition was accomplished before his departure the following spring. One day, while sitting beneath Lanier's Oak, he penned what many people consider his best poem, "The Marshes of Glynn." A few days later at a meeting of a literary club at the home of a friend, Mrs. James Maxwell Couper, this poem was read aloud for the first time and from the original manuscript. However, its publication did not take place until three years later — 1878.

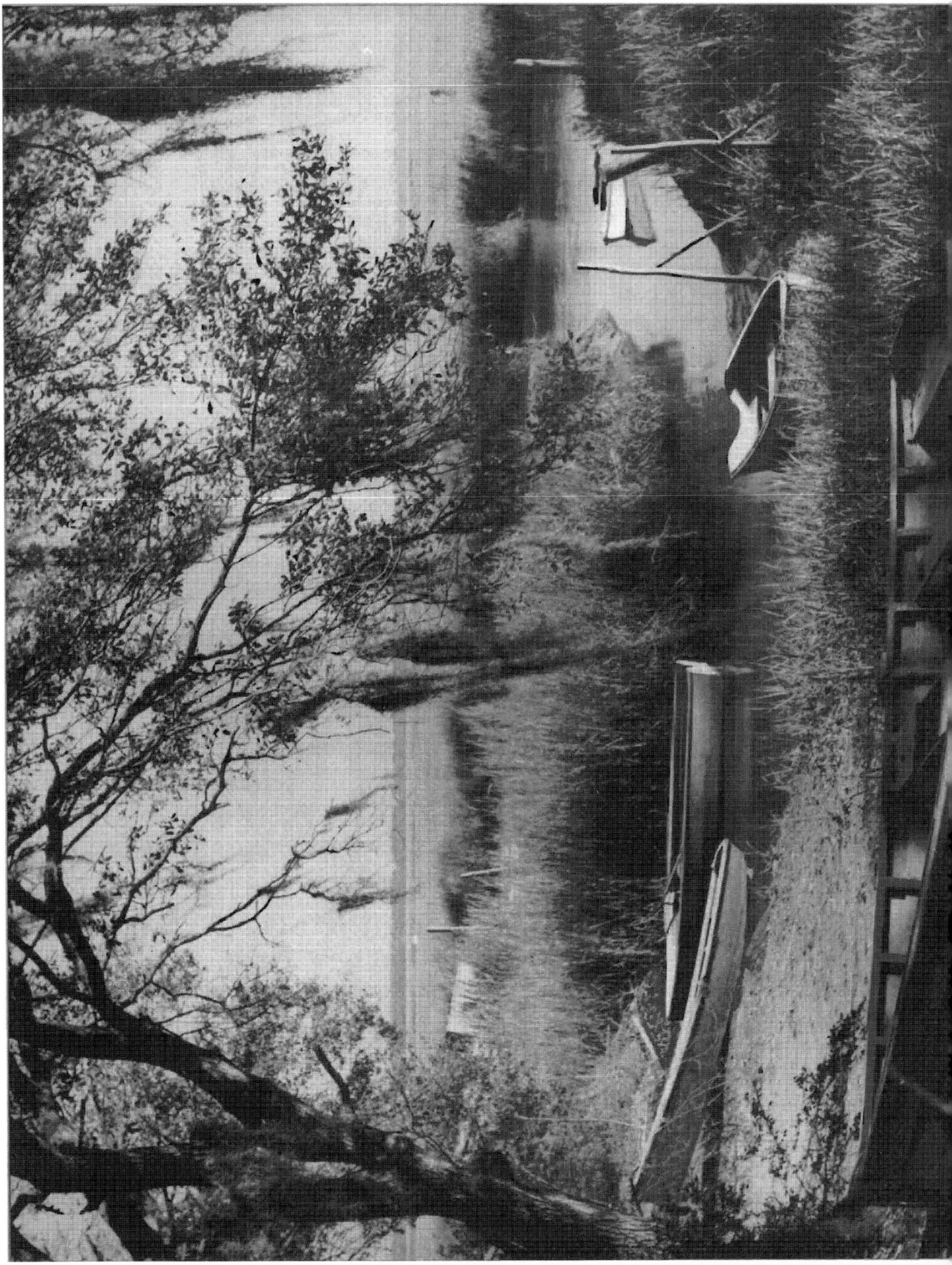

Lanier's Marshes

It was from this scene that Lanier received inspiration which was to remain with him permanently and to culminate in two poems which are conceded to be among the finest in the English language — "The Marshes of Glynn" and "Sunrise".

The hectic years that intervened between his departure from Brunswick and his death in 1881 did not affect the impressions which "the marvelous Marshes of Glynn" made upon the poet. "A Marsh Song," "At Sunset," "A Marsh Hymn," "Between Dawn and Sunrise," and another poem, entitled "Individuality," written during the period, show this conclusively.

But a more striking proof comes from his last days, when he seemed to fear he would die with his thoughts unuttered. Too feeble to raise food to his mouth and with a fever temperature of 104 degrees, he wrote his last poem, "Sunrise," which in the estimation of one critic, marks the culminating point, the highest vision of Sidney Lanier.

Lanier's last days were spent in the mountains of North Carolina. There, in 1881, the gentle soul of the poet came to rest. His body was returned to the Baltimore which had given him the life he desired — a life devoted to music and to poetry. On a boulder marking his grave in Greenmount Cemetery there is a line from "Sunrise," one of his marsh poems, *"I am lit with the sun."*

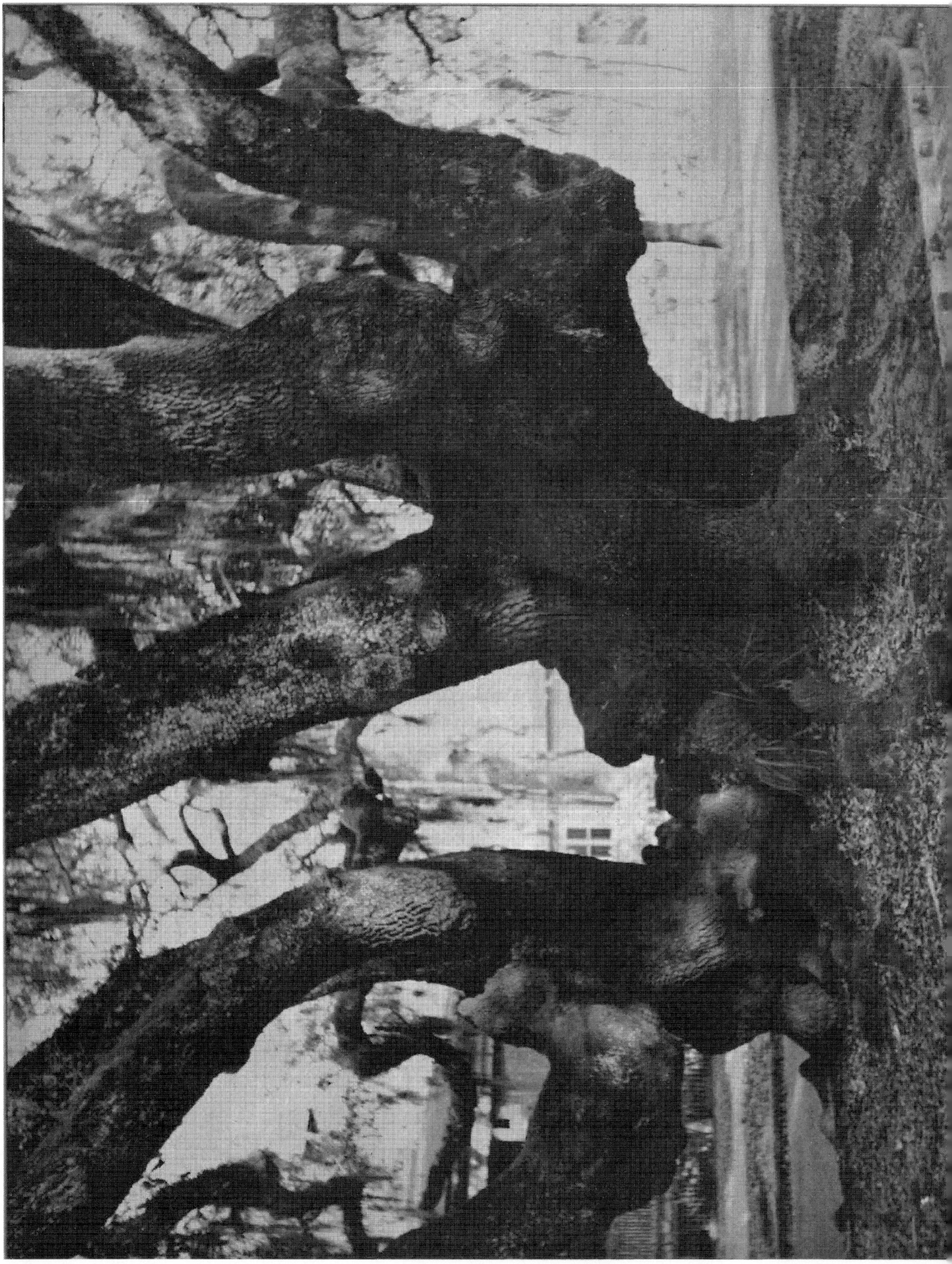

Lovers' Oak

This giant live oak *(Quercus virens)* is known as Lovers' Oak. The traditional story of the Indian maiden and her lover has many variations, but it is certain that Indian children would have played in it as have generations of white and Negro children. These live oaks grow to great size and live for centuries. The native habitat of the live oak is from Virginia south along the Atlantic Coast and the Gulf Coast to Texas.

Lovers' Oak measures thirteen feet in diameter three feet above the ground, where it branches into ten limbs, some of which measure thirty inches in diameter. In several instances limbs some distance from the body of the tree have crossed and formed a natural graft.

The beautiful moss *(Tillandsia usneoides)* which festoons the oaks and other trees is a member of the pineapple family, and has the same habitat as the live oak. It is not a parasite, but an epiphyte, and grows as well on electric wires or wire fences as it does on trees.

Throughout the ages this moss has been valuable. The Indians made rope of it, they used it for their couches, the women dressed in it, and it was mixed with mud and used to cover their wattle-work houses. During the Revolutionary War it was used to wad the guns and during the Plantation Era mattresses were made of the moss. Today, it is used in upholstery, as a filter in air-conditioning machines, and as the basis of a powerful astringent used in plastic surgery.

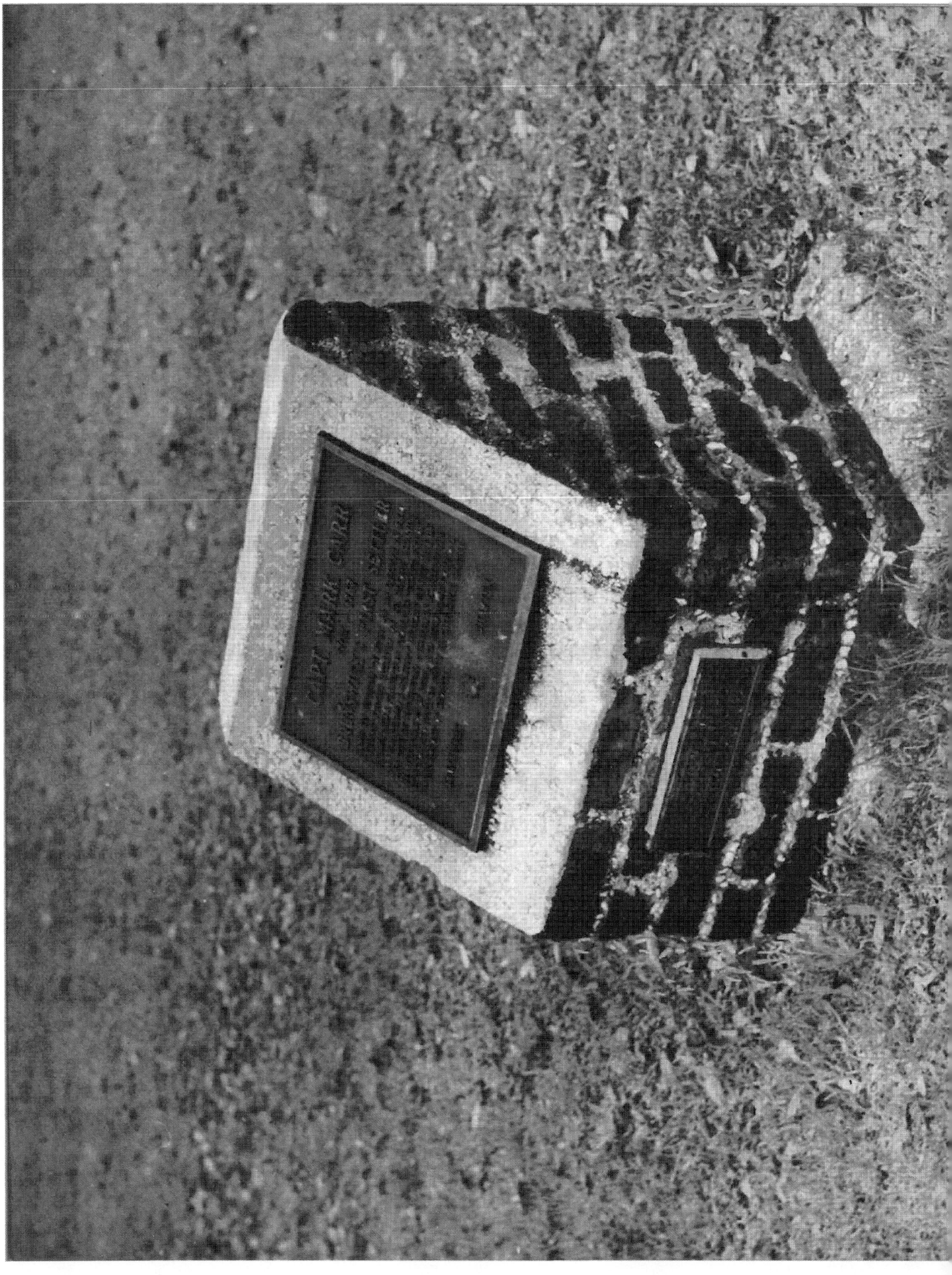
CAPT MARK CARR

Capt. Mark Carr, Brunswick's First Settler

In 1738 Mark Carr came to Georgia with Oglethorpe's Regiment and about a year later was granted five hundred acres of land on the present site of the City of Brunswick. Here he had his plantation which was said to be as fine as any in Virginia. This plantation produced corn, tobacco, and other staples and, incidentally, gave Brunswick its first name, "Carr's Fields."

A detachment of the Regiment was stationed here to protect the settlement. Capt. Carr commanded a Marine Company of Boatmen, who were stationed at the Hermitage, a few miles up Turtle River above Brunswick, where he was granted a thousand acres of land on which he had a sawmill with four saws.

Capt. Carr assisted in repelling the Spanish Invasion of 1742 and served the Colony in many important positions. It was agreed that his "industry in improvements had not been outdone by any."

When it was decided to lay out a town on the site of Carr's Fields, the owner relinquished these lands and was granted a tract on Blythe Island where he built a two-story brick house and made his home.

In 1771 the Colonial Council at Savannah ordered that the town laid out on the site of Carr's Fields be called Brunswick in honor of the British royal family, who were of the House of Hanover or Brunswick.

In 1938 the Brunswick Chapter, Daughters of the American Revolution erected this marker to the memory of Capt. Carr and in celebration of the bicentennial of his arrival in Georgia. The brick used in building the marker came from the ruins of his house on Blythe Island, which was burned by Indians in 1788.

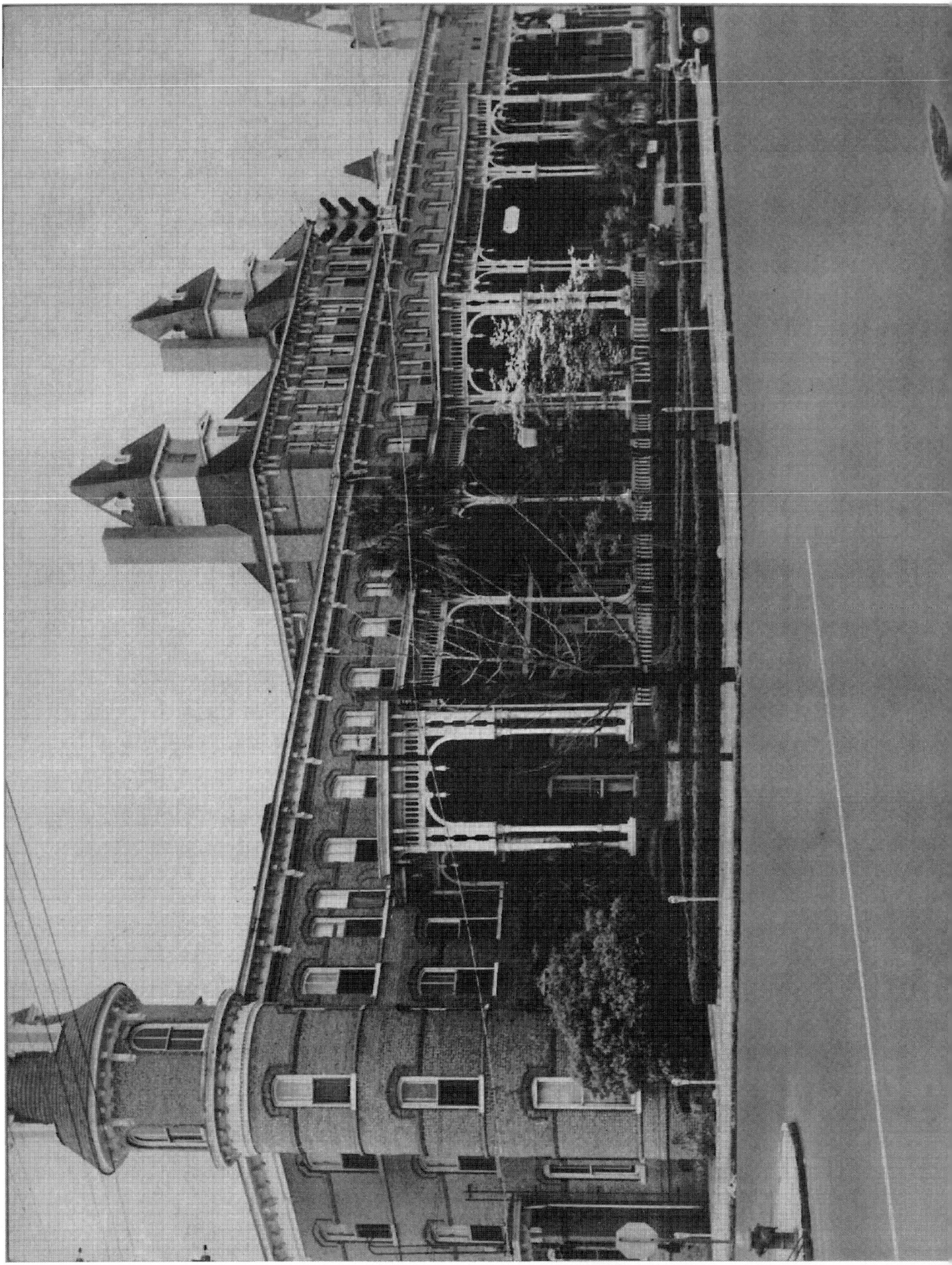

Oglethorpe Hotel, Brunswick

The building of the Oglethorpe Hotel and the Jekyll Island Club House marked the beginning of the resort era for this section. They were erected about the same time, one of the leading spirits in the building of the Oglethorpe Hotel being James F. O'Shaughnessey, a member of the Jekyll Island Club. The Oglethorpe occupied the site of the old Oglethorpe House erected in 1837 and burned by accident during the Civil War.

The Oglethorpe Hotel was opened in January, 1888, and was pronounced one of the finest resort hotels in this section. A planned program of events for the entertainment of the guests included walks to Hanover Park, Lovers' Oak, and Windsor Park; and drives in carriages from the livery stable connected with the hotel to Sulphur Springs, to Camp Walker, to Cypress Mills, to Belle Point, to Freedman's Rest and around the Boulevard. Rowboats, sailboats, and a naphtha launch were used for boating and fishing. Arrangements were made for hunting parties and for excursions to the nearby islands of St. Simons, Jekyll and Cumberland.

So marked was the success of this opening season of the Oglethorpe that it was decided to build a summer hotel on St. Simons Island. This St. Simons Hotel, patterned after the Oglethorpe, was three stories high and built of wood. It was located on the South End of the island on lands belonging to James Postell, later known as the Massengale Tract, and now a County Park. Passengers from Brunswick on the steamboats *Ruby, Egmont, Hessie, Pope Catlin,* or *City of Brunswick,* landed at the pier which had been built near the lighthouse, and were transported to the hotel in mule-drawn street cars whose tracks ran down Railroad Avenue.

This hotel corporation, operating the Oglethorpe Hotel in winter and the St. Simons Hotel in summer, used the same equipment for both hotels, moving the furniture to the St. Simons Hotel for the summer and back to the Oglethorpe for the winter. They purchased Sea Island, then known as Long Island, for a hunting preserve. It was stocked with pheasants, which in addition to the native deer and turkey, offered ideal sport. Hunting parties went to Sea Island on "maroons," camping in tents and enjoying the beach as well as the hunt.

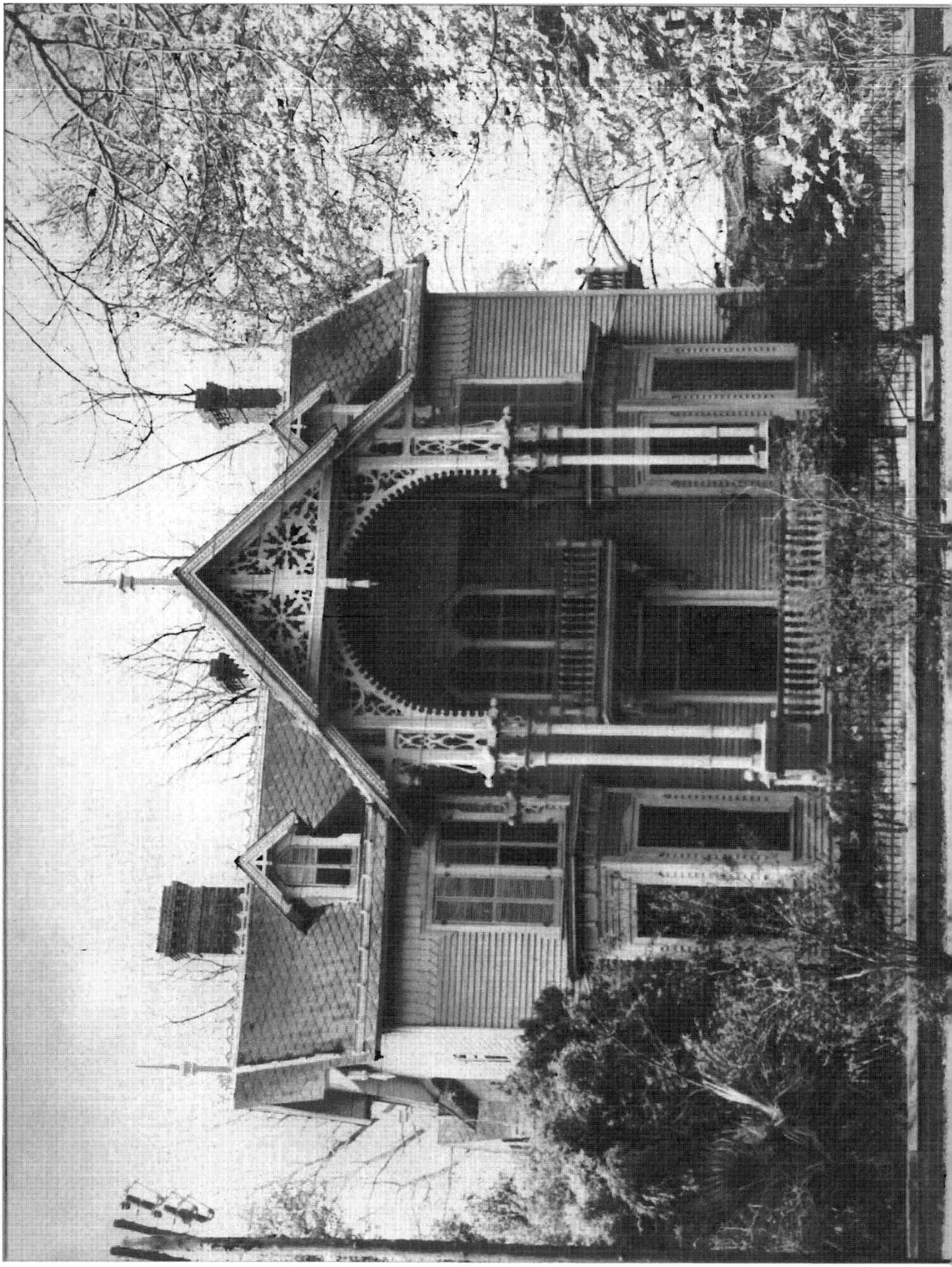

Mahoney House

Built the same year as the Oglethorpe Hotel and designed by the same architect, this Mahoney house is a perfect example of period architecture, sometimes called Victorian. It was erected by Timothy Mahoney as his family residence and has never been occupied by any other family.

Mr. Mahoney was a native of Ireland who came to Brunswick soon after the Civil War. During the war he was an engineer on Confederate troop trains; he and his son, William Mahoney, were railroad men all their lives.

Timothy Mahoney and his wife, Mary (Dunn) Mahoney, had two sons and three daughters. One of the sons married and moved away, but the parents and the other four children lived and died in this home.

Too often houses of this type are allowed to fall into bad repair; sometimes they are remodelled and some of the characteristics of the period removed. Luckily, nothing of this sort has happened to the Mahoney house for it has been kept in good repair and has gone unchanged throughout the decades. Even when a new roof was put on the house some years ago, the trim which had decorated the ridgepole, the gable ends, and the edge of the roof was replaced on top of the new roof.

In the office of the architect who designed the Oglethorpe Hotel and the Mahoney house there was a young apprentice by the name of Stanford White; so Brunswick has two buildings on which this well-known architect worked.

After the death of the last surviving member of the Mahoney family, their residence became the property of Miss Virginia McGarvey, a friend of the family, to whom it had been willed. Miss McGarvey plans to keep the house exactly as it was built so that it will continue to be a perfect example of Victorian architecture.

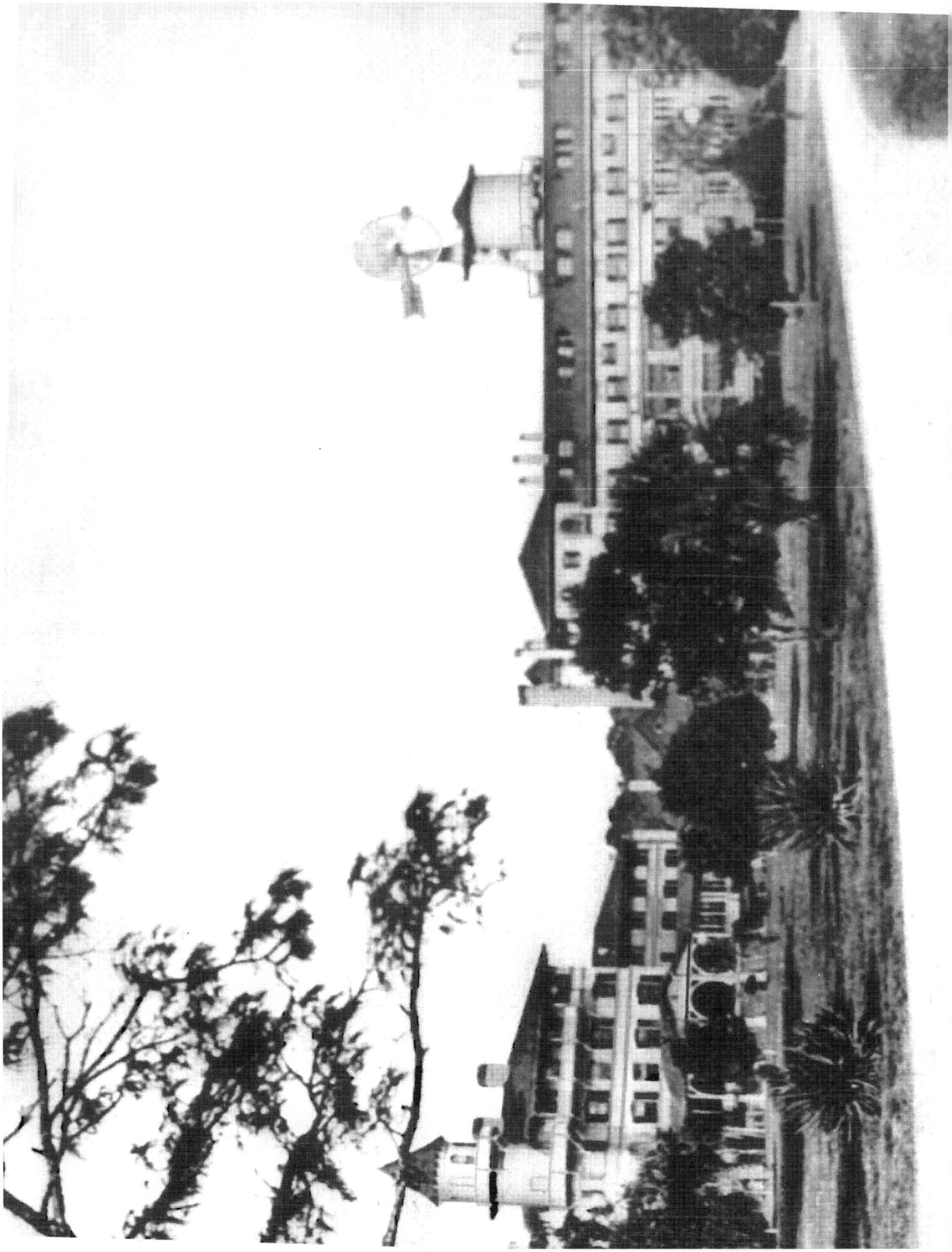

Jekyll Island Club

The Island, known to the Indians as Ospo, was named "Jekyll," by Gen. Oglethorpe in honor of his friend, Sir Joseph Jekyll, who, with Lady Jekyll, had contributed six hundred pounds toward the founding of the Colony of Georgia.

Major William Horton, an officer of Oglethorpe's Regiment, had his plantation here. After the Revolutionary War the island came into the possession of Christopher Poulain du Bignon, in whose family it remained for a century. In 1886 Jekyll was purchased by a group of men who organized the Jekyll Island Club. This Club was composed of the social and business leaders and included the Gould's, Astors, Vanderbilts, Rockefellers, Morgans and other leading men of that day, who established here a place where they could rest from the cares and worries of the busy world.

The Club season opened the middle of January and closed at Easter. The Club House and Annex; the San Souci Apartments, built by J. Pierpont Morgan, George F. Baker, James J. Hill, Frederick G. Bourne, William Rockefeller and Robert C. Pruyn; and about a dozen cottages, built by members of the Club, were all located on the western shore of Jekyll on the Inland Waterway. The Golf Course was across the Island near the beach.

These Jekyll cottages included those built by Charles S. Maurice; Frank H. Goodyear; Walter Rogers Furness; Edwin Gould; Frank M. Gould; Walter T. Jennings; M. Bayard Brown; Gordon McKay, who sold to William Rockefeller, who in turn sold to Mrs. Helen Hartley Jenkins; H. K. Porter, who sold to John Claflin; William Struthers, who sold to V. Everit Macy; Joseph Pulitzer, who sold to J. J. Albright; Mrs. George F. Shrady, who sold to Dr. Walter B. James; N. K. Fairbank, who sold to Walton Ferguson; and Frederick Baker, whose cottage was occupied by President and Mrs. William McKinley on the occasion of their visit to Jekyll and was later burned, the site then being used by the R. T. Crane cottage.

The Jekyll Island Club's last season was 1941. The attack on Pearl Harbor in December of that year cancelled all plans for the opening of the Club and, in 1947, Jekyll Island was purchased by the State of Georgia for a State Park.

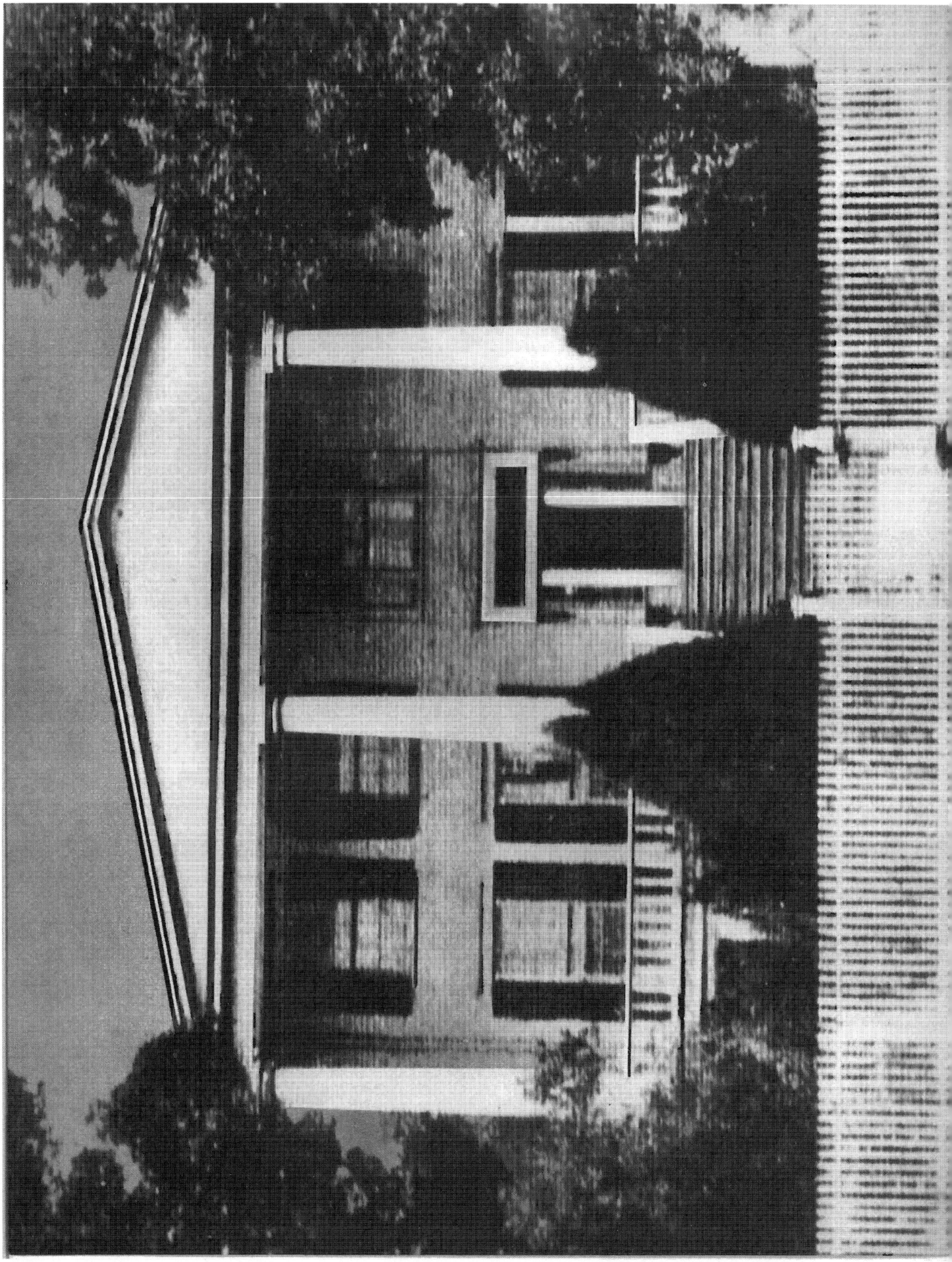

Orange Hall, St. Marys, Georgia

This beautiful ante-bellum mansion, the home of the Rev. Mr. Horace Pratt and his wife, Jane (Wood) Pratt, stood just across the street from the St. Marys Presbyterian Church, of which the Rev. Mr. Pratt was the minister.

The building was constructed for Jane (Wood) Pratt by her mother, Mrs. John Wood of St. Marys. John Wood (1752-1829) and his wife, Laila (Drysdale) Wood (1743-1830), together with their daughter, Jane (Wood) Pratt, are buried on the grounds of the St. Marys Presbyterian Church.

Orange Hall is considered a perfect example of the Greek Revival type of architecture. Every detail is correct — the doors, the windows, the fluted columns with their Doric capitals. It is the sort of house which would have been built in town; on the plantation such a house would have had the kitchen in the separate building a short distance from the "big house."

Such a house, with its spacious rooms, calls to mind the day when social life was centered in the home, when living itself was an art, and the home told of the occupants, of their way of life and of the joy of such living. Its style was reserved and in the good taste and simple elegance which has been cherished by cultivated people throughout the ages.

These were people who enjoyed the hospitality of their friends and delighted in entertaining; their doors were open to friend and stranger alike; and each, according to his rank — the gentleman in the drawing room or the humble traveler in the kitchen — was always welcome.

It was a charming life. There was no great wealth as we know it to-day, but everyone had food and raimant, and there was peace. There was no splendor, no style, no show, but sincerity, with gaiety and heartiness, genuineness and refinement. In this picture of Orange Hall the memory of this era still lingers.

[103]

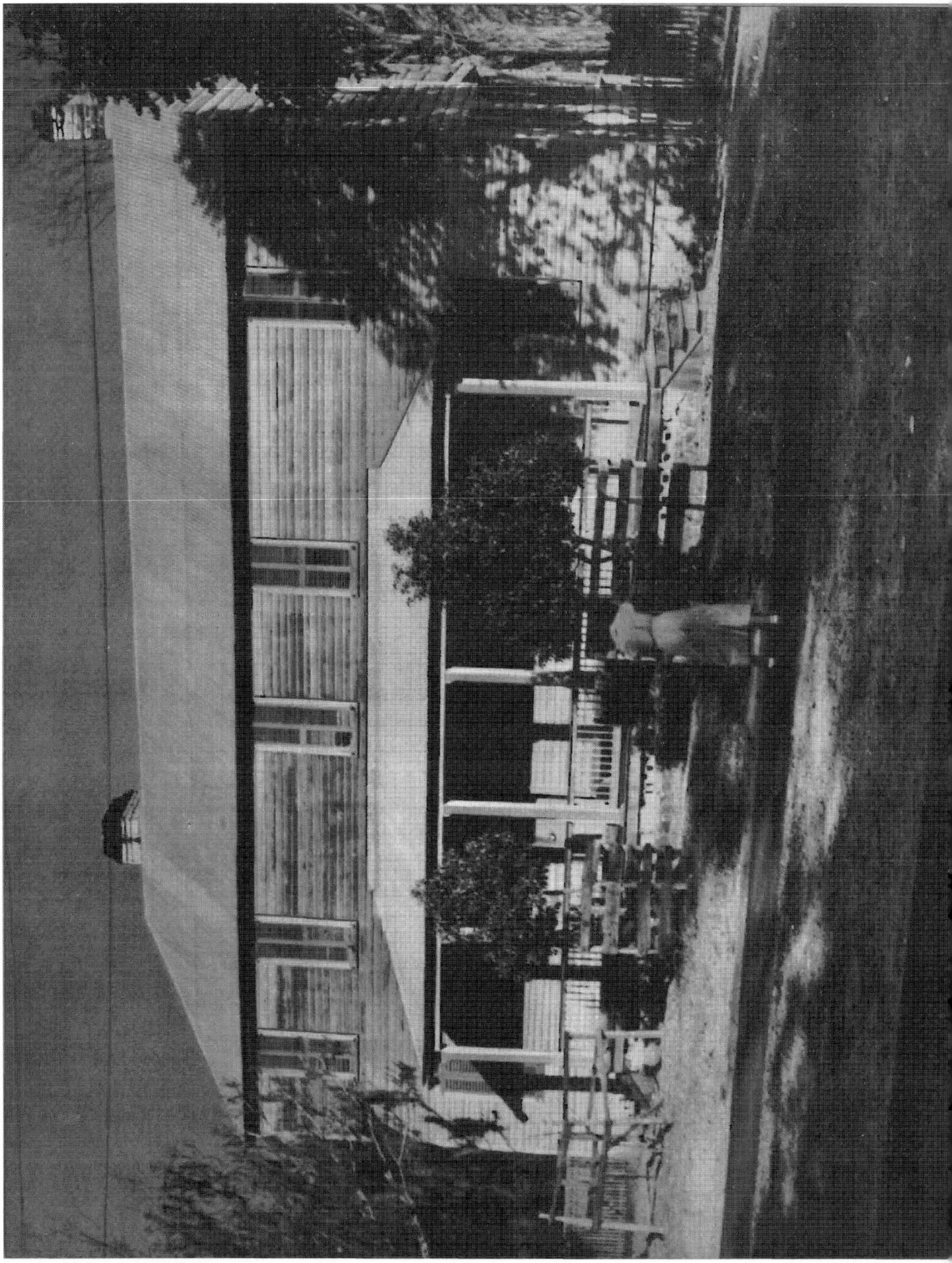

Residence of Major Archibald Clark, St. Marys, Georgia

This house, standing across the street from Orange Hall, was the home of Major Archibald Clark. Major Clark was a native of Savannah and attended the famous Litchfield Law School at Litchfield, Conn. Settling in St. Marys in 1802, he began the practice of law and a few years later was named by President Thomas Jefferson as Collector of the Port of St. Marys.

At that time this was a position of importance since St. Marys was the most southern port in the United States (Florida was then a Spanish Province) and through it came the commerce from the West Indies. Clark held this post under nine presidents, serving until his death in 1848.

While living here Major Clark entertained many notables, including Aaron Burr, Vice-President of the United States, and Gen. Winfield Scott of the United States Army.

Clark and Burr had been friends for many years, having attended the Litchfield Law School together. In 1804, following the duel with Alexander Hamilton, which resulted in Hamilton's death, Burr sought refuge on St. Simons Island where he spent five weeks at Hampton, or Butler Point, the Sea Island cotton plantation of Major Pierce Butler. During this time Burr went to St. Marys to visit Major Clark, making the trip by boat down the Inland Waterway and, after his St. Marys visit, continuing his journey south as far as the St. Johns River, before returning to St. Simons.

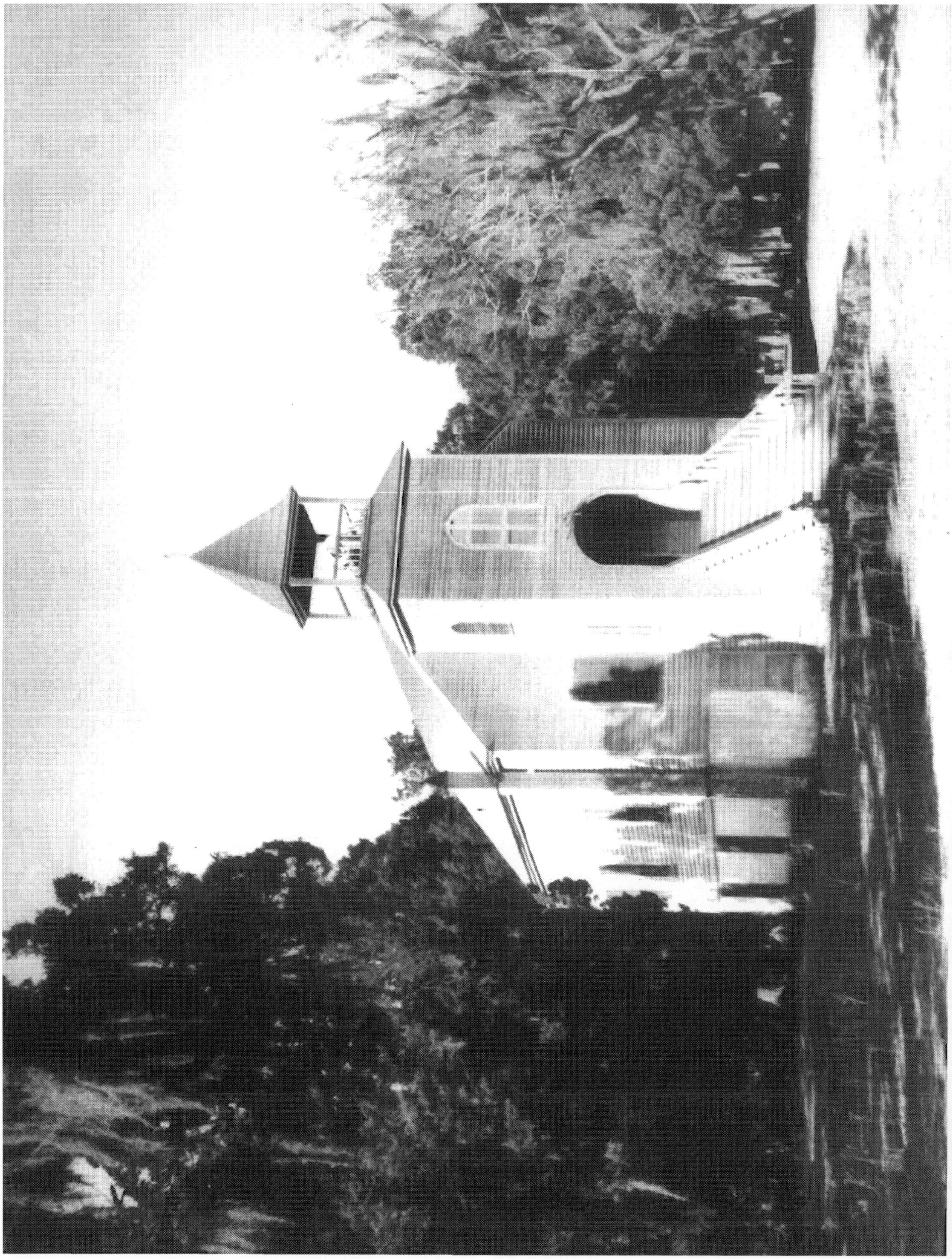

St. Marys Presbyterian Church

Built in 1808, this church was used by all the denominations who cared to worship there. In 1828, it was incorported as the Independent Presbyterian Church of St. Marys. It is one of the oldest churches still in use in our State.

Georgia's oldest church building is the Salzburger Church, Jerusalem Lutheran Church, at Ebenezer, Effingham County, which was completed in 1767. Our second oldest church, built in 1792, is Midway Congregational Church in Liberty County, and this Presbyterian Church at St. Marys is next, being the third oldest.

One of the early ministers of this St. Marys Presbyterian Church was the Rev. Horace Pratt, who lived across the street from the church in the beautiful mansion, Orange Hall.

In those days St. Marys was a thriving port with commerce from the West Indies and other foreign ports. Then, as now, efforts were made to smuggle goods into port so as to avoid the payment of duty.

There is a story which has been handed down from generation to generation that tells of the successful evasion of these charges by a group who used a unique method. As the story goes, one night they took the minister's horse from his stable. Leading the animal up the steep steps of the church to the vestibule, they tied the bell rope to his head. The horse in his efforts to free himself shook his head thus pulling the bell rope and causing the bell to ring. The ringing of the bell brought the townspeople to the church. While they gathered around, wondering how the horse got into the vestibule and speculating as to how to get it safely down the steps, the smugglers landed their goods.

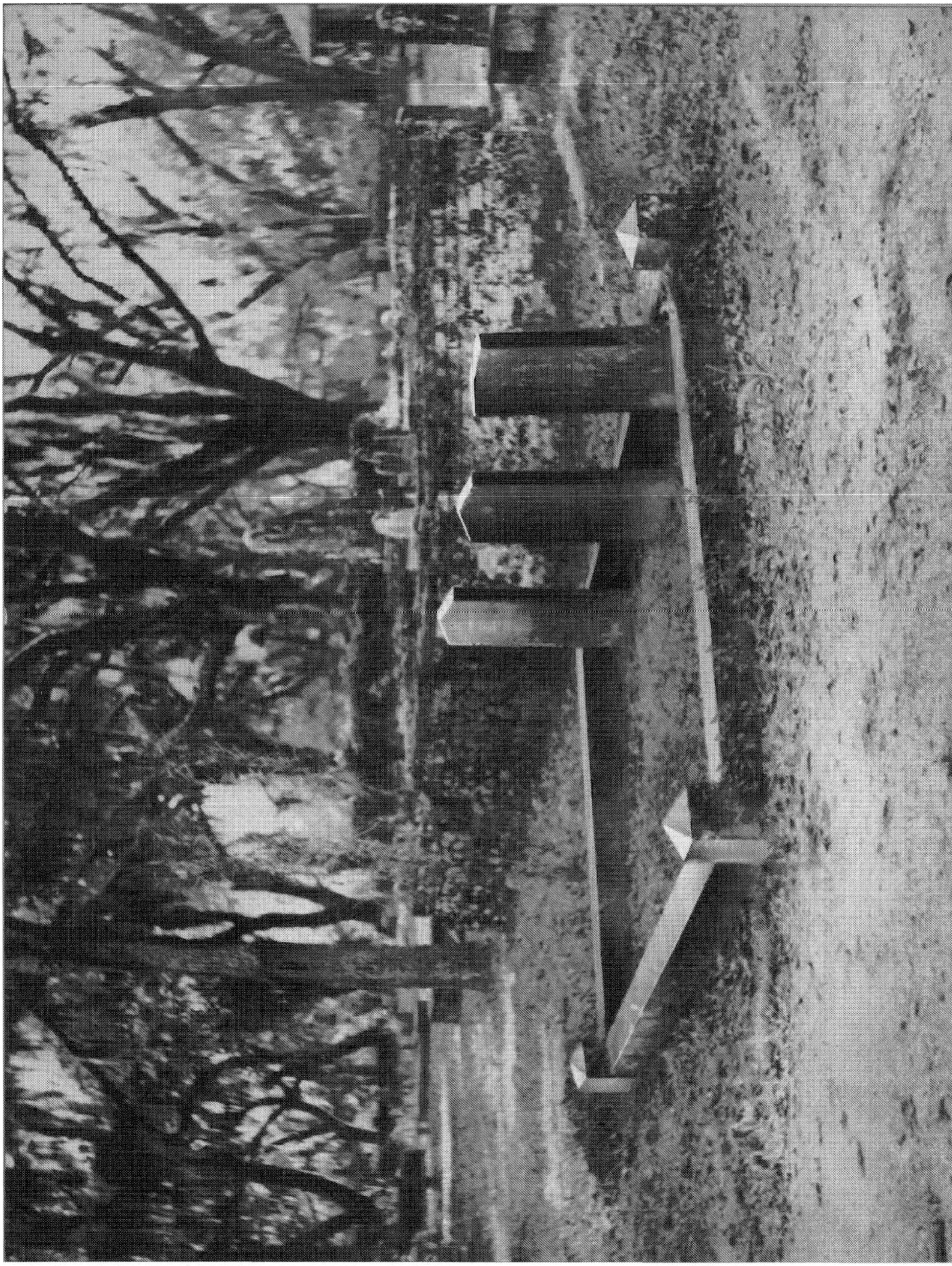

Oak Grove Cemetery, St. Marys, Georgia

Set in a grove of moss-draped live oaks, this silent City of the Dead presents a restful and peaceful scene. Here, for more than a century and a half have been interred the bodies of the citizens of St. Marys. Among its sleeping members there is a soldier of every war this country has ever fought. The inscription on the tombstone of one of these Revolutionary soldiers states that he was "at the memorable Battle of Little York which terminated the War."

Throughout the cemetery the tombstones tell the history of St. Marys and its people. Here one learns of the terrible yellow fever epidemic of 1801, which wiped out a family whose bodies were placed in a single grave and their names engraved on one stone.

Another marker, with an inscription that covers all four sides, tells of a lady who, "AFTER TRAVELLING DURING THE SUMMER, . . . IN UN-USUALLY FINE HEALTH HAD REACHED NEW YORK ON HER RETURN TO THE SOUTH. WHILE THERE SHE WAS URGENTLY SOLICITED TO COMFORT BY HER PRESENCE A SICK (DYING) FRIEND WHO WAS ALSO ON A VISIT TO THE NORTH. SHE HASTENED TO COMPLY AND IN TWO HOURS WAS ON HER WAY TO NEW JERSEY. HER BENEVOLENT ATTENTIONS WERE SOON AR-RESTED BY DISEASE, THERE CONTRACTED WHICH SHE EARLY BELIEVED TO BE UNTO DEATH. IN ONE BRIEF MONTH (NEAR NEW MARKET, N.J.) WITH HER MIND PERFECTLY UNCLOUDED, WITHOUT A GROAN, OR A SIGH — SHE PEACEFULLY RESIGNED HER SPIRIT TO HIM WHO GAVE IT."

Scattered throughout this cemetery are small enclosures surrounded by solid brick walls. These are family burial plots of persons who were members of the Roman Catholic Church, these individual plots having been blessed as holy ground. In the enclosure pictured here there are two interesting tombstones, with the inscriptions in French, which are shown in the next picture.

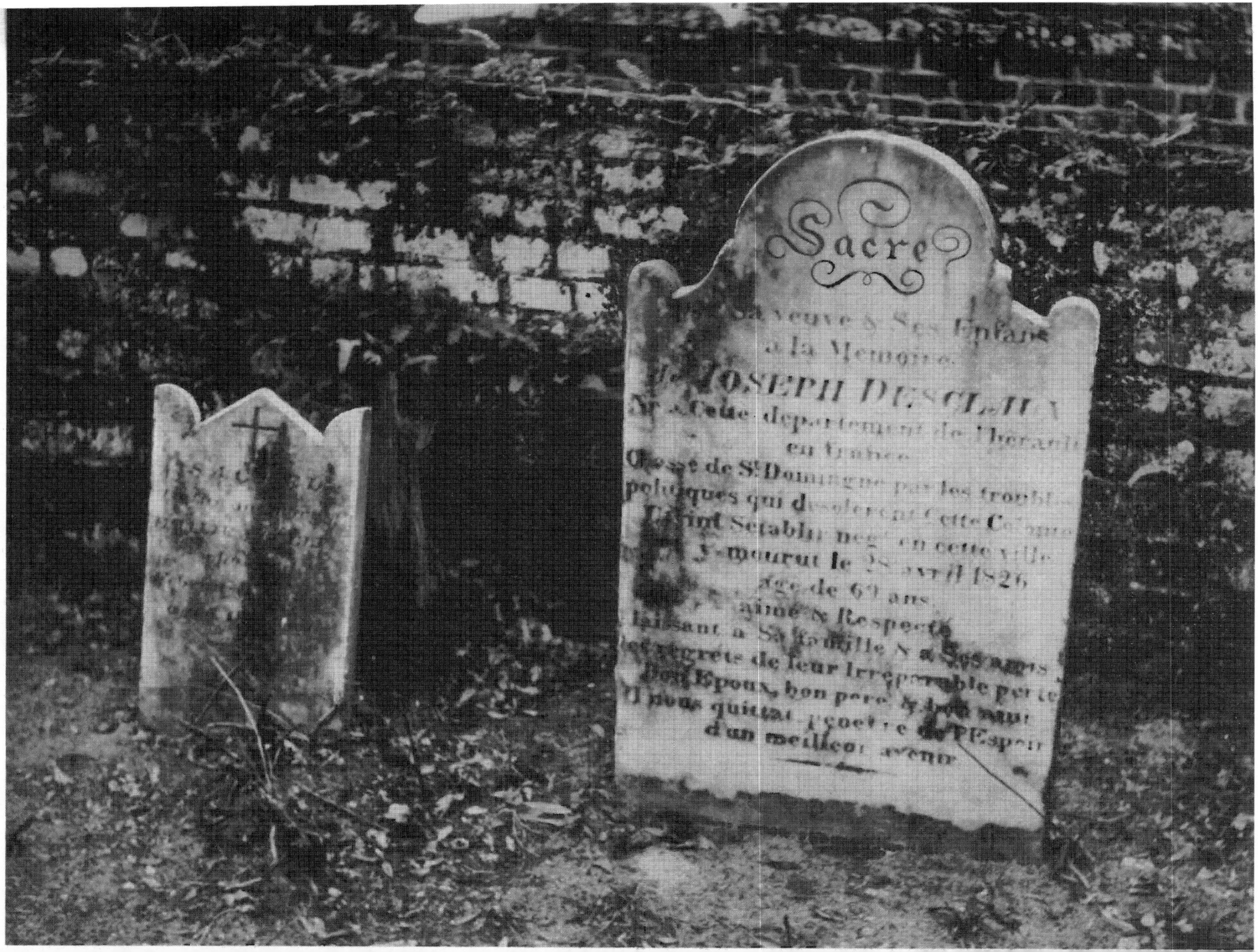
Sacre
a la Memoire
JOSEPH
en France
age de 69 ans
d'un meilleur avenir

The French at St. Marys

The smaller stone, to the left, marks the grave of Marguerite Comeau, a native of Acadia — one of Evangeline's people.

Driven from their homes in Nova Scotia, these people were loaded into vessels and scattered along the coast. Two vessels, one loaded with 120 women and children and the other with 280 men, came into Savannah in December, 1755. Governor Ellis supplied them with provisions and hired boats to carry some of them to plantations throughout Georgia; others built huts for themselves near Savannah. They proved to be "... useful to the Colony as they employed themselves making oars, hand spikes, and other implements for sea craft that are readily bought up ..." Many built boats in which they left the Colony, though several years later there were about one hundred Acadians still in Georgia. Not wishing to dwell among "another race with other customs and language," these unhappy French people left Georgia and joined others of their group in searching for a home to replace the one they had lost. Some found refuge in San Domingo and other French Colonies, while others settled in various parts of our nation.

"Written their history stands on tablets of stone in the churchyards."

The larger stone, on the right, marks the grave of Joseph Desclaux, one of those driven out of San Domingo by the slave insurrection of 1791. Fleeing from their plantations, with only those possessions they were able to gather in haste, these San Domingan refugees were landed at various ports up and down the coast, where they settled down to a new life in a new land. Many of them had no experience or qualifications which would enable them to earn a living, except that they were well educated, and so they taught school. In these schools the youth of our land learned not only the essentials of the education of the day; but they absorbed the culture of the Old World from a people who had lost all their worldly possessions, but who never lost their spirit and whose contribution to the Nation that gave them refuge was most valuable.

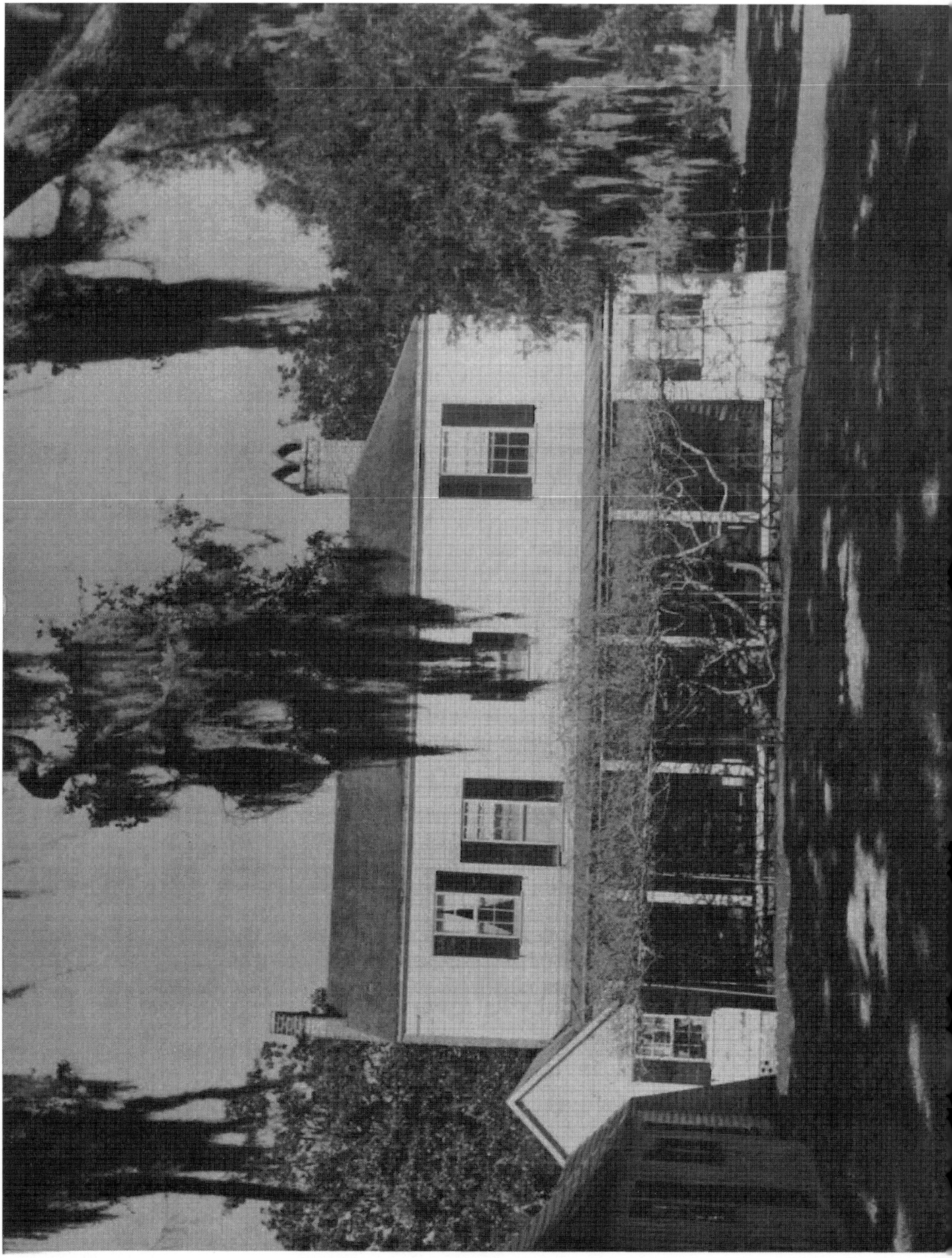

Hofwyl Plantation

Hofwyl Plantation is part of a large rice plantation, known as Broadfield, which was the property of William Brailsford and his wife, Maria (Heyward) Brailsford. It later came into the Troup family through the marriage of their daughter, Camilla Brailsford, to Dr. James McGilvary Troup. A daughter of this marriage, Ophelia Troup, married George C. Dent and her portion of the estate was called Hofwyl in honor of the school in Switzerland where Mr. Dent was educated.

This house, built in 1851, is the oldest residence in Glynn County. It was intended for the use of the overseer, but the plantation house at Broadfield having burned, the family moved here.

During the summer months rice plantations were not considered safe at night for white people since it was believed that breathing the "miasma" which rose at sunset would cause malaria fever. Therefore, families left the rice plantations in April and did not return until after a heavy frost. Many of the plantation families spent the summer at Waynesville, a popular resort nearby. However, the Dents spent the days at Hofwyl and the nights at a cottage located on salt water and in the "pine barrens," a situation considered safe.

Every afternoon, before sunset, the family left Hofwyl to drive four miles to "The Parsonage," carrying the evening meal which Fibby had prepared at Hofwyl to be served by Fanny Proudfoot, the cook at The Parsonage. Breakfast was eaten at The Parsonage before starting back to Hofwyl. Each and every day during the "dangerous" months of summer this trip was made.

James T. Dent, having read of the experiments which were being conducted to prove that mosquitoes were carriers of fevers, concluded that if his home could be thoroughly screened it would not be necessary to leave Hofwyl at night. Accordingly, he screened this house and, in 1903, for the first time the family spent the entire summer at Hofwyl. Mr. Dent was the first person in this section to demonstrate that malaria was contracted through the bite of the mosquito.

Hofwyl has remained in one family for a century and a half, through five generations. It is the last of the old plantations of this area; rice was planted here on a commercial scale as late as 1912.

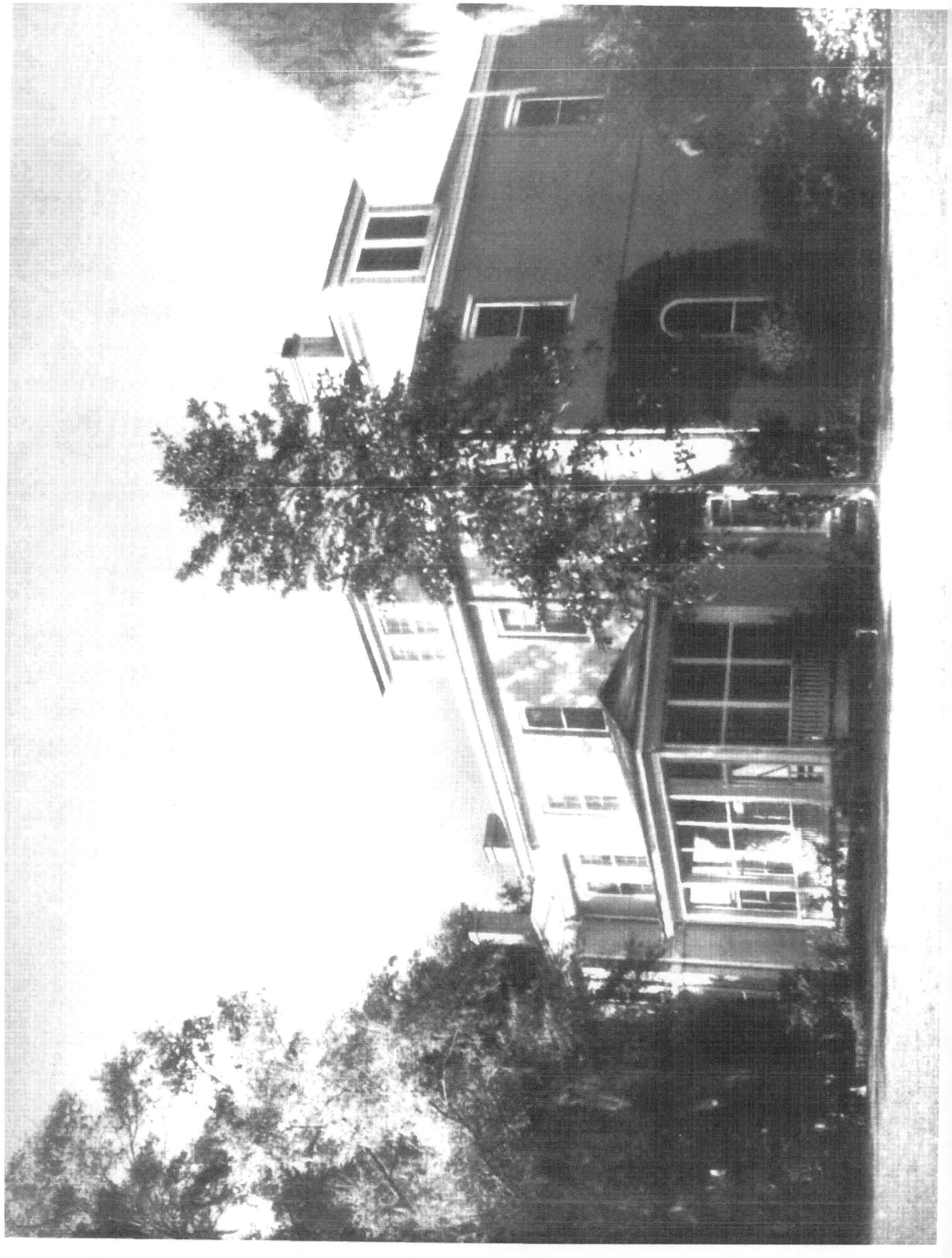

Altama

Altama was formerly part of Hopeton Plantation which had been granted to William Hopeton of South Carolina, who sold it to John Couper of Cannon's Point Plantation, St. Simons Island. John Couper, in turn, sold Hopeton to his friend James Hamilton, and to his son, James Hamilton Couper. James Hamilton divided his time between his residence in Philadelphia and Hopeton Plantation, while James Hamilton Couper resided at Hopeton and managed the plantation.

After the death of Mr. Hamilton, James Hamilton Couper negotiated with the Corbon heirs, grandchildren of Mr. Hamilton, for the purchase of their part of the southern part of Hopeton. Here, in 1857, he built this tabby residence, Altama, which was his home for the remainder of his life. Altama is the only plantation residence built of tabby still standing in Glynn County.

James Hamilton Couper was one of Georgia's distinguished sons. A Yale graduate of the Class of 1814, he was a recognized authority on scientific subjects and one of the leading agriculturists of the South. His library was one of the finest in the country; he was a conchologist, an ornithologist, a paleontologist, a herpetologist, his opinions being sought by specialists in these fields. Many of these scientists visited Mr. Couper and wrote of their visits, giving an intimate picture of life on his plantation. He was a pioneer in the production of sugar and molasses. His sugar mill, built in 1829, was the finest ever erected in the State of Georgia and was pronounced "equal to any . . . in the West Indies or Louisiana."

However, James Hamilton Couper was to enjoy his beautiful Altama estate for only a short time. In a few years war brought great changes and Mr. Couper lived to experience the full extent of this tragedy. He died here in 1866.

In 1914 Altama and Hopeton became the property of William Du-Pont, who remodelled the Altama house to its present state. These plantations were acquired in 1933 by Cator Woolford of Atlanta, who built the Playhouse and landscaped the grounds. In 1945 Altama and Hopeton were purchased by Mr. and Mrs. Alfred William Jones of Sea Island.

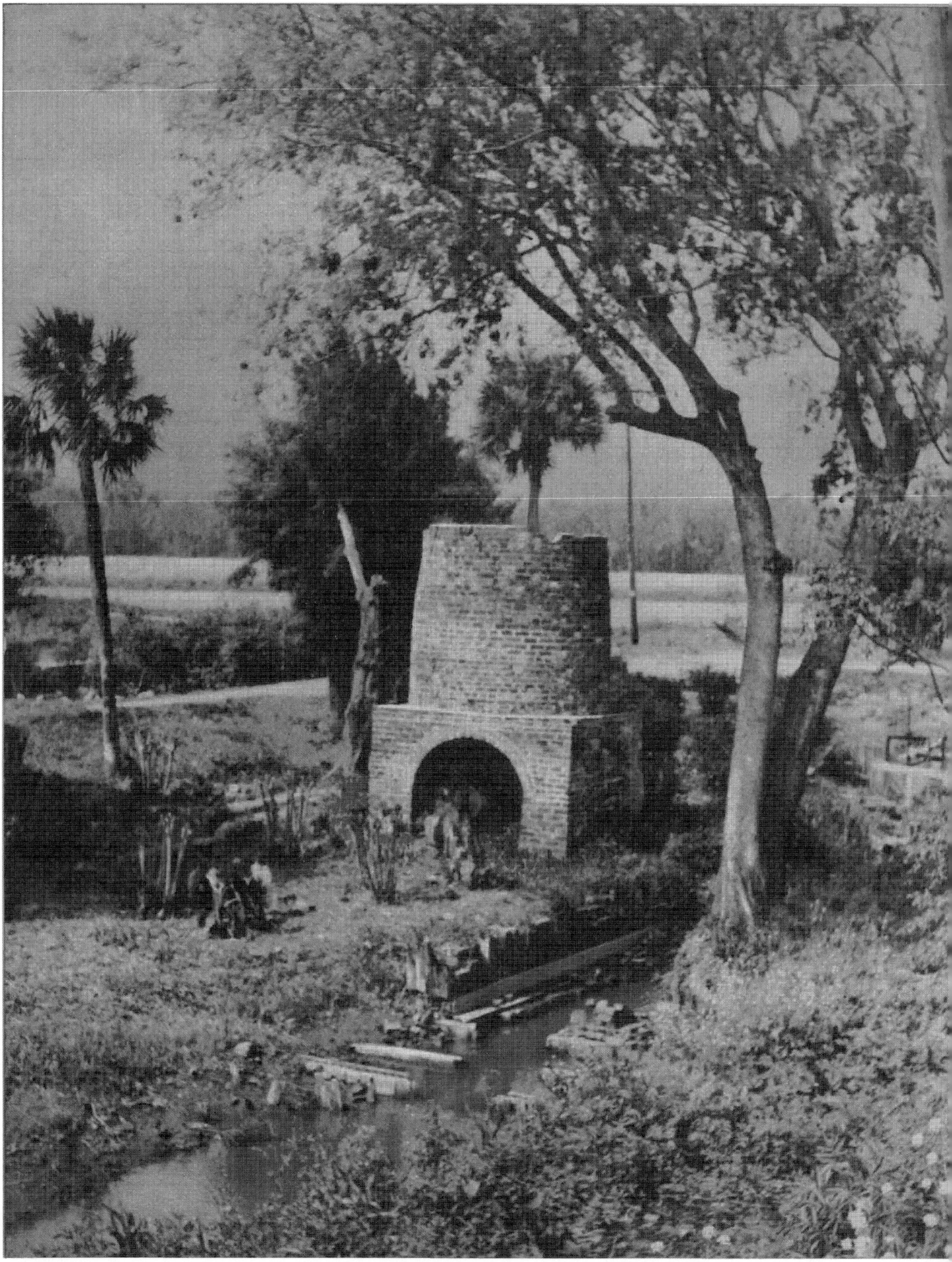

Old Rice Mill on Butler Island

This old rice mill brings to mind the contrast between the use of machinery and the primitive method used by the Negroes in preparing rice for cooking. To thresh the grain the sheaves of rice were spread on a sheet and beaten with a flail so as to break the grain from the stalk. This was a most picturesque operation, with the worker swinging the double-jointed flair-stick high in the air, bringing it down on the sheaves, and singing the words of the "Flail Song":

Blow, Tony, blow; O, blow, Tony; Blow, Tony; Blow, Tony, blow!
I whip dis rice an' I whip 'em so; Blow, Tony, blow!
I whip dis rice and I whip 'em so; Blow, Tony, blow!
Blow, Tony, blow; Blow, Tony; Blow, Tony, blow;
I whip dis rice, go down to de groun';
Blow, Tony, blow; Blow, Tony; Blow, Tony; Blow, Tony, blow;
O, blow, Tony; Blow Tony; Blow Tony, blow!

Next, the grain and straw were scooped up into a large round tray with a slanting rim, known as a "fanner," and "fanned" to separate the straw from the grain. Since the wind was needed to blow away the light straw, the Negroes whistled and called for the wind; and, to all the Negroes of this area, the wind was "Tony."

Each grain of rice is encased in a tough fibrous husk and to remove this they used a hand-made mortar and pestle. A small amount of rice was put into the mortar and beaten with the pestle. Sometimes one worker used two pestles; but more often two workers or even three, could keep as many pestles operating in perfect unison. Always, as they worked, they sang:

Peas, peas,
Peas an' rice, peas an' rice, peas an' rice, dun dun.
O shucks!
Peas dun dun; O, peas dun dun.
O, peas an' rice; Peas an' rice; Peas an' rice, dun dun.
O, peas dun dun; O, peas dun dun;
O, peas an' rice; Peas an' rice dun dun.

Again the fanner was used to separate the rice from the husk, to the accompaniment of whistling and calling the wind:

O Wind; Come, Wind; Come blow my rice; Come, Tony;
Come, Tony!

[117]

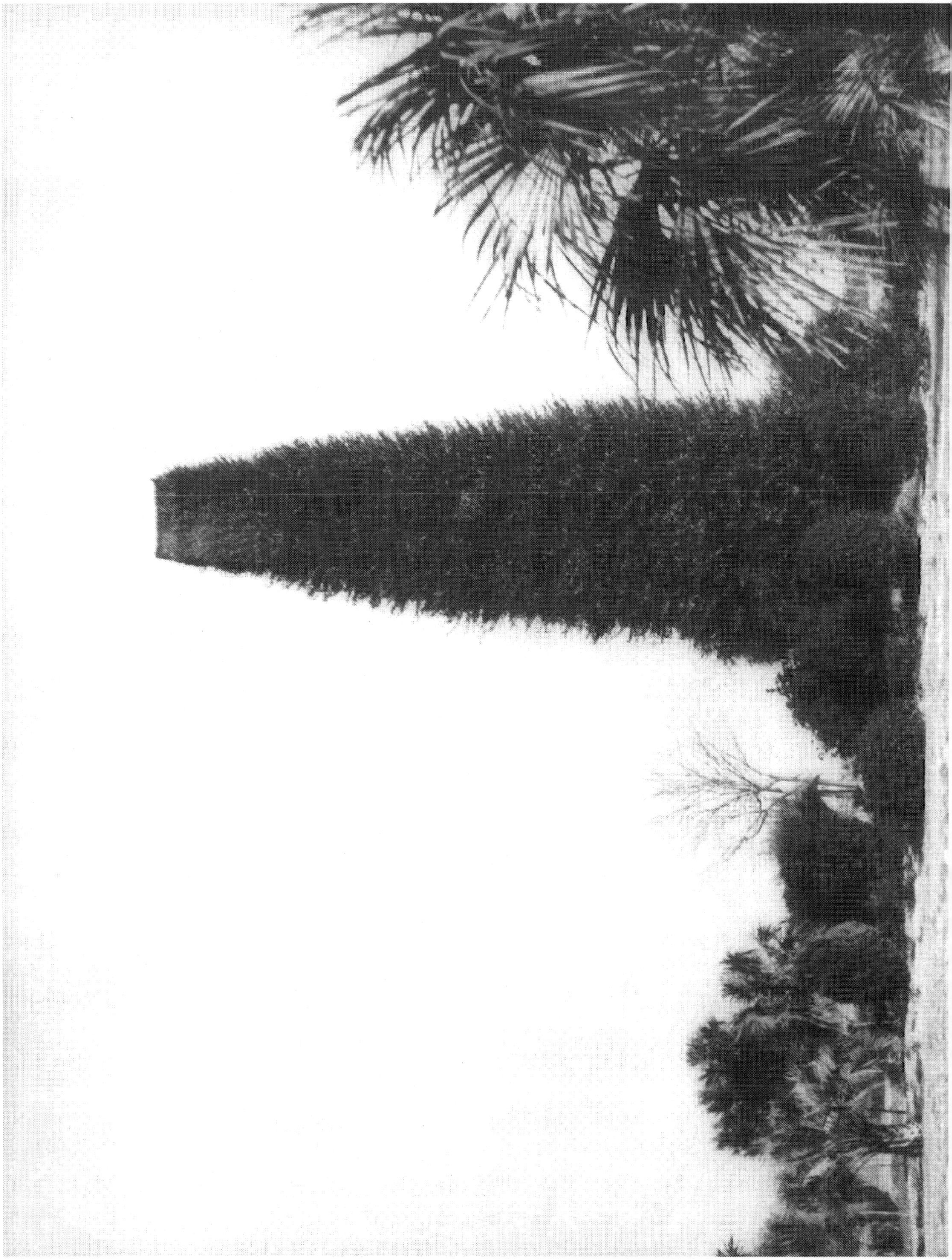

Rice Mill Chimney on Butler Island

Soon after the Revolutionary War this island came into the possession of Major Pierce Butler, whose grandson of the same name married Fanny Kemble, noted English actress and violent abolitionist. It was on this island that Fanny Kemble spent two months. Arriving at the close of the year 1838, she left in February 1839 to go to the Sea Island cotton plantation of the Butlers on St. Simons Island.

Butler was one of the finest rice islands in the delta of the Altamaha River. The rich alluvial soil found on these islands and the banks of the river was utilized for the culture of rice, the golden grain which brought wealth to this section long before cotton was "king."

The planter chose a location up the river far enough to get away from salt water, for salt water kills rice; yet, not so far from the ocean but that the tide would influence the height of the waters of the river, as he depended on the daily rise and fall of the tide to flood or drain the fields. Generally this meant that the lands along the river for a distance of about ten miles were devoted to the culture of rice. These rice plantations were located on all the large streams of this coastal area from the Cape Fear River in North Carolina to the St. Johns River in Florida.

Even before the Revolutionary War, steam mills were in operation along this Rice Coast for the preparation of the grain for market. On Butler Island there were three mills — one run by steam, one by the tide, and one by horse. This chimney of the old steam mill and a portion of the mill shown in the next picture, along with the canals, are all that is left of Butler Island's rice era.

In 1926, Butler and its neighboring island, Champney, were acquired by the late Col. T. L. Huston, who repaired the old "banks," installed modern flood gates, and planted the fields in lettuce and other truck crops. Butler and Champney Islands became the property of Richard J. Reynolds in 1949. In 1954 nine of these islands in the Altamaha Delta, formerly rice plantations — Butler, Champney, General's, Broughton, Rhett, Camber's, Vivian, Wright's, and Carr's Islands — were made a waterfowl reservation under the name, Butler Island Waterfowl Management Area.

[119]

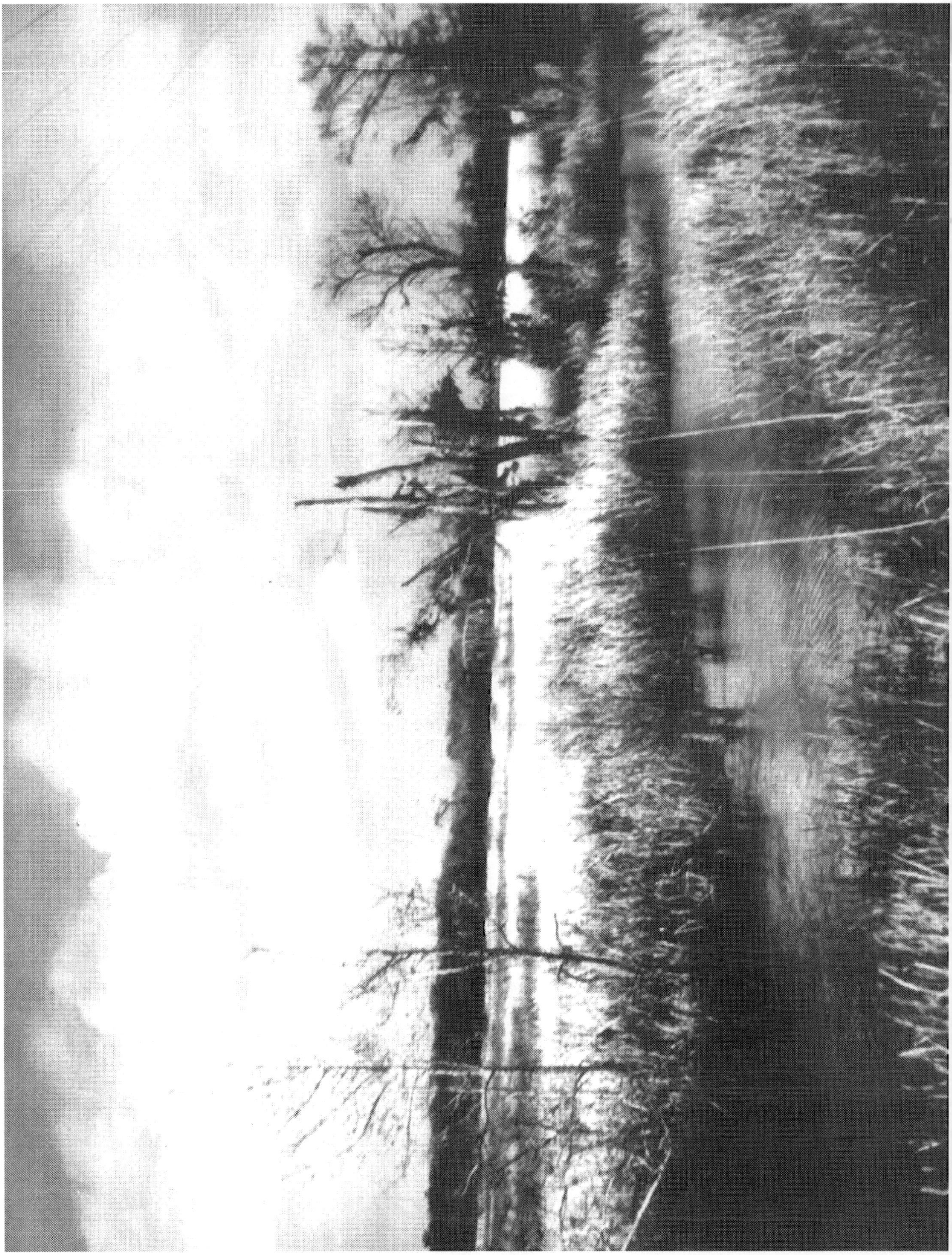

Rice Field Canal

Today, as one looks down from the air on these abandoned rice fields, the checkered pattern of the canals and "drains" stands out so clearly that it would seem the lands were ready for planting again. These canals and smaller drains were dug by slave labor, working with a shovel and a wheelbarrow; and the earth removed in making the canal was used to make the "banks." The larger canals not only brought water to the fields but furnished navigation for the flat boats on which the rice was transported from the fields to the barnyard, while the banks were broad enough to be used as roads.

The flood gates, known as "trunks," were wooden culverts with a hanging door at either end. These were installed in the banks and through them the water flowed with the doors at either end controlling the flow.

Seed was planted on the new moon and the full moon to take advantage of the higher tides which prevailed at those times, since this would guarantee sufficient water to flood the fields.

The planting of a field was completed without delay and the lands were flooded immediately. This was done to hasten the sprouting of the grain, to keep birds from eating the seed, and to kill grass. Fields were flooded when the tide was high and drained when the tide was low. This first flow, known as the "sprout flow," remained on the fields from three to six days, depending on the warmth of the weather; then the fields were drained and the crop cultivated. Next, the "stretch flow" held the water on the crop for about two weeks and was followed by a period of dry cultivation of about forty days, though the length of time for these "flows" and for the dry cultivation varied with the whim of the planter. Finally, came the "harvest flow" which remained on the crop until time for the harvest, which ran from late August through October.

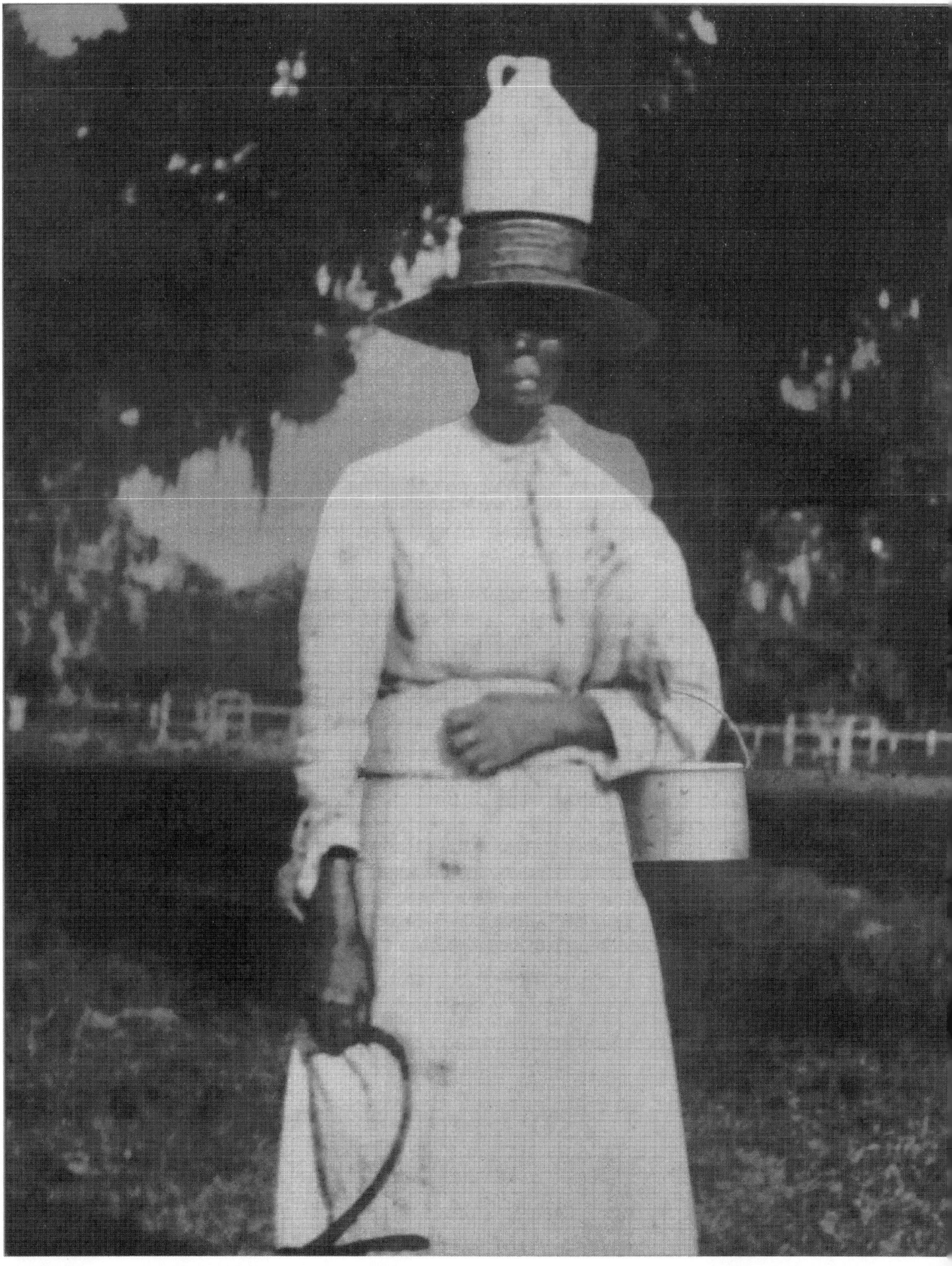

Dido, a Rice Field Worker

Dido is ready for her day's work in the rice field. She has her lunch in the bucket on her arm, drinking water in the jug on her head, and carries in her hand the "rice hook," or sickle, with which she will cut the rice. Since the rice fields were wet and boggy and women's dresses of that day were ankle-length, women working in the fields shortened their skirts by tying a string around their hips and pulling their skirts up. This formed a bloused portion which looked like a bustle all around their body.

When the fields were ready for the harvest, the water was drawn off and the workers went in to cut the rice. Grasping a handful of rice with the left hand and using the rice hook with the right, the worker cut the stalks about a foot above the ground laying them on the stubble to dry. Later, these bunches of rice were tied in sheaves and stored in the barnyard until such time as they were carried to the plantation mill and threshed.

Ships came to the plantation wharves to load the rough rice (with the husk on the grain) in bulk into the hold and carry it to market, where the factor handled the sale for the owner. In the large rice centers, Savannah and Charleston, pounding mills removed the husk from the grain. Butler Island, however, had a pounding mill of its own. The grain, after husking, was placed in tierces — large barrels, averaging about seven hundred pounds net weight. Some of the Butler rice was shipped to the members of the Butler family in Philadelphia, but the bulk was marketed in Charleston. In 1845 Butler Island sold 7500 bu. of rough rice and 1157¾ tierces, a total of 998,717 lbs.

Rice was a crop that gave employment to the plantation workers the year around. The planting, cultivating and harvesting of the crop occupied the spring, summer and fall months, while the threshing and preparing the crop for market was winter's work. As soon as this was completed, it was time to give attention to cleaning the ditches, repairing the banks, and rebuilding trunks.

The plantation blacksmith made the plows, shovels, hoes, rakes, nails, bolts, and any other iron goods needed on the plantation, while the carpenter built the wooden trunks as well as the tierces and any and every other piece of needed equipment.

[123]

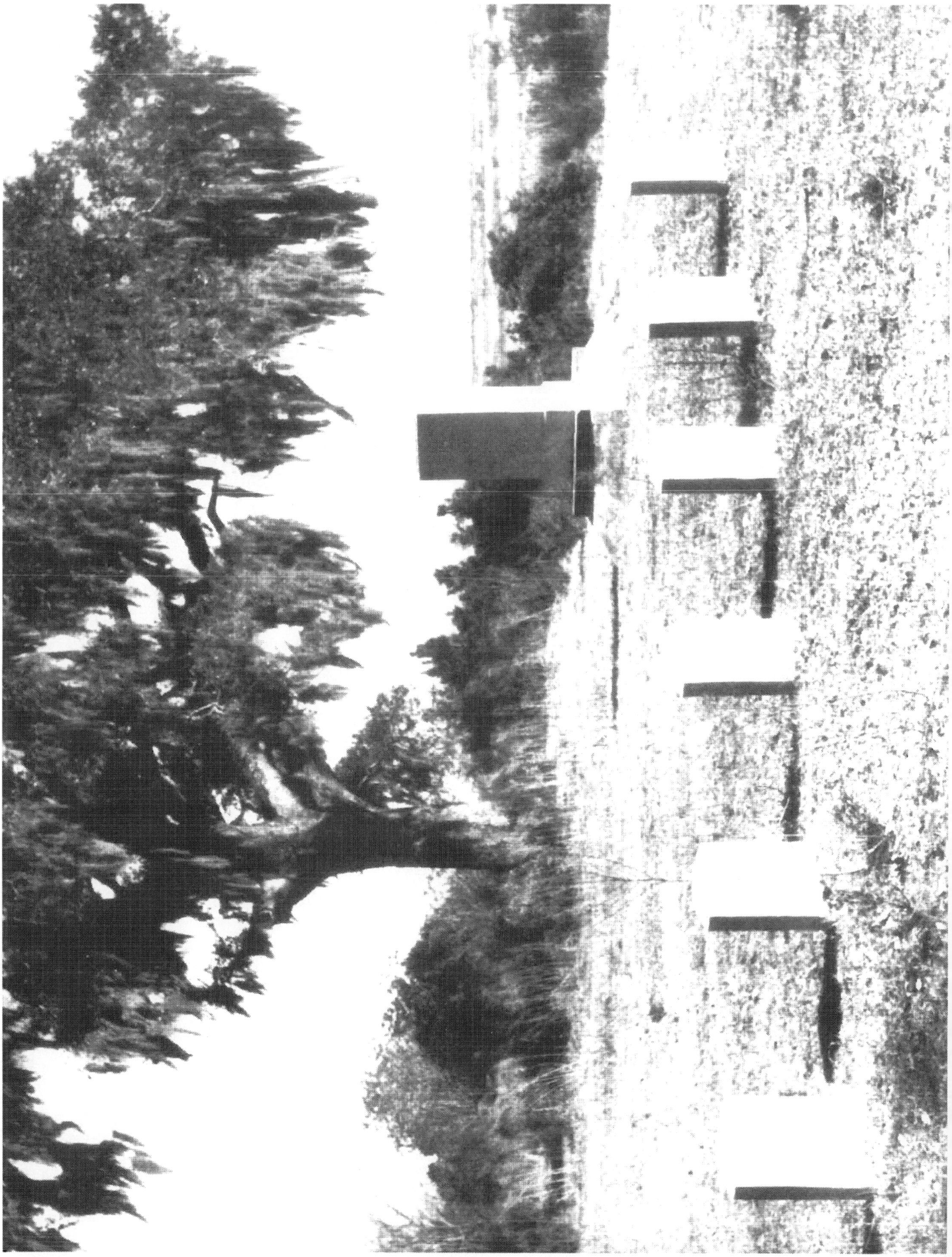

Fort King George

Situated on a bluff just east of the present site of Darien, Fort King George was the first British settlement in what is now the State of Georgia and represented Great Britain's first effort to establish her claim to The Debatable Land, that strip of the Atlantic Coast between Port Royal and South Carolina and St. Augustine in Florida. Its construction in 1721 by Capt. John Barnwell and his South Carolina scouts, marked the initial step in the long chain of events which led finally to bringing this southeastern section of our country under the British flag.

Barnwell, the greatest planter of the Port Royal District and a veteran of the Indian Wars, was known as "Tuscarora Jack." For the building of his fortification, he chose a high bluff near the salt marshes and a short distance from the northern branch of the Altamaha River. This place had formerly been the site of an Indian village where the Spaniards had maintained a mission, which, in the opinion of Mary Ross, Georgia's historian for this Spanish Era, was Mission Santo Domingo de Talaxe (Talaje). Here Barnwell found extensive fields. He wrote ". . . that all the Land for 4 or 5 mile Round this point being old Indian fields, and lately grown up with Thickets . . ."

Fort King George was a cypress blockhouse twenty-six feet square and twenty-three feet high, with palisaded earthworks and a moat. Palmetto-thatched huts served as barracks for the soldiers of His Majesty's Independent Company stationed here.

During the six years that Fort King George was maintained 140 soldiers died of sickness and disease. They were buried on the bluff near the fort and some of the graves, uncovered in the course of archeological excavations begun in 1940, have been marked. Each grave is that of an "Unknown Soldier," the marker bearing the inscription, *"Soldier of Fort King George"* and a likeness of the British flag of that day.

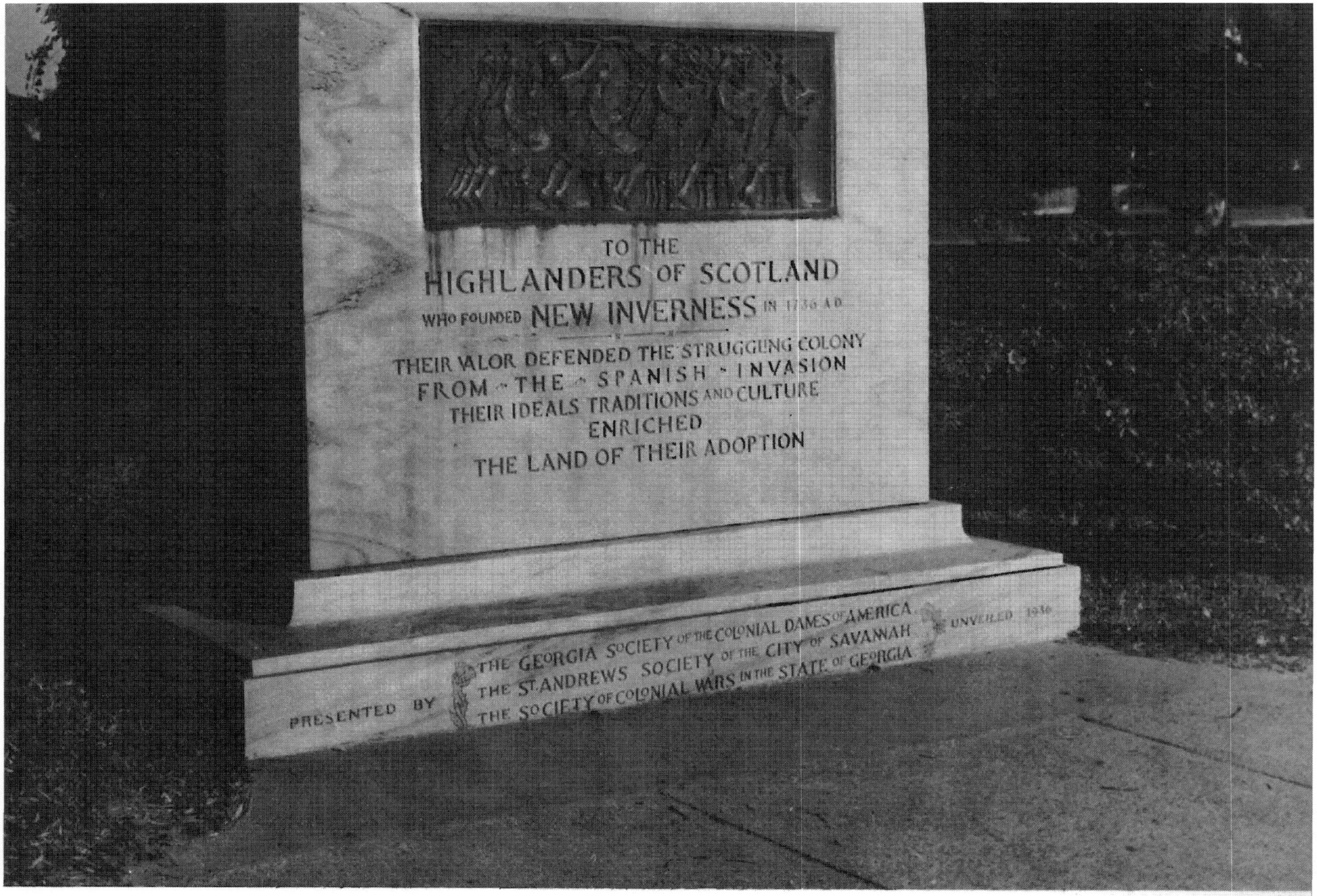
TO THE
HIGHLANDERS OF SCOTLAND
WHO FOUNDED NEW INVERNESS IN 1736 A.D.
THEIR VALOR DEFENDED THE STRUGGLING COLONY
FROM THE SPANISH INVASION
THEIR IDEALS TRADITIONS AND CULTURE
ENRICHED
THE LAND OF THEIR ADOPTION
PRESENTED BY
THE GEORGIA SOCIETY OF THE COLONIAL DAMES OF AMERICA
THE ST. ANDREWS SOCIETY OF THE CITY OF SAVANNAH
THE SOCIETY OF COLONIAL WARS IN THE STATE OF GEORGIA
UNVEILED 1936

The Highlanders of Darien

In commemoration of the bicentennial of the founding of Darien by the Highlanders from Scotland, this beautiful pink Georgia marble marker was erected in 1936 by the Georgia Society of the Colonial Dames of America, the St. Andrews Society of the City of Savannah, and the Society of Colonial Wars in the State of Georgia. The bronze plaque, *Pipes of War,* is the work of the late Dr. R. Tait McKenzie of the University of Pennsylvania and shows the Scottish band with banners flying and bagpipes skirling.

Under the leadership of John Mackintosh Mohr this group of Highlanders from Inverness settled here on the north bank of the Altamaha River, in what was a relocation of old Fort King George. They called their settlement Darien in memory of the ill-fated settlement of their kinsmen on the Isthmus of Darien.

Darien was one of a string of fortified posts which formed this Southern Frontier and these Darien Highlanders were a part of the brave band of fifty men who brought about the victory at Bloody Marsh and made possible the defeat of the Spaniards in the Invasion of 1742.

By the time Darien had reached her centennial, she was the metropolis for the prosperous plantations of the area, whose rice, Sea Island cotton, and sugar were shipped through this port, along with the commerce from Middle Georgia which came down the Altamaha River to the Darien market.

The stage coach from Savannah had regular schedules down the Post Road to Darien and up to the river to Fort Barrington where it was ferried across the Altamaha and continued the trip down the Post Road to Florida.

During the Civil War the town of Darien was burned and after the war its rebirth and prosperity were based on lumber. Floated down the river from the interior of Georgia, rafts of pine logs were cut into lumber by the numerous mills located in Darien and on the islands nearby. Darien was one of the leading lumber ports in the nation and continued to hold this place until all the trees were cut and, lacking raw materials, the mills closed.

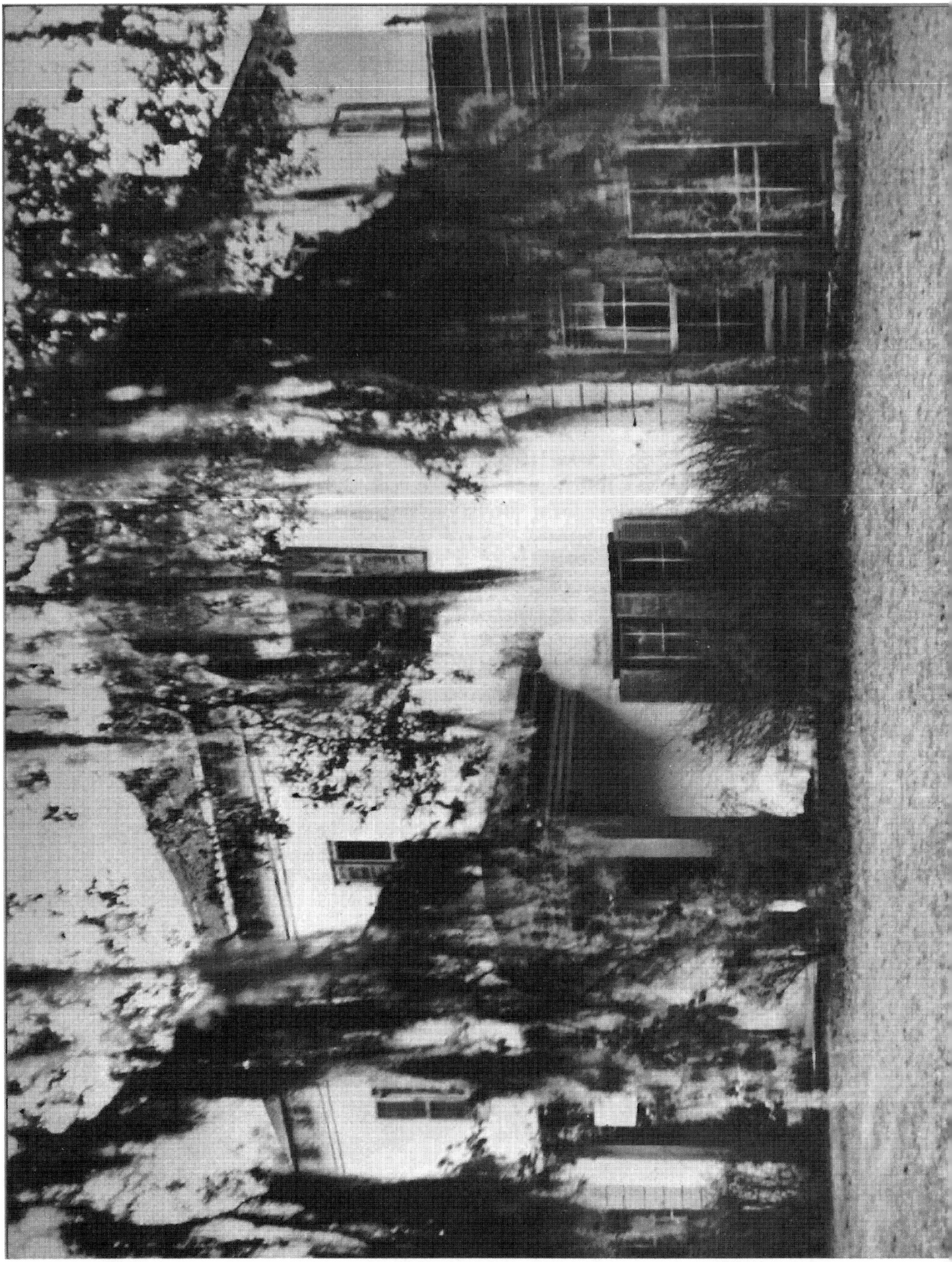

Ashantilly

This beautiful tabby house was built about 1815 by Thomas Spalding of Sapelo to be used as the family home on the mainland. As the Spaldings were heirs of the Barony of Ashantilly in Perthshire, Scotland, he used this Old World name for his New World home. It is now the home of the W. G. Haynes family.

In 1802, Thomas Spalding had purchased Sapelo Island and made it his plantation home. Always experimenting with a new crop, or a better method with an old one, he was ever ready and willing to share all valuable information.

Born in the tabby house which had been Oglethorpe's home on St. Simons, Thomas Spalding grew up amid the vine-clad ruins of Fort Frederica. His great-grandfather, John Mackintosh Mohr, one of the founders of Darien, was captured in the 1740 Invasion of Florida, and spent many months in Spanish prisons. From his grandfather, William McIntosh, who fought at Bloody Marsh, Spalding heard stories which bred in him a veneration for his State. Spalding believed that a man should build for permanence and with him this meant building with tabby. He wrote articles for agricultural journals and demonstrated its use in practically all of the buildings he erected. He was born in a tabby house and it was in a tabby house that he died. Even the tombs of those members of his family who had preceded him in death were built of tabby, though Spalding's own tomb was built of brick!

A member of the 1798 Convention which framed the Constitution of the State of Georgia, he was the last survivor of that body. He served in the Georgia Senate and in the U. S. Congress. Though he served his State and Nation well in many and varied capacities, perhaps he will be remembered best for his work in the Georgia Convention of 1850. Elected president of that body, he threw the full force of his power as its presiding officer, as well as the weight of his influence as Georgia's "elder statesman," to steer the Convention on a course that would keep Georgia in the Union. Thus, Georgia is credited with having postponed secession by a decade. No man worked harder to accomplish this than did Thomas Spalding. As he himself said, "It is perhaps an appropriate termination of my long life." Returning from the Convention, he lived to reach Ashantilly, where he died Jan. 4, 1851.

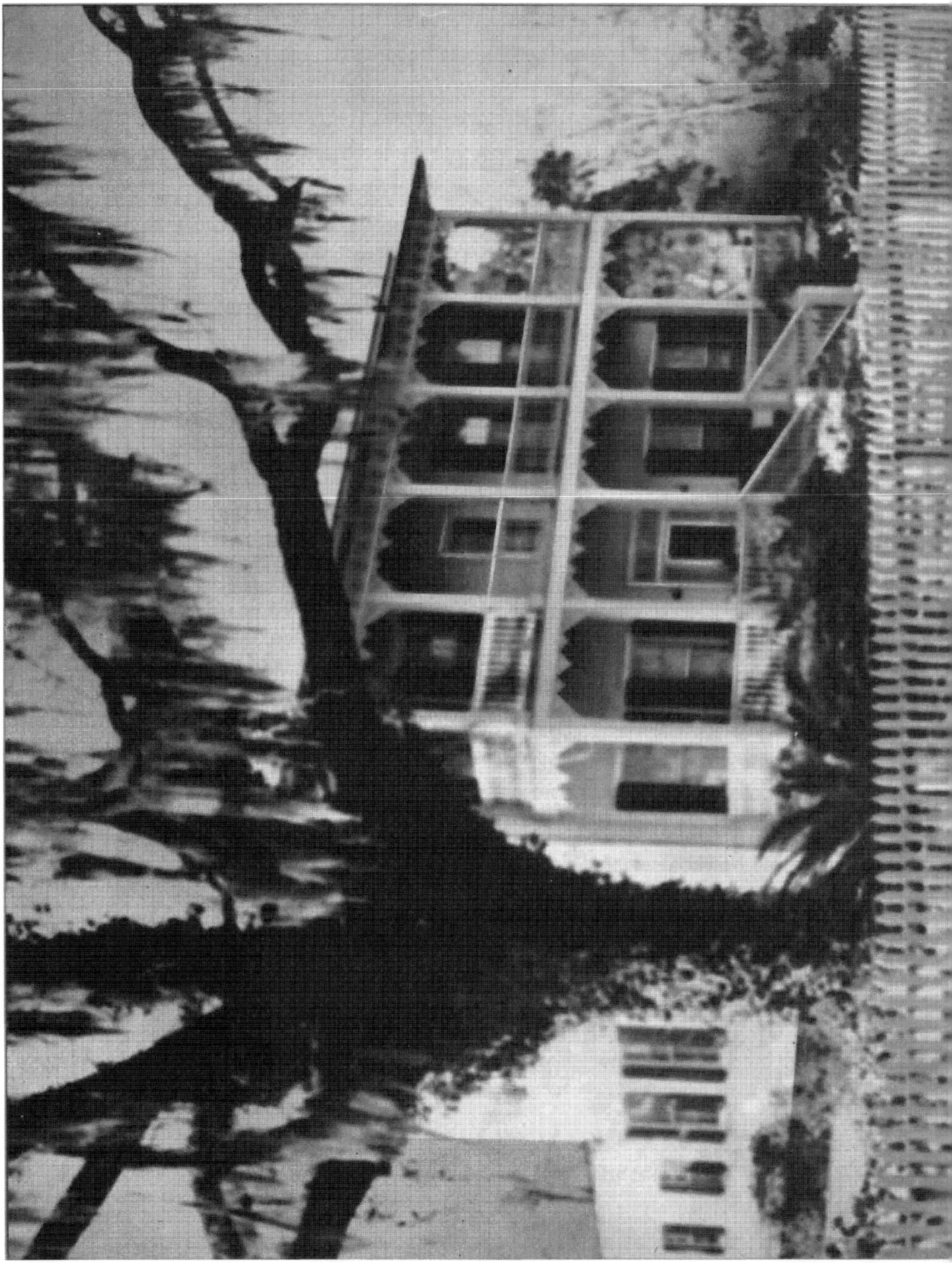

Downey Home, the Ridge, Darien

This and the other beautiful homes on The Ridge, a short distance from Darien, are typical of Darien and its lumber era. Built in 1882 by William Downey, it has been the family home all these years and its timbers are as sound today as the day it was built.

Darien's timber era began soon after the founding of our nation. Great rafts of long leaf yellow pine, cut in the interior of Georgia, were floated down the Altamaha River to Darien. Stored in log booms which lined the waters for miles, the logs were carried to the mills as needed, where they were cut into lumber and shipped to all parts of the world in wooden sailing vessels, which crowded the wharves of the mills waiting for their cargoes.

Generally a raft was made up of about fifty to seventy-five logs. Two of these logs were fastened together to form a V-shaped bow into which the logs were wedged tightly and held in place by cross binders laid on top of the logs. A long piece of timber, called a sweep, dressed to resemble the blade of an oar, and mounted at the bow and a similar piece at the stern, were used to steer the raft around the bends and curves of the river.

Each raft was manned by a crew of three who lived on it during its three or four days' journey down the river. Planks covered with sand were laid on the logs, where a fire could be built and food cooked.

The "raft hands" were a hardy race and lived a rough life. As they moved around the streets of Darien, they could be *heard* even before they were *seen*. Their approach was heralded by the jingle of the tin coffee pot knocking against the iron "skillet." These utensils were fastened to the belt on one side, an axe fastened to the other side, and a great piece of manilla rope coiled over the shoulder. On the streets these "raft hands" mingled with sailors from foreign vessels who made music on their harps and accordions and sang their native songs, all of which gave Darien a cosmopolitan air, very different from that of an inland Georgia community.

But times change! Railroads supplanted river traffic and the close of the century saw the end of Darien's timber era. But this beautiful house, serves as a link with the day when lumber was "king" and Darien led all Georgia in its production.

[131]

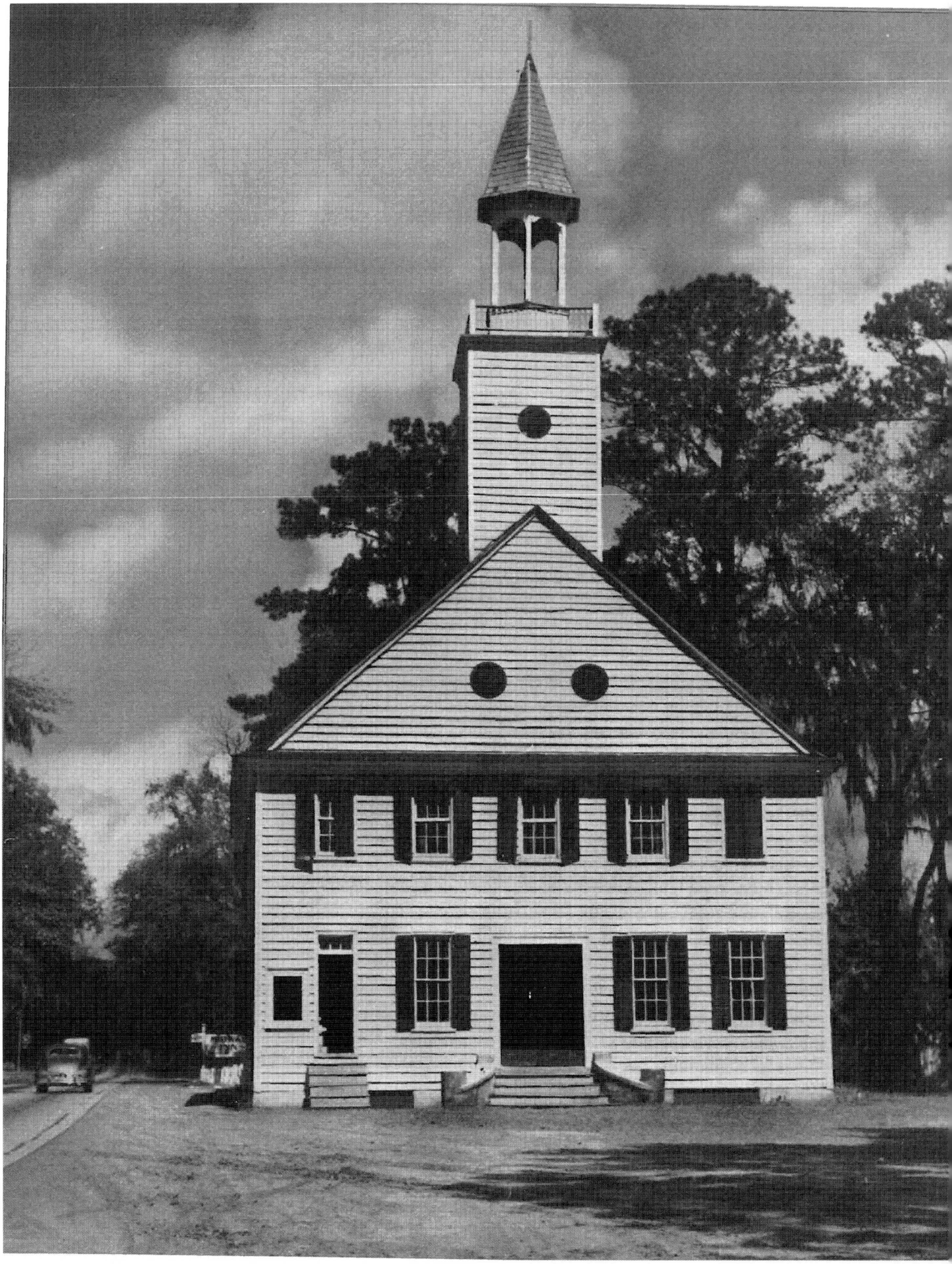

Midway Church

Driving north from Darien toward Savannah, at about the half-way mark, you round a curve in the road and this building looms up directly ahead. With its steep roof, your first thought is of New England for it seems out of place in sub-tropical Georgia.

This is Midway Congregational Church, built by a group who were descended from those who came to America in 1630 on the *Mary & John* and settled on the shores of Massachusetts at a place they called Dorchester. Some of them moved to Connecticut and settled another Dorchester, which today is Windsor. In 1695, a part of the group moved to South Carolina and founded another Dorchester. In 1752 some of the South Carolina colony moved to Georgia, settled on the Midway River and, again, called their settlement Dorchester, naming their house of worship, Midway Church. This building was erected in 1792 to replace the original, burned by the British during the Revolutionary War. These settlers were Puritans and brought to Georgia an element much to be desired. They "were the moral and intellectual nobility of Georgia."

During the several decades just prior to the Civil War, Liberty County sent to the University of Georgia more than double the number of students sent from any other county in the State, with the exception of the county in which the University is located.

During its 113 years of existence Midway Church counted a total of 752 members and boasted that she sent out eighty-six ministers, among them being the Rev. Abiel Holmes, father of Oliver Wendell Holmes; the Rev. Jedidiah Morse, father of Samuel F. B. Morse; and the Rev. I. S. K. Axson, grandfather of Ellen (Axson) Wilson, wife of President Woodrow Wilson.

The gallery which extends around three sides of this church was used for Negro slaves, who attended worship with their masters. During the Plantation Era, Midway had a white minister, as well as Negro preachers, who worked among the slaves of this district. When a Negro developed ability as a preacher and gave time to this work, the church provided him with food, clothing, and a horse and paid his master for such time as he spent in this work. In one instance, a slave was purchased by the church so that he might be free and give himself wholly to the work of the church among his own people.

[133]

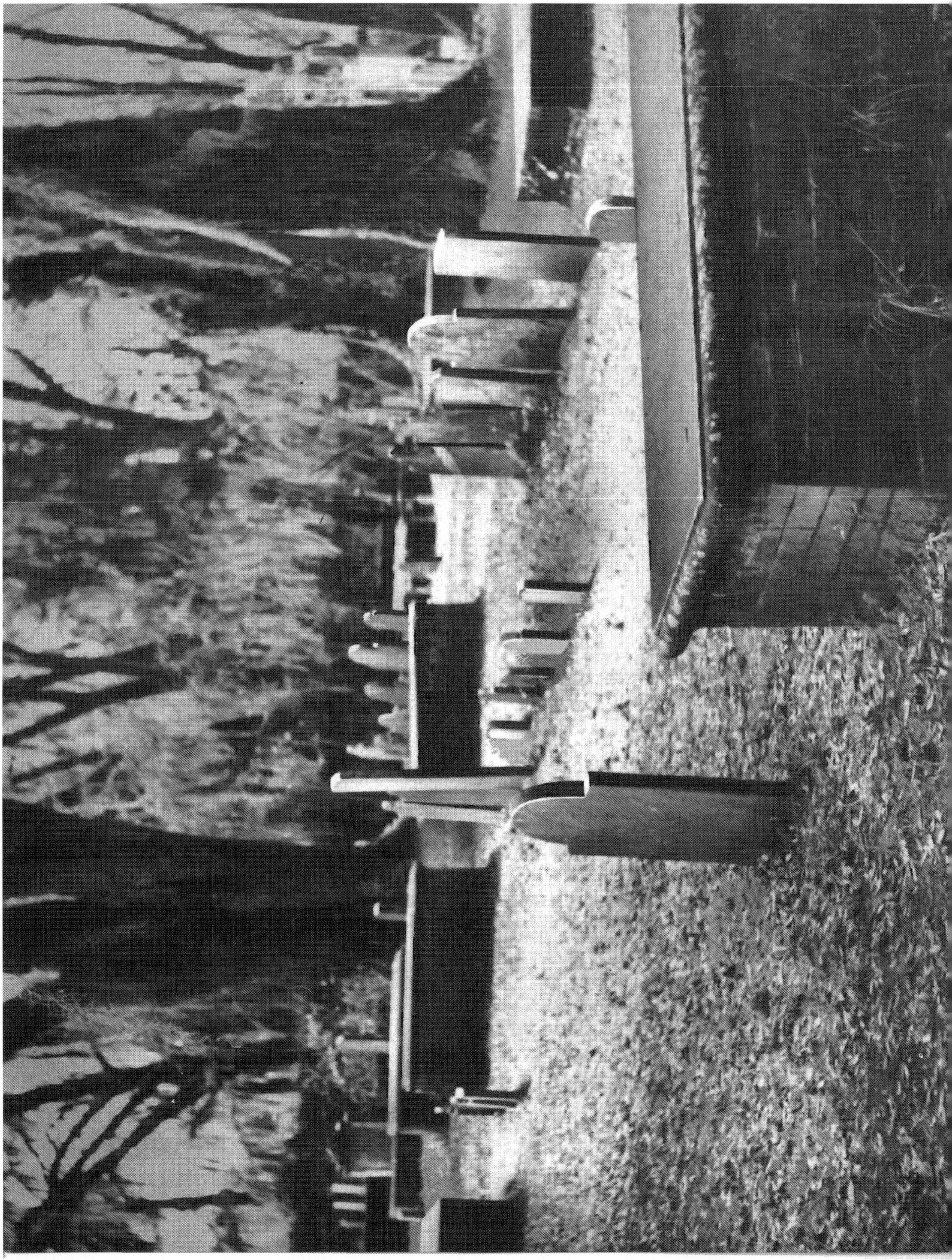

Midway Cemetery

In the cemetery across the road from the church lie the bodies of many noted men and women, Midway's sons and daughters. Among them are eleven ministers, a governor, a senator, high-ranking Army and Navy officers, about two score Revolutionary soldiers, doctors, lawyers, and persons prominent in every walk of life.

Here lie the ancestors of John and Joseph LeConte, founders of the University of California, as well as the bodies of two Revolutionary generals, Gen. James Screven and Gen. Daniel Stewart, the ancestor of President Theodore Roosevelt and of Mrs. Franklin Delano Roosevelt.

This Midway District, the Parish of St. John, was labeled "the cradle of the Revolutionary spirit in Georgia." The youngest of the Thirteen Colonies, Georgia was slow to take steps which would alienate the Mother Country and, when she refused to send delegates to the First Continental Congress, Midway sent her own representative, Dr. Lyman Hall, who was seated "as a delegate from the Parish of St. John in the Colony of Georgia." By the time the Second Continental Congress met, Georgia, had fallen in line and sent regularly elected delegates. Three of these achieved immortality by becoming Signers of the Declaration of Independence, and two of these Signers, Lyman Hall and Button Gwinnett, were from Midway.

As a tribute for its devotion to the cause of freedom from British rule, the first Constitution of the State of Georgia designated this area as Liberty County.

The service rendered by these people in the founding of the Nation was recognized in 1915 when the United States erected in this cemetery a monument to the memory of the two Revolutionary generals who are buried here.

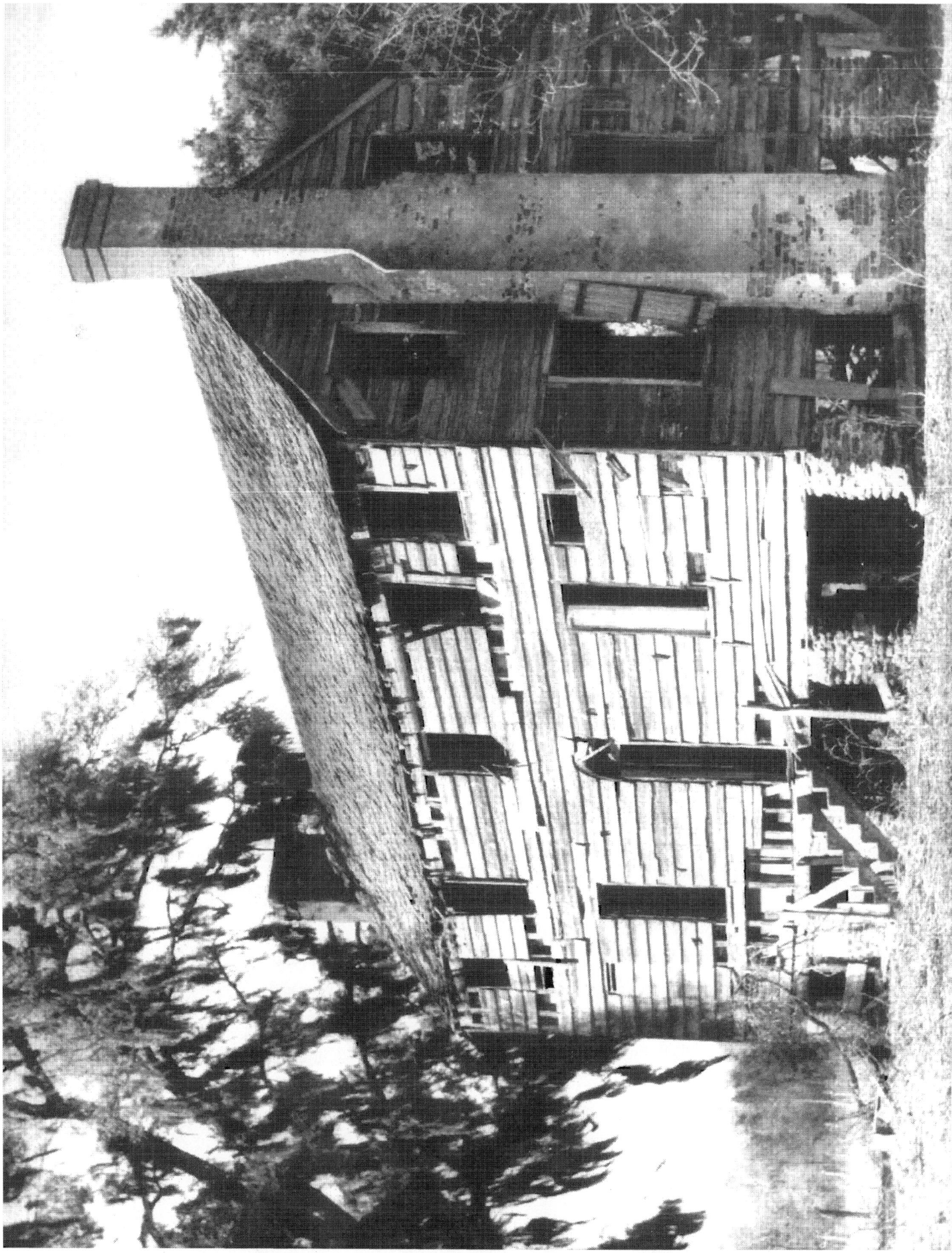

Old Screven House at Sunbury

Standing as a lone survivor of Sunbury's former glory, this old Screven house, built about 1815, surveys a scene of quiet beauty where once the bustle of trade and commerce held sway; for Sunbury was the port for prosperous Midway District which, in the 1770's, possessed nearly one-third the wealth of Georgia.

In 1758 Capt. Mark Carr, one of Oglethorpe's officers and Brunswick's first settlers, gave the land for the town of Sunbury. Located on a bluff overlooking the waters of Midway River and across the Sound from the Islands of Ossabaw and St. Catherine, Sunbury soon became a place of importance.

A small earthwork, Fort Morris, situated just below Sunbury, was built for the protection of its inhabitants. In 1778 this fort was commanded by Col. John McIntosh, who successfully defended it against an attack by the British. To their demand for its surrender he replied, "Come and take it!" Fort Morris fell the following year, being the last spot in the State to surrender when Georgia was overrun by the British.

Dr. Lyman Hall, one of Georgia's Signers of the Declaration of Independence, made his home in Sunbury and was the medical doctor for the community, though his plantation was located on the Post Road (now Route #17) a few miles north of Midway Church. It was from this port of Sunbury that he carried 160 barrels of rice and sixty pounds sterling, as a contribution from its citizens to relieve the condition of the patriots at Boston.

Button Gwinnett, Georgia's other Signer from Midway District, had his plantation home on St. Catherine's Island, within sight of Sunbury where he transacted business and moved among its citizens as one of them.

Only this old house remains of the town that had a population of about a thousand just before the Revolutionary War, and was considered a rival of Savannah in commercial importance. Today, Sunbury is a "dead town."

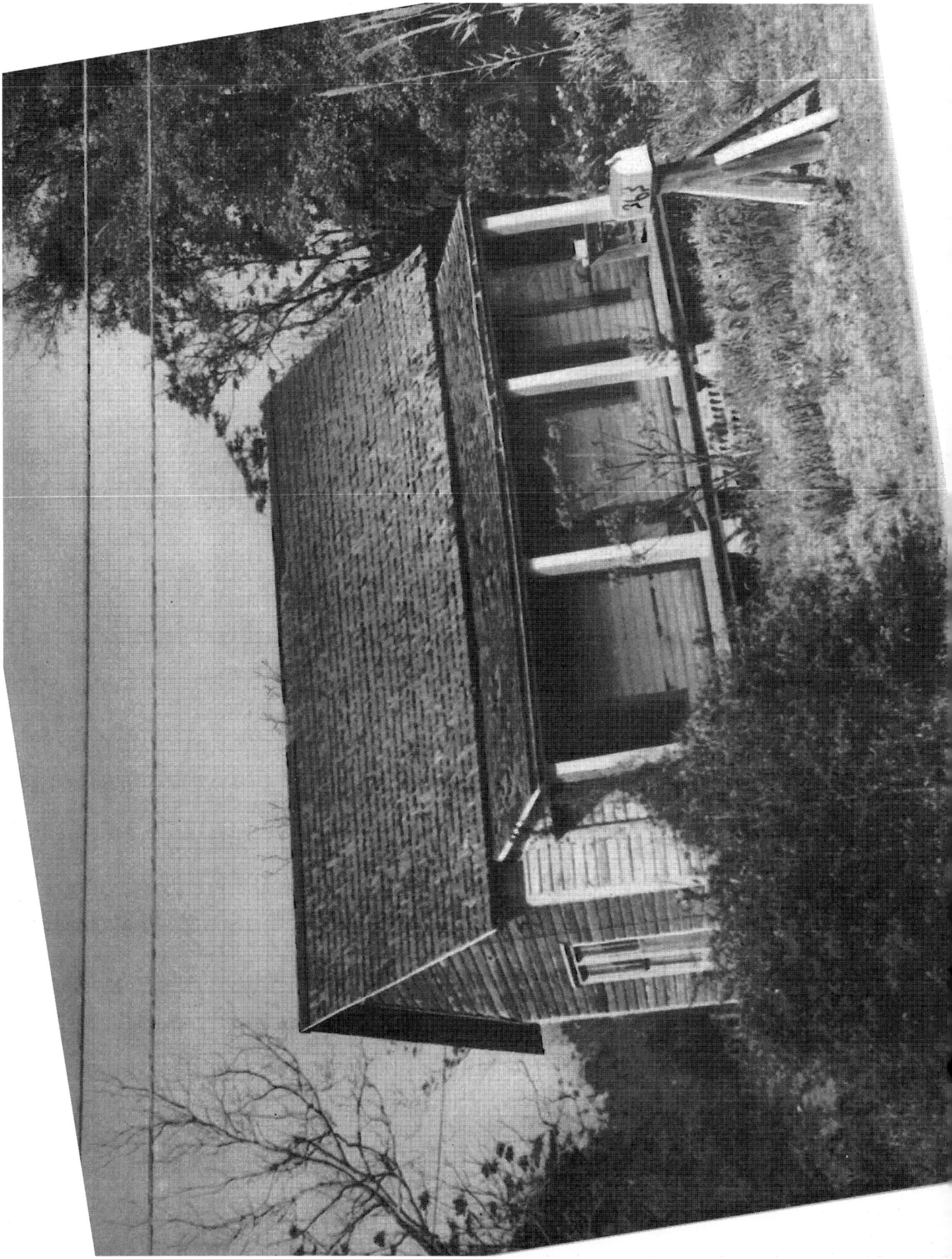

A Negro Home in Jewtown

After the Civil War the former slaves of the St. Simons plantations settled themselves in several communities. Those from the plantations at the North End acquired land and settled in Harrington, while the Negroes from the plantations on the lower part of the island grouped themselves in an area which they called the South End. Another settlement was located east of Gascoigne Bluff and near the site of the Hilton Dodge Lumber Company mill.

At this mill, of course, there was a commissary, where the workmen purchased their supplies. Soon, a Jewish merchant named Levison located his store just off the mill property and between the mill and the Negro settlement. He called the area Levisonton, but the Negroes called it "Jewtown"; and so it is till this day, even though Levison moved away in 1880.

In these settlements each Negro secured a small plot of ground and built his home. Among these people the ambition to own their homes is very strong. Furthermore, they want that home to have a sufficiently large piece of land around it so that they will not feel they are hemmed in.

In these homes they keep alive many of the old practices of their ancestors. They paint the doors and windows blue, believing that, since blue is the color of Heaven, the devil will not come near the blue opening in the house, so they will be safe and secure.

Another custom which is thought to be a protection is the practice of papering the walls with newspapers for when the "ha'nts" come at night, they have to read every word on the wall before they can go to work on the people in the house. When the walls are not papered in this fashion, the newspapers may be spread on the tables, the mantels, or even the floor. No matter where they are, the "ha'nts" have to read them. Since they could not possibly finish them in one night and have to start over the next night, the persons in that house are safe; for no "ha'nt" can work in the day. "Ha'nts" are creatures of darkness!

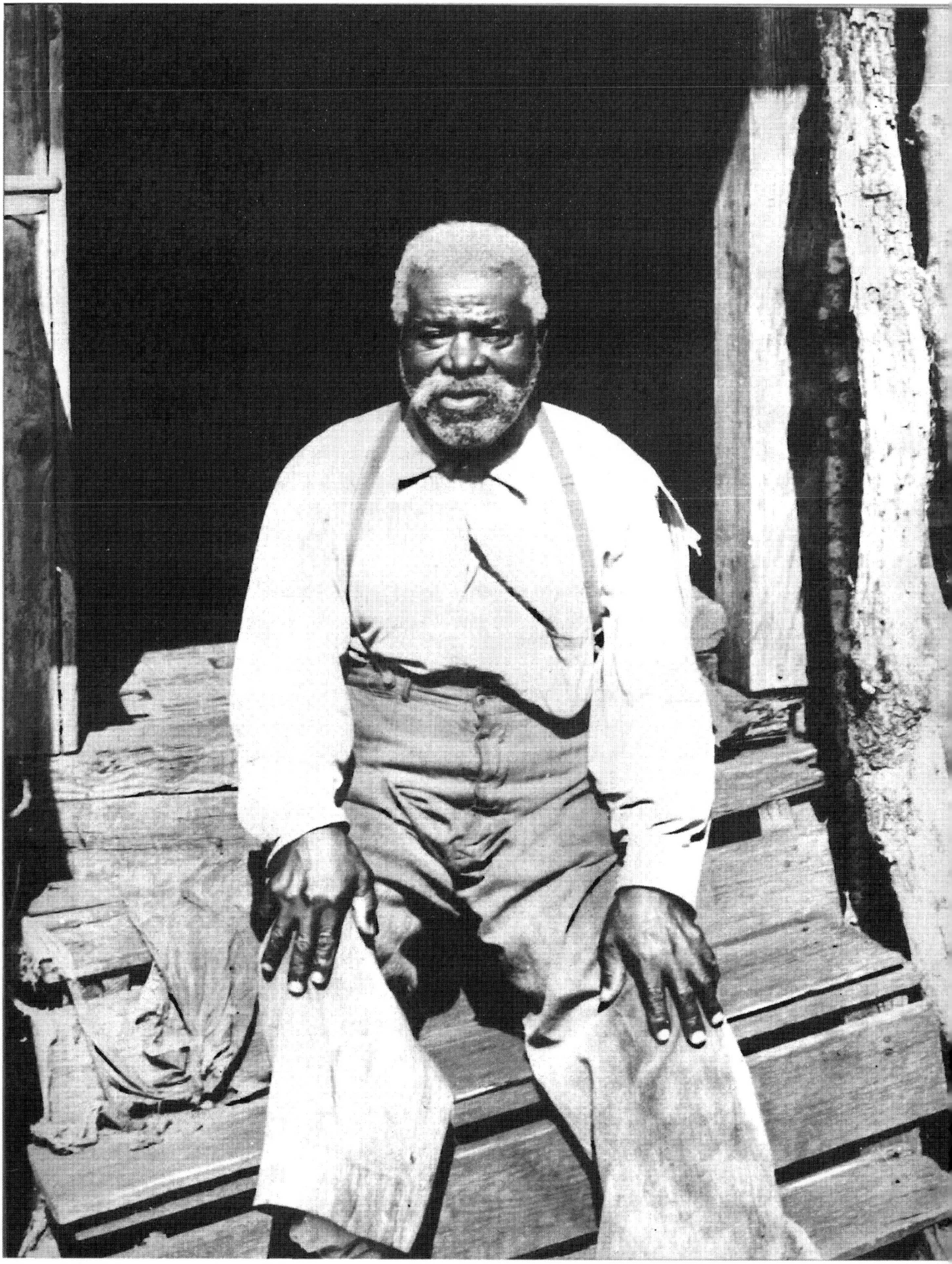

Bacchus Magwood

A familiar figure among the Negroes of Jewtown for almost his entire life, Bacchus was an interesting person and made himself a good neighbor in the finest sense of the word.

When Liddy who lived next door became ill, he took her to his house and cared for her until she died.

Years later Bacchus' house burned and he was left homeless. A friend who inquired where he was staying was told, "I move over an' stay wid Lily."

"Bacchus, I knew someone would give you a home for I remember when you took Liddy into your home and cared for her when she was sick and helpless."

Back came reply, "You cas' your bread!"

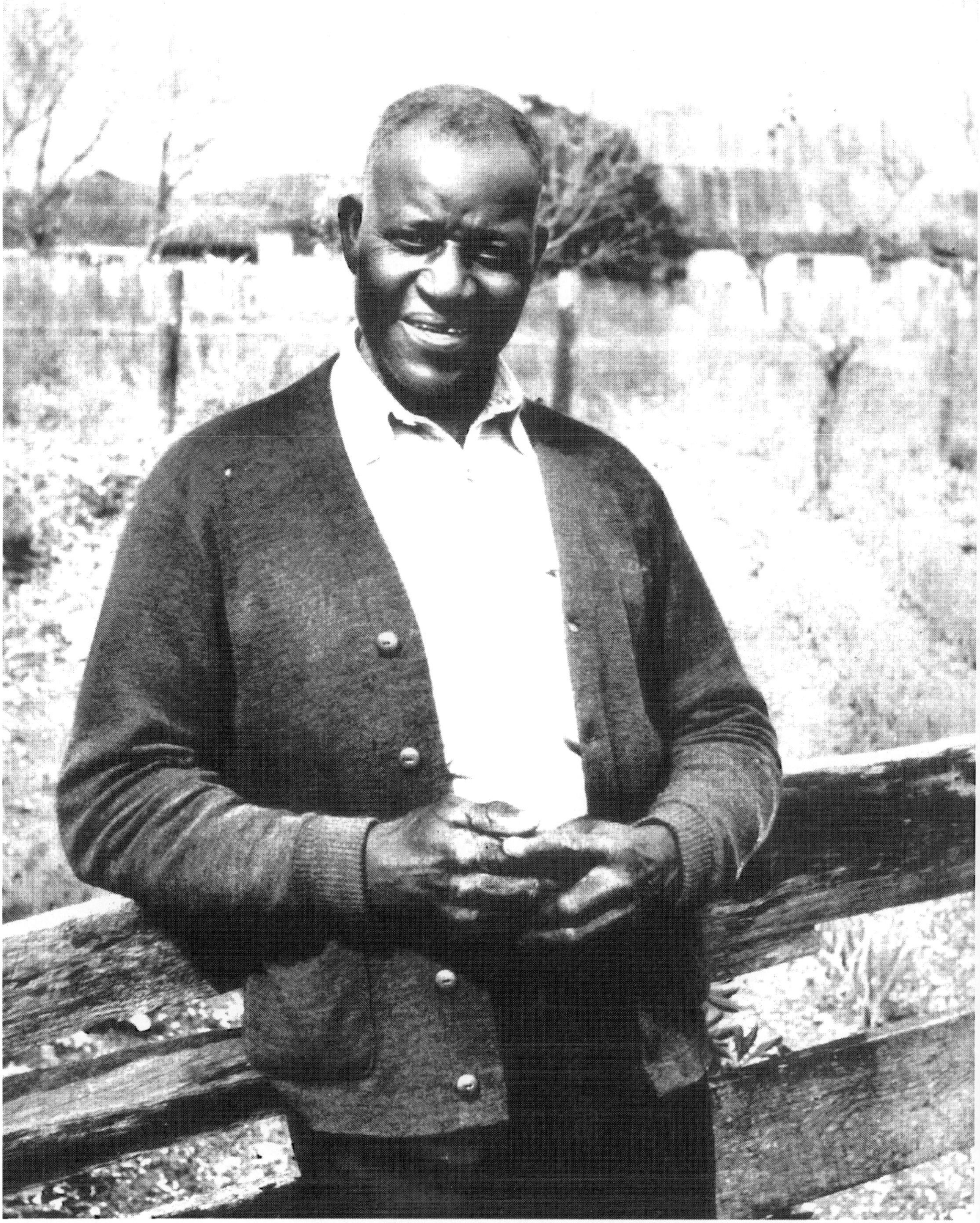

Willis Proctor

Willis Proctor belongs on St. Simons Island where his ancestors have lived for many generations. His mother was Mina, the daughter of Robert Merchant, who was one of the Retreat "people," as Mrs. King called her slaves. It was Robert who, in 1848, planted the beautiful avenue of live oak trees which formed the entrance to the plantation. Robert Merchant and Mina are buried in the old Retreat burying ground just north of the Sea Island Golf Club House. There, for a century and a half, the Negroes of this plantation have been buried—and there they still bury their dead. Willis' father, Adam Proctor, who belonged to the Goulds of Black Banks Plantation, is buried in the cemetery belonging to the people of that plantation, located just south of Harrington.

Willis is a capable man and has held many responsible positions. For ten years he had charge of the dining room at the Arnold House on St. Simons and held a similar position at the Georgia Military Academy at College Park. He later worked for the Jekyll Island Club and became the personal valet of William Rockefeller at his Indian Mound home on Jekyll. Now, for many years, he has operated his own store near his home in the South End section of St. Simons.

Willis has made himself outstanding among the members of his race. His honesty, his integrity, and his dependability are the qualities which have made him a leader and highly regarded by all who know him. He is a leader, too, among the singers who keep alive the old songs of his people. Of all of these songs, his specialty is:

> One o' these days, my people; One o' these days, my people;
> One o' these days, When the Lord call me home.
> Well, we soon shall be done with the crosses;
> Well, we soon shall be done with the troubles o' the world;
> Well, we soon shall be done with the crosses.

Shaking hands with each "Sister" he in turn sings:

> Sister Charlotte, One o' these days;
> My sister, One o' these days, My sister, One o' these days,
> When the Lord call me home.

Going on down the line to "Sister" after "Sister," he sings to each as he shakes her hand.

[143]

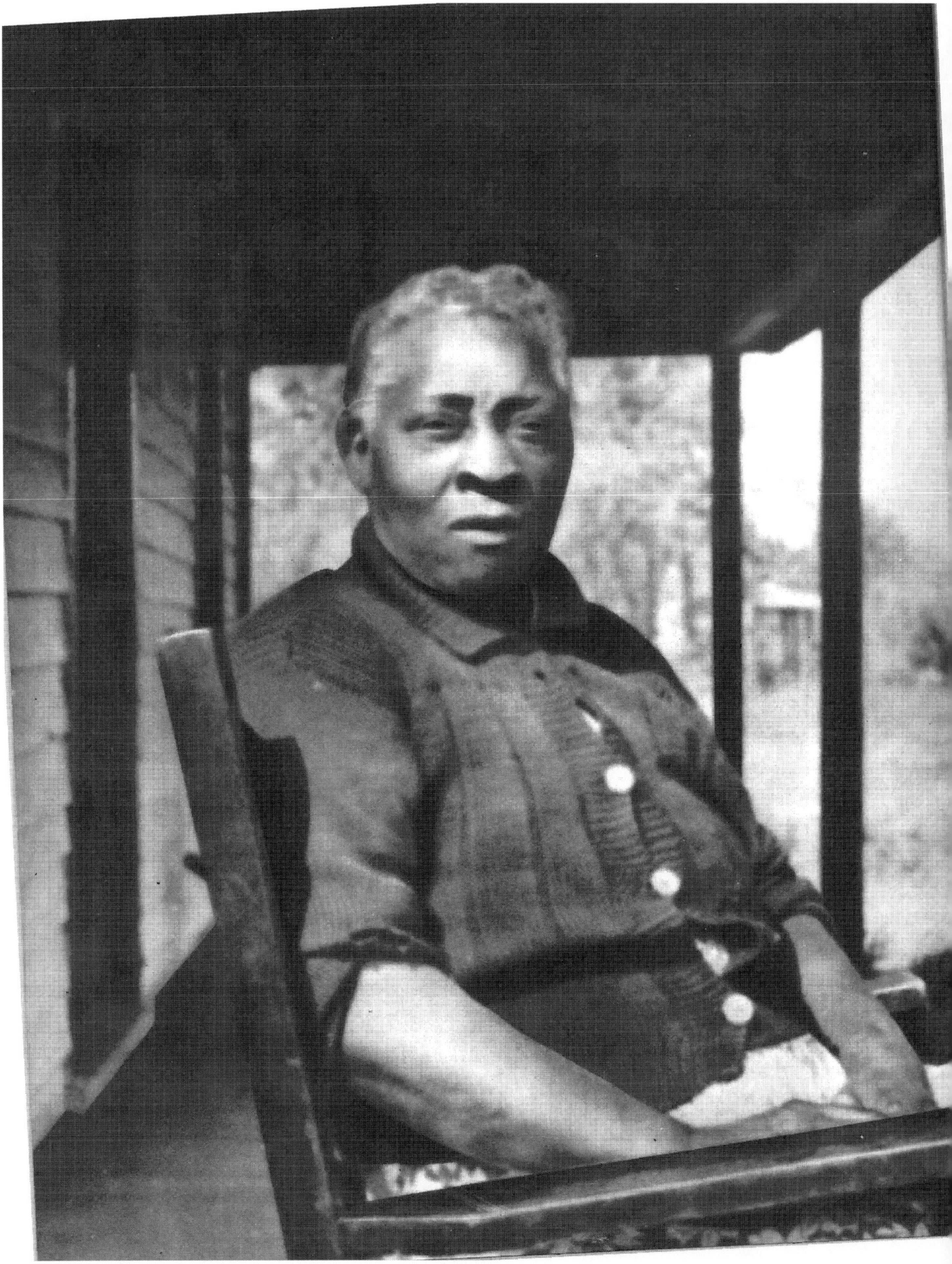

Julia Armstrong

Willis' sister, Julia, the wife of Joe Armstrong, was employed by the late Mrs. Maxfield Parrish when Mrs. Parrish first came to St. Simons. Mrs. Parrish became interested in the singing of the Negroes and Julia found the men and women who could sing the old songs in the old way. Mrs. Parrish recorded these spirituals and "shouts" and saved them for posterity in the publication of her excellent book, *Slave Songs of the Georgia Sea Islands.* By insisting that the Negroes sing in the old-fashioned way Mrs. Parrish created in their minds a feeling of respect for the songs of their ancestors. She held "sings" at the cabin she built for this purpose and made it possible for visitors to enjoy them. Now, these "sings" are held regularly at The Cloister Hotel on Sea Island.

The spirituals are American music, having been developed on the plantations of the South, but the "shouts" are of African origin. These religious dances were brought from Africa and kept alive by the Negroes who performed them in their churches. The "shouters" go round and round with a shuffling motion of the feet and a tap of the heel on the floor, singing all the while. In Africa they would have used with these shouts a drum, but in the South this instrument was denied them. This came about because of a slave uprising in South Carolina in 1739, known as the Stono Rebellion, which, led by a Negro with a drum, resulted in the death of dozens of people, black and white. So, to take the place of the drum, they tap on the floor with a broomstick.

The words sung with these "shouts" can have no connection with the words used for their dances in Africa. One is "Knee Bone Bend" and as they sing, they bend their knees in supplication. Another is "O Eve, Where Is Adam? Down in the Garden Picking up Leaves". As they sing, they go through the motion of picking up leaves. Still another is "On the Eagle's Wing" in which they hold their arms out as if they were the wings of the eagle.

In all of this the Negroes give an authentic production without modern innovations and free from any touch of the white man's influence. A picture from the past!

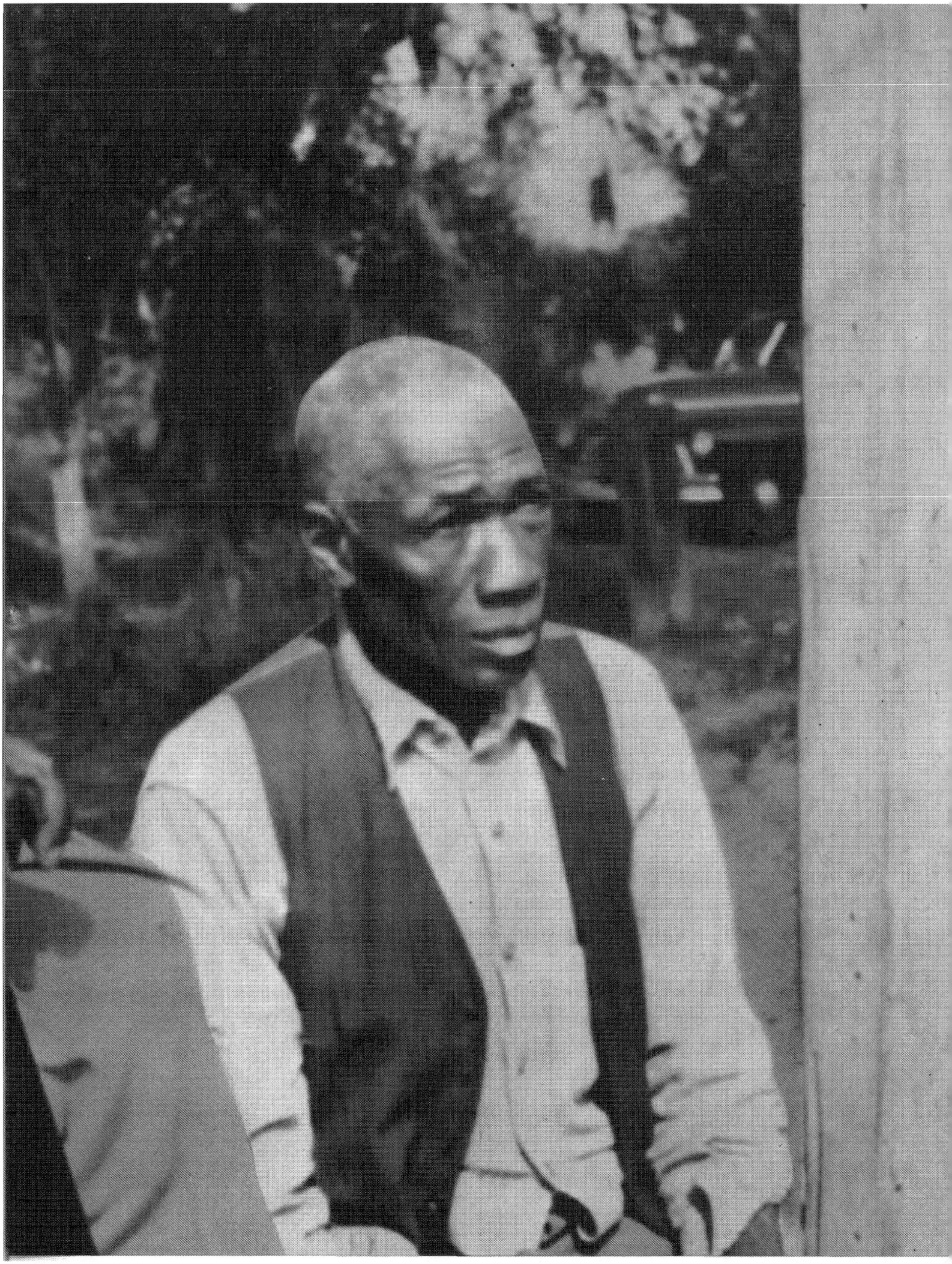

Joe Armstrong

Joe, who is Julia's husband, is also one of the singers. However, he specializes in work songs or chanteys. For many years he was a stevedore at the Hilton Dodge Lumber Company mill, located at Gascoigne Bluff on St. Simons Island, on the site of Hamilton Plantation, now the location of the Methodist Center, Epworth-By-The-Sea.

The long-leaf yellow pine which supplied this mill was cut in the interior of Georgia and floated down the Altamaha River in great rafts. The mill operated from 1874 until it closed in 1903 and vessels from all parts of the world tied up at the wharves to load this lumber.

Among the Negroes engaged in the loading of these vessels, those who had the ability and could direct the work of others were known as stevedores. These stevedores played an important part in the successful loading of the vessels, for the heavy timbers had to be carefully stowed away so that they would not shift and cause damage to the vessel during the ocean voyage. As a stevedore, Joe had charge of a gang of men who moved these heavy timbers from the wharf and stowed them in the hold of the vessel. In order that they might all pull together to move these timbers, they sang as they worked and, at the proper place in the song, gave a great pull.

One song which was very popular with the workers — and is still used when men are moving a house or doing work of that sort — was:

Oh pay me, pay me, Pay me my money down;
Pay me or go to jail; Oh pay me my money down.
Think I hear my captain say Pay me my money down,
Tomorrow is my sailing day, Oh pay me my money down.
Oh pay me, pay me, Pay me my money down;
Pay me, Mr. Stevedore, Oh pay me my money down.
One o' these days I'm goin' away, Pay me my money down,
Won't be back till Judgment Day, Oh pay me my money down.
Oh pay me, pay me, Pay me my money down,
Pay me or go to jail, Oh pay me my money down.
Wish I wuz Mr. Alfred Jones' son, Pay me my money down,
Stay in de house and drink good rum, Oh pay me my money down.

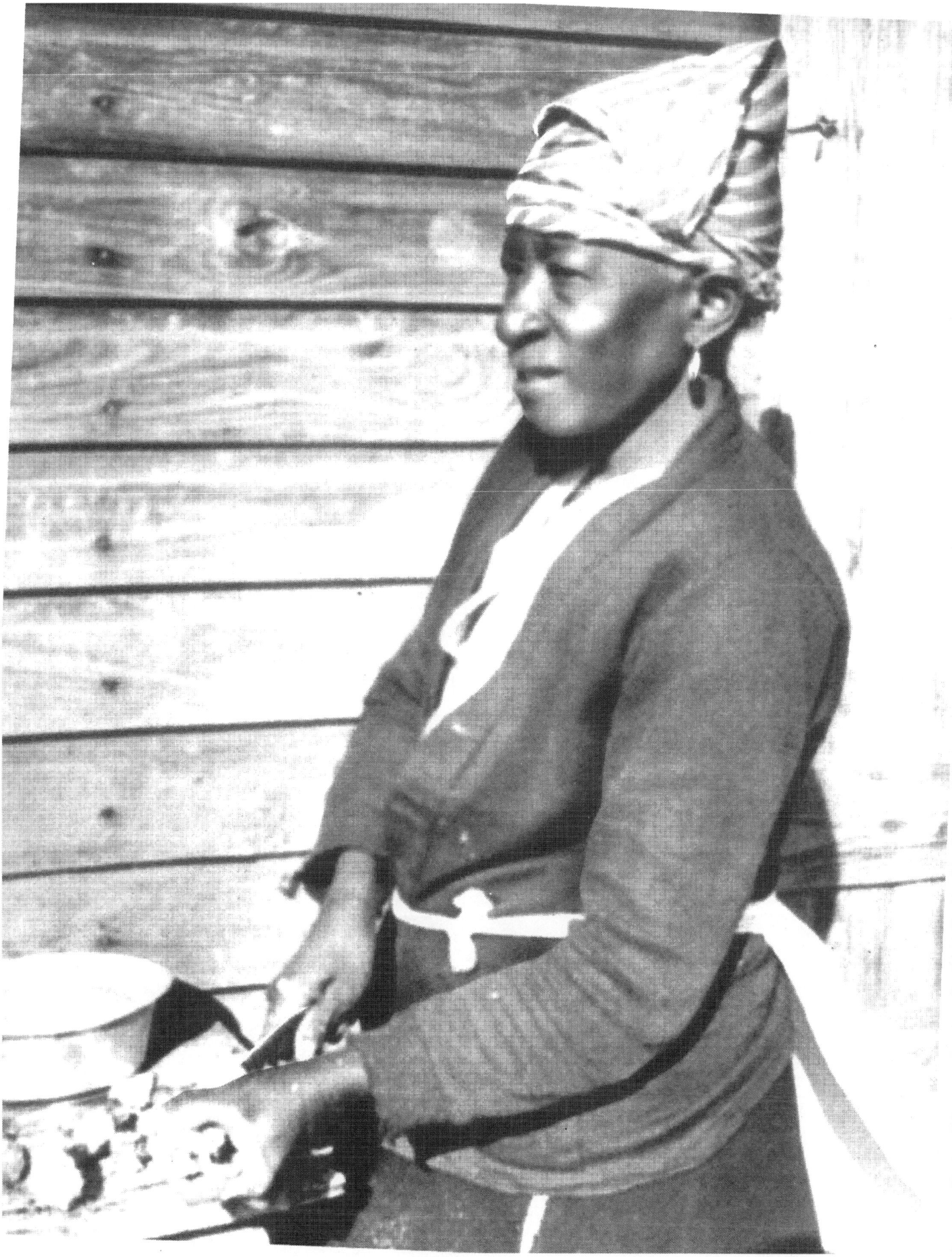

Edith Murphy

Edith Murphy is a St. Simons Island woman whose ancestors for many generations belonged to the Demere family.

Capt. Raymond Demere, the first of his family to come to America, was a native of France who had seen service with the British at Gibraltar and came to Georgia in 1738 as an officer in Oglethorpe's Regiment. He was granted lands near Frederica where he built his home "rather in the French taste than the English." He called his home Harrington Hall in honor of his friend, Lord Harrington, under whom he had served at Gibraltar. Later, the Demeres moved to Mulberry Grove at the South End of St. Simons, a plantation which took its name from the fact that here were planted thousands of white mulberry trees. These were to feed the silk worms of the industry which was planned in the early days of the Colony.

The Demeres have not lived on St. Simons since the Civil War. Gone are the plantation house and the slave cabins. The only evidence of their occupation of the place was the family burial ground, enclosed in a tabby wall and containing the bodies of several generations, including three Raymond Demeres. When the airport was enlarged, these tombstones were moved to Christ Church Burying Ground at Frederica.

Edith lived on land which was a part of Mulberry Grove and on the site occupied by the slave cabins which housed her ancestors. She is one of the group of singers who sing the spirituals and "shouts" in the authentic manner and is one of the best of these singers, her specialty being "Hush, Hush, Somebody Callin' My Name."

Here, Edith is opening oysters. The empty shells will go into a tin can on the ground and the aluminum pan on the table is almost full of oysters. Most people wear an apron to keep a dress clean. Evidently, Edith's apron is clean and she does not want to get it dirty!

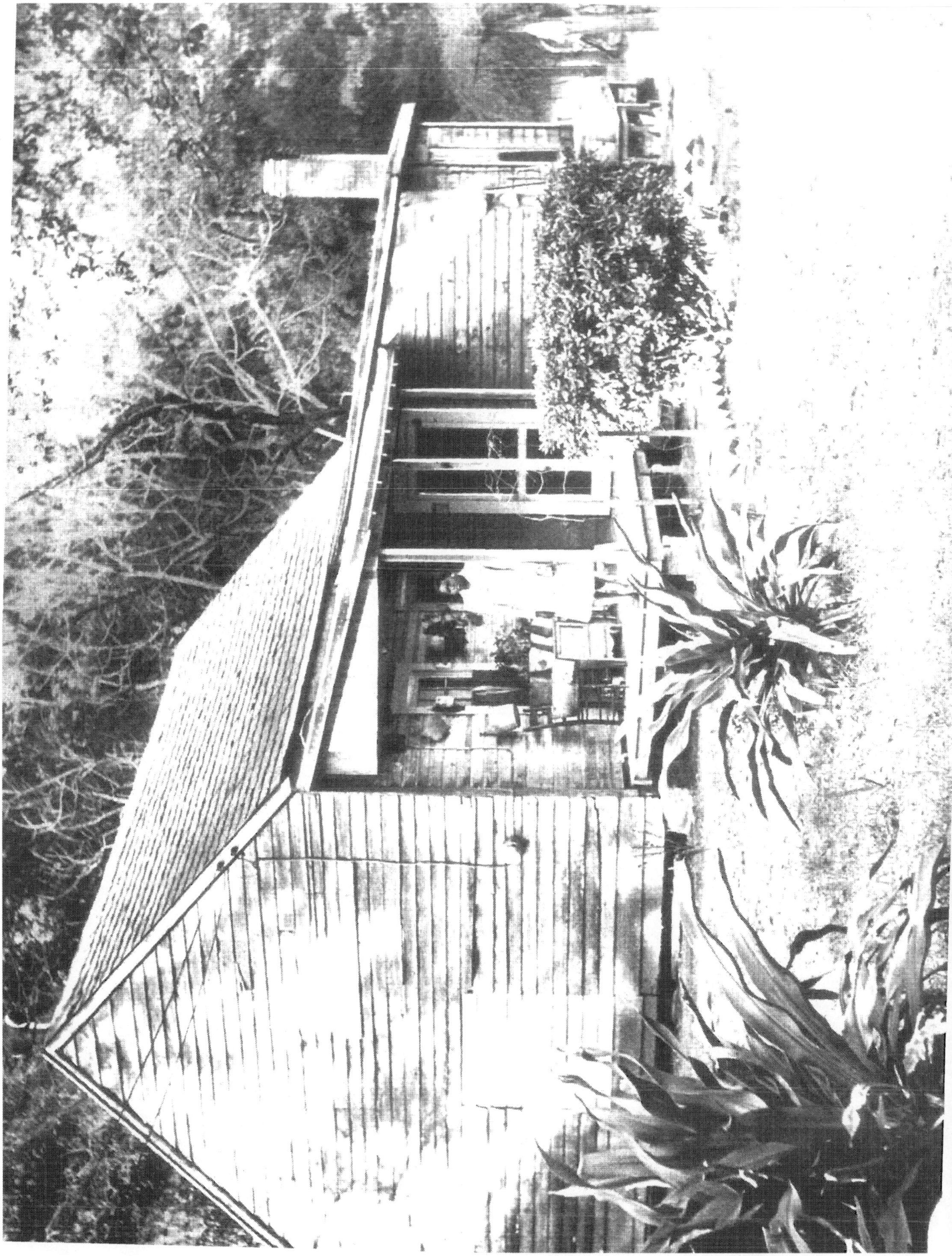

The House that Neptune Built

Neptune was the faithful servant of the Thomas Butler King family of Retreat Plantation. When the son of this family, Capt. Henry Lord Page King, enlisted in the Confederate Army and went off to war, Neptune went along to act as his body servant. In Virginia at the Battle of Fredericksburg, Capt. King was killed. When night came on and the master did not return from battle, Neptune went out to search for the body, found it, and brought it home — all the way from Virginia to Georgia. Today, Capt. King's body lies in the family burial plot in Christ Church Burying Ground, Frederica.

After the war, Neptune was given a piece of ground on the southern edge of the Retreat lands where he built this house and made his home. During the remaining years of his long life — for he died around the turn of the century — "Daddy" Neptune was honored and respected by all who knew him. (In this area old Negroes were called "Maum" and "Daddy" not "Aunt" and "Uncle.")

Looking around for a family name, for there were no surnames in use among the Negro slaves before the war, Neptune took the name Small, because of his own small stature. His descendents living here now are very proud of their ancestor and proudly relate the story of his heroism.

Neptune is buried in the old Retreat Burying Ground at the Sea Island Golf Course, his grave marked by a bronze tablet which tells the story of his heroism. Set in a base of tabby, such as Neptune would have built, his marker is a most appropriate memorial.

Neptune's daughter, Cornelia, lived with him even after her marriage to Cassius Murphy; and a daughter of Cornelia and Cassius, Charlotte (Murphy) Reese, was born in this house and lived there until recently.

A visitor who knew the house and had seen it many times during the eighty-five years that it had been occupied as a home, drove around in the area looking for it. Failing to find it, she stopped in a Negro settlement and asked what had become of the house and was told, "Neptune house been tore down. Yes, ma'am, Charlotte wuz libin' dere in a nes' o' white folks an' she sell out an' move ober here wid us."

[151]

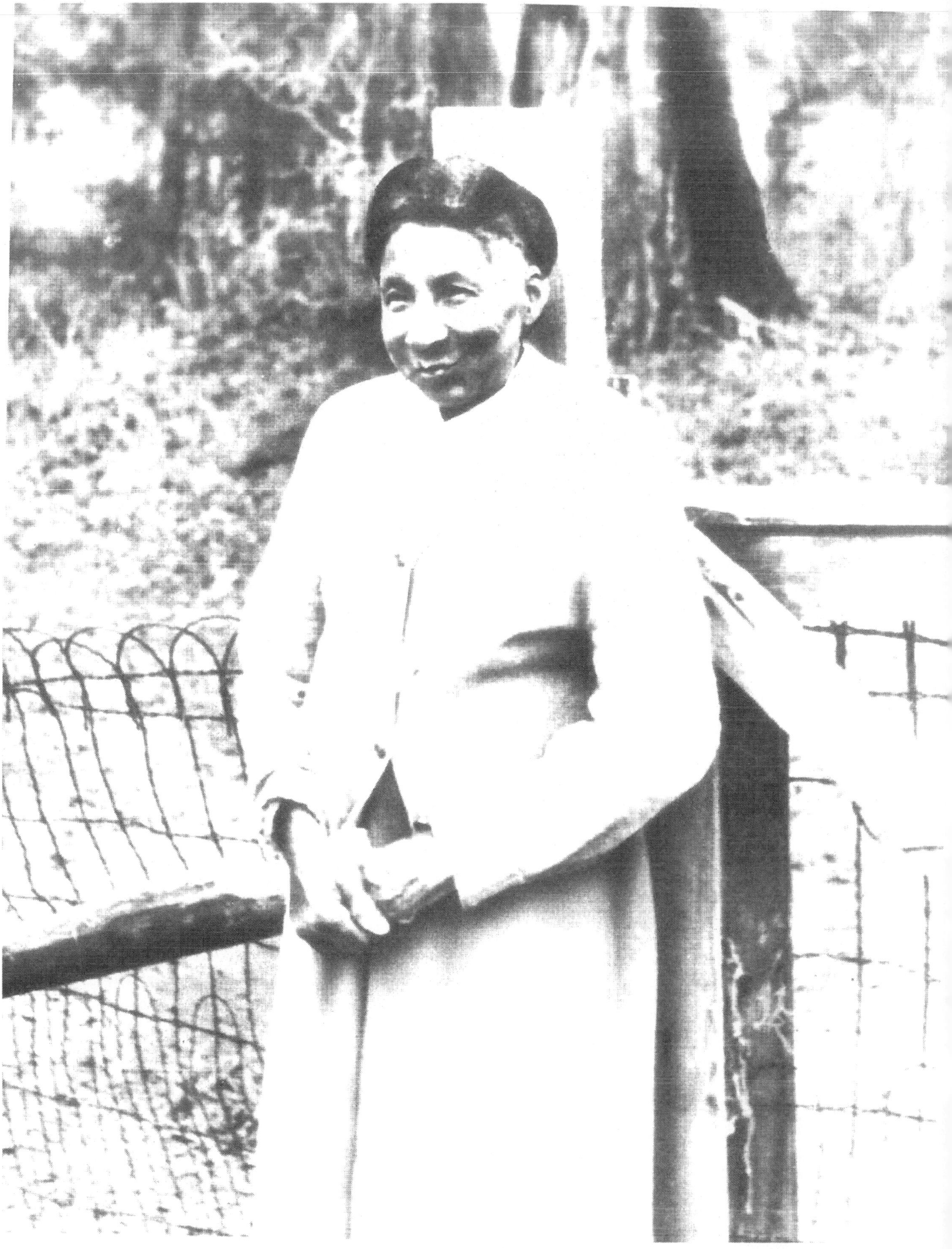

Lavinia Abbott

This woman, Lavinia (Sullivan) Abbott, and her brother, Ben Sullivan, whose picture appears on the next page, are from a well-known St. Simons Island family of Negroes, being the grandchildren of old Tom, whose African name was Sali-bul-Ali. Tom, who was of the Foulah tribe, was purchased in the Bahama Islands about 1800 by John Couper of Cannon's Point Plantation, St. Simons. Mr. Couper and his son, James Hamilton Couper of Hopeton and Altama Plantations, were high in their praise of Tom's industry, his intelligence, and his honesty.

Tom was given positions of trust on the plantation, finally being made the head man of Hopeton Plantation, a position he held for three decades. James Hamilton Couper wrote that he left Tom in charge of the plantation and its 450 Negroes, without an overseer, for months at a time and found him fully capable of managing the estate.

Tom, who was a Mohammedan, abstained from the use of spirituous liquors, kept the fasts, and was free of the African belief in evil spirits. He had a Koran and could read but not write Arabic. His African home was on the Niger River, where he was a native of the Town of Kianah in the District of Temourah in the Kingdom of Massina. He said his parents were farmers and were possessed of considerable property. In 1785, when he was fourteen years of age, he was captured and sold into slavery.

During Tom's lifetime there were a number of Negro slaves on the plantations along the Georgia coast who were Mohammedans. One of the best known of these was Bilalli of Sapelo Island. His owner, Thomas Spalding of Sapelo, made him the head man of the Sapelo Plantation. This Bilalli of Sapelo could read and write Arabic and a manuscript which he wrote in that language is preserved in the Georgia State Library in Atlanta. Though these men kept their faith and were strict Mohammedans, their children were Christians.

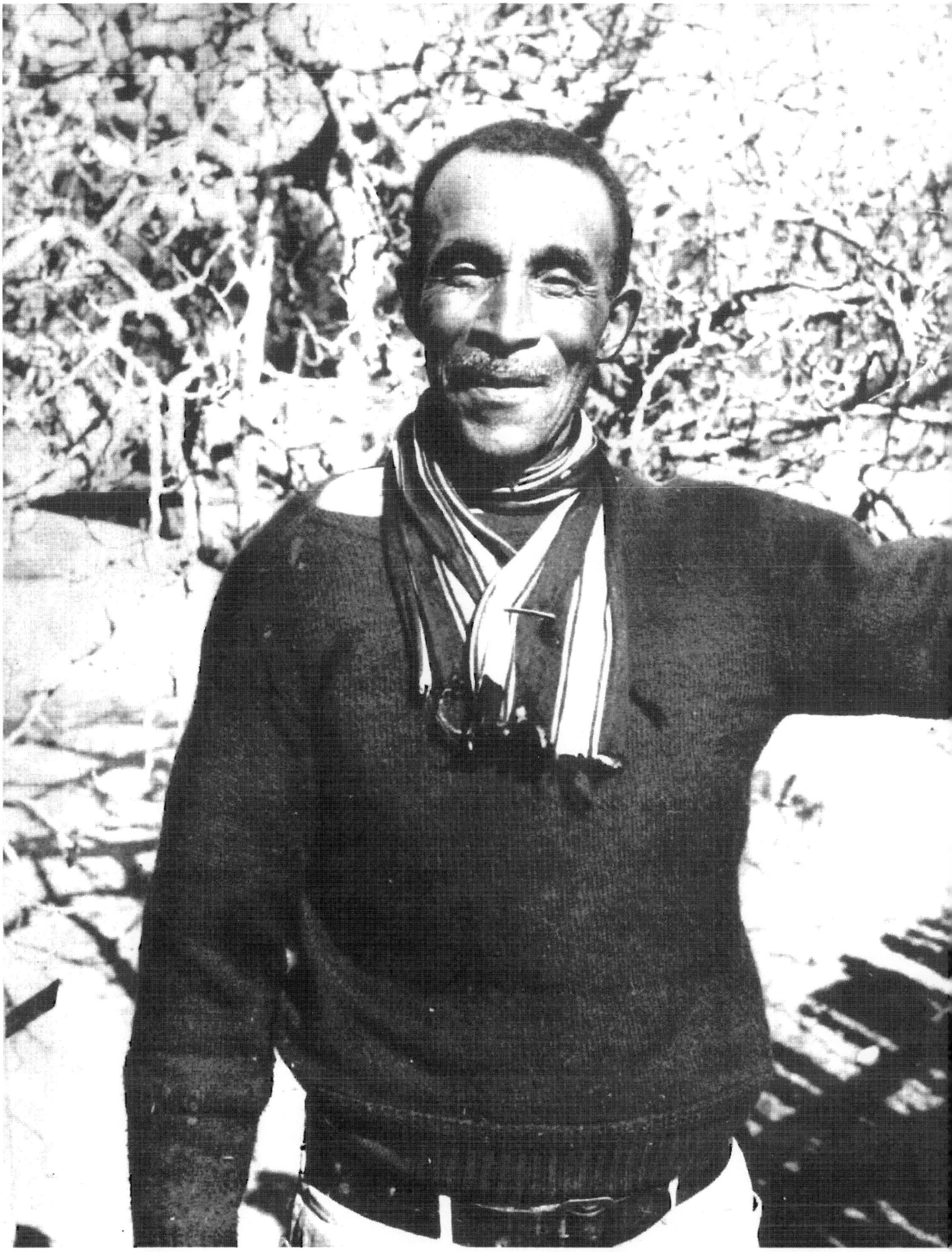

Ben Sullivan

Ben Sullivan comes of a family that can trace its ancestry back to a definite spot in Africa, being one of the very few Negro families in this country who can do this.

Old Tom — or, to use his African name, Sali-bul-Ali — had a son who was called Bilalli. After the emancipation of the Negro, Bilalli adopted the family name of Sullivan and his numerous descendants now living on St. Simons are a superior group of Negroes who own their homes and operate their businesses or follow some trade or profession with the same good judgment and attention to duty which characterized their grandfather, old Tom.

Many of these descendants, like the ones pictured here, possess the same physical characteristics described as belonging to old Tom. James Hamilton Couper wrote that Tom was "tall, thin, but well made. His features are small, forehead well developed, mouth well formed, with lips less protruding than is usual with the Negro race, the nose flat, but not thick. His eyes are peculiar, being like those of a Chinese, without their obliquity . . ." Mr. Couper further stated that Tom's hair was woolly and his skin a brownish black.

Many of the Sullivan family on St. Simons live in a settlement known as "Harrington". During the Colonial Era these lands were granted to Capt. Raymond Demere of Oglethorpe's Regiment, who called his home "Harrington Hall" in honor of Lord Harrington under whom he had served at Gibraltar. After the emancipation of the Negro many of the former slaves of the old St. Simons plantation began to settle here in a group. They acquired small tracts of land which gave them sufficient space for a garden, a cow, hogs and chickens; and, with the money they made at "The Mills," they were able to live comfortably. Today, this entire settlement of about a hundred houses is occupied by Negroes who own their homes and are respected citizens.

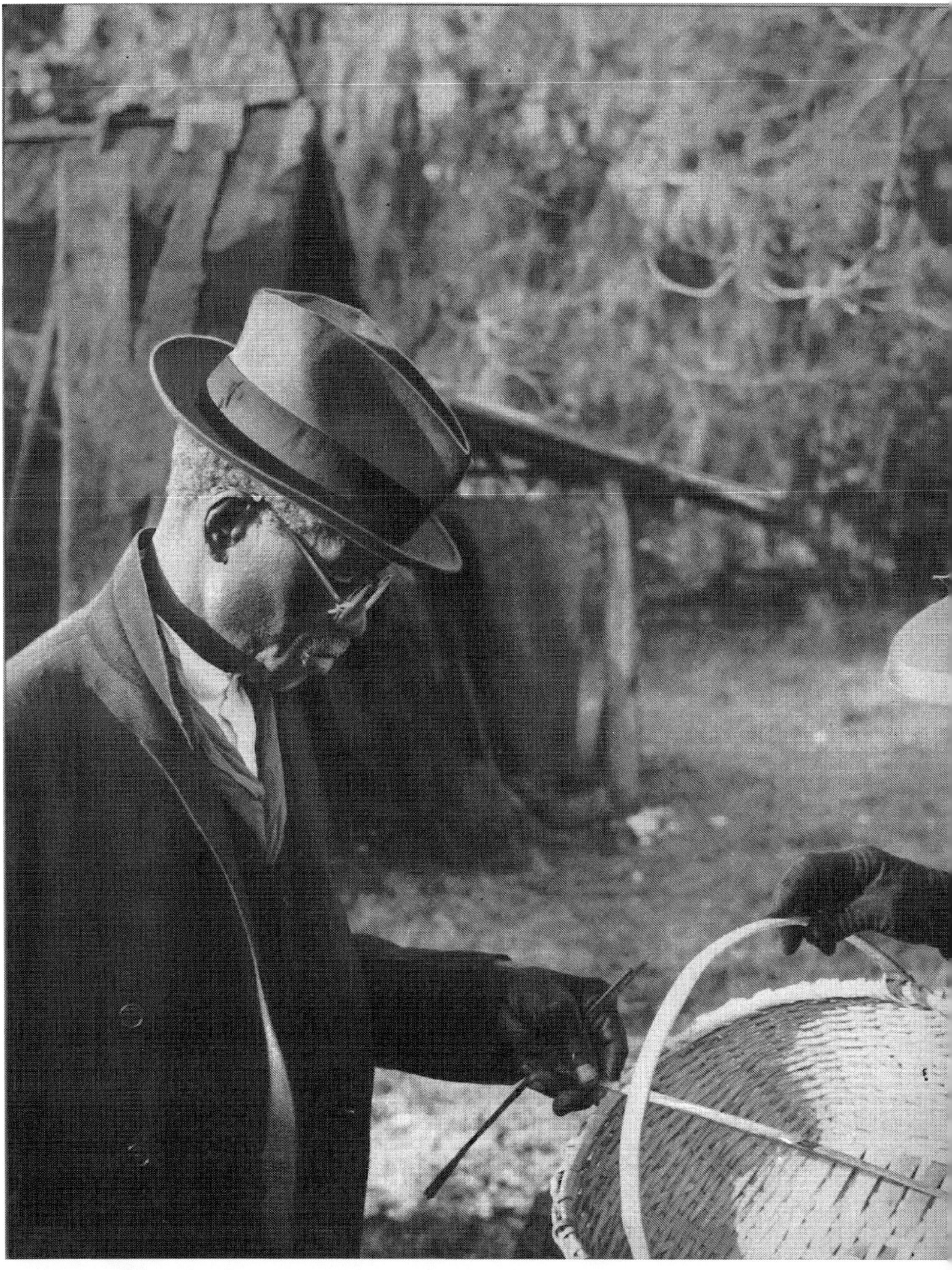

Charles Wilson, The Basket Maker

Charles Wilson was the last of the old basket makers to ply his trade in this area.

His baskets were beautifully made and no shoddy piece of work ever came from his hand. To make his baskets Charles used the leaf stem of the cabbage palmetto, or sabal palm. He split these leaf stems and worked them to a uniform width and thickness with a pocket knife. As he wove these pieces into baskets he turned the outer surface of the stem to the outside so as to give the baskets a highly polished finish.

Once, when he was asked to duplicate a basket, he started looking around on the ground for his "ya'd stick." Thinking he meant a thirty-six-inch ruler, which most people call a "yard stick," the visitor was surprised to see him pick up a stick which he kept in the yard and was, therefore, his "ya'd stick." With this he measured the basket and scratched on the stick with an oyster shell to make the dimensions!

On the table is a rice "fanner," made of light weight grasses and used to fan the rice to separate the chaff from the grain.

In the background is the house where Charles lived almost half a century. He built this house and was very proud of it. The original shingle roof had rotted and Charles had patched the roof with tarred paper, layer after layer piled one on top of the other. Finally, he lived in one room and did all the repairs to that room, but he was careful to keep the door closed so that visitors never saw inside.

Charles owned the ten-acre tract of land he occupied and lived just as he wanted to. His younger brother lived nearby and Charles fared well with the care he received from this brother and his family.

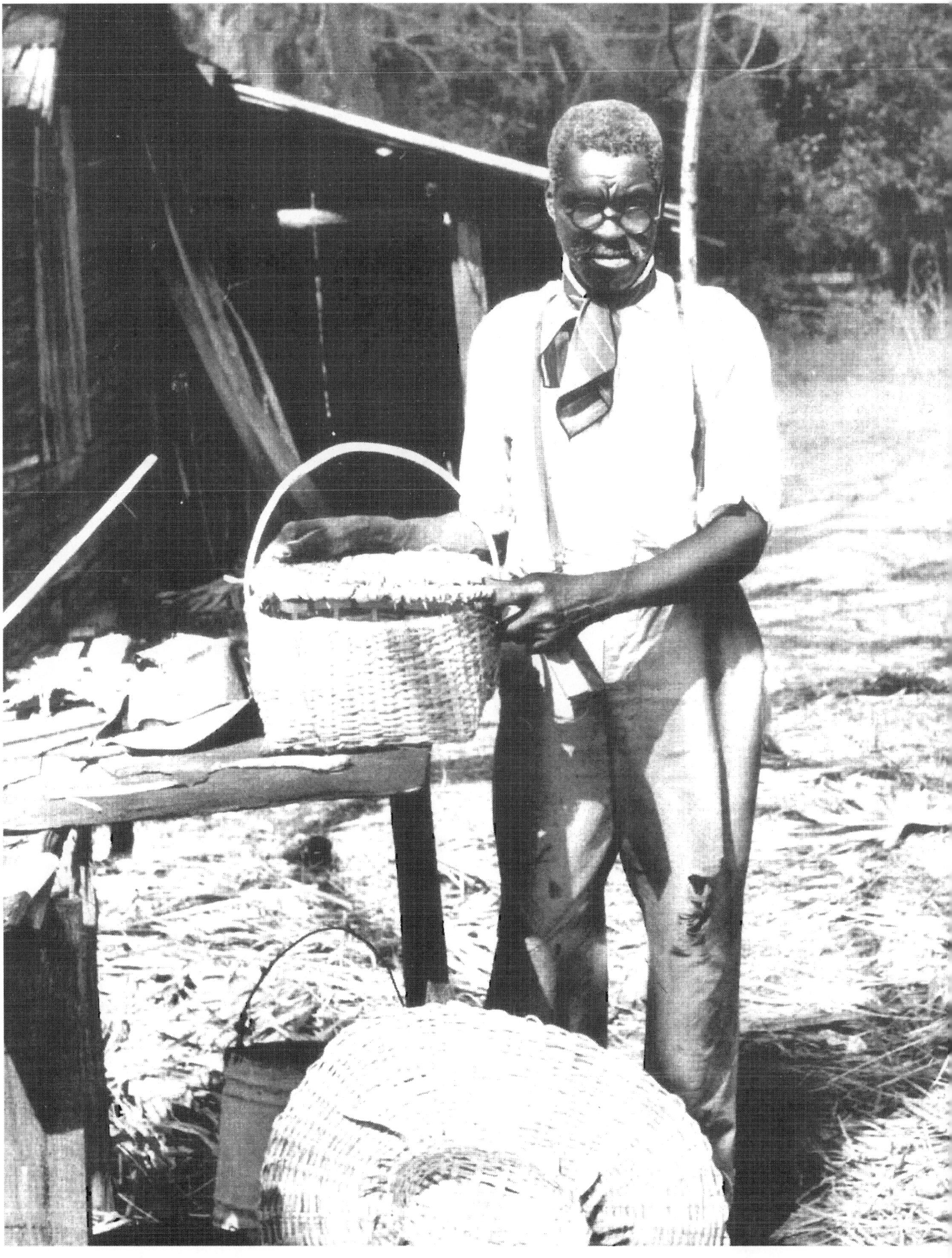

Charles Wilson

Charles did all of his cooking out of doors. He never made a fire in his house for he was afraid it might burn down. He rigged up a fire bucket and across the top placed pieces of green wood or bricks and some iron bars to hold his pot or frying pan. A piece of tin formed a screen to keep the wind from blowing the fire.

He used a "Dutch oven" for baking bread or roasting potatoes but said that a hoe cake cooked in the frying pan was as good bread as any and that potatoes roasted in the ashes were better than any other.

He always had a garden from which he got his vegetables. His poultry flock supplied a pot of chicken quite often and, when a 'possum began to feast on his chickens, Charles put the mother hen and her "biddies" in a basket and hung them up in a tree, set a trap for the 'possum, and Charles ate the 'possum!

Charles had much trouble with his eyeglasses. He wore the variety that would fit anyone and they were always falling off. When the side pieces (bows) were broken he used wire to make a new bow and, in order to insure against their falling off, he bent the wire into the shape of a ring which went over and around his ear.

Generally the lens in his spectacles, one or both of them, was cracked, even broken into many pieces, but he continued to use them; and it did not seem to make much difference, for he looked over the top of his glasses most of the time.

Charles was ingenious; he learned early in life "ter mek what yer hab do!"

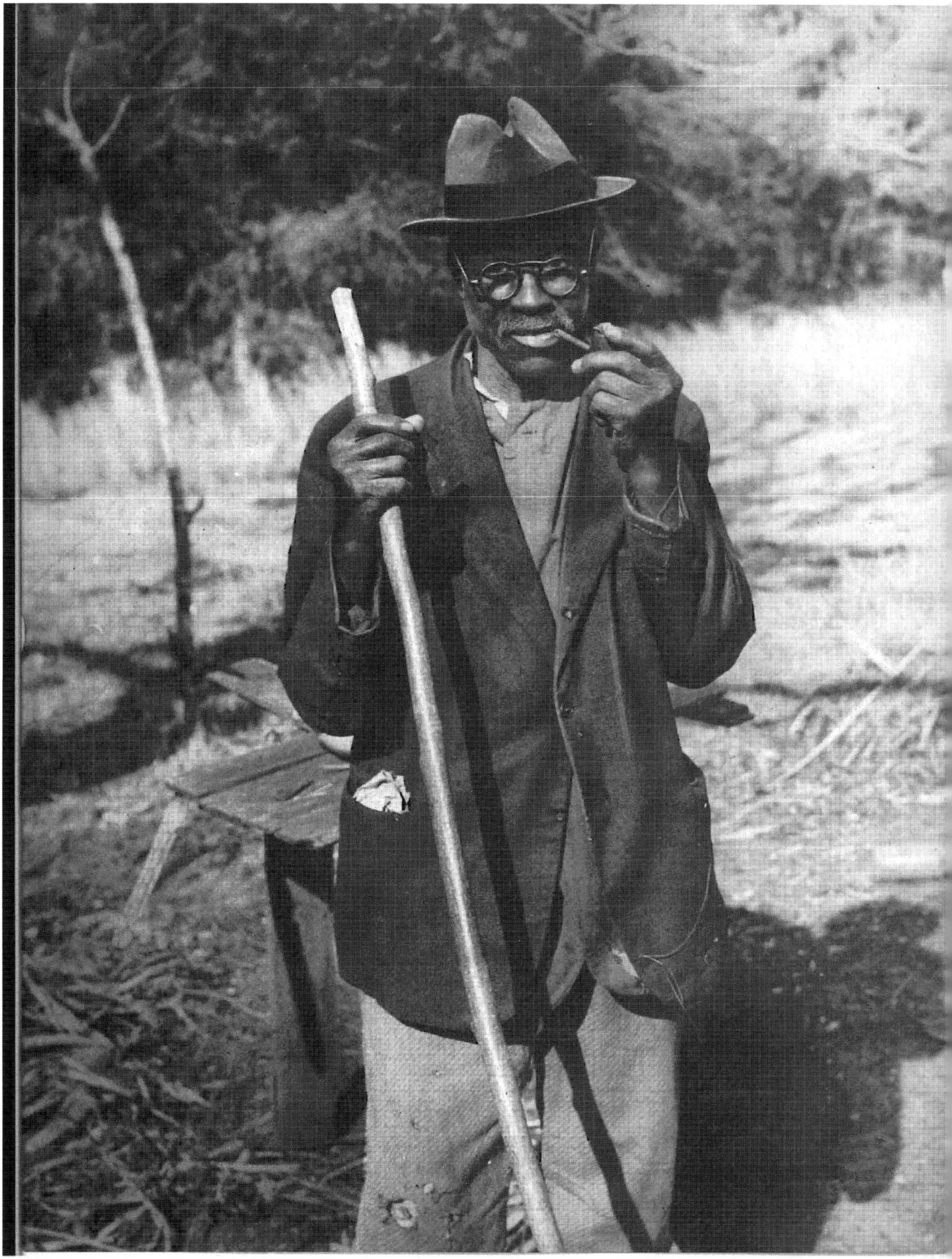

Charles Wilson and His Pipe

Charles said that, when he went out in the woods to gather palmetto leaves for making his baskets, he always lost his pipe, so he never bothered with a "boughten" pipe, but made his own. He gathered the tuberous root of the briar (*Smilax lanceolata* or Florida *smilax*), dried them, hollowed out the bowl and bored the hole of the stem. When asked what he used for a stem, he replied, "Chicken leg bone make a good pipe stem."

Just as Charles went to the woods to get the material for his pipe, so he did for remedies to cure any ailment. Around the door of his little cabin were various herbs, barks, and berries, which he had gathered and hung to dry. He explained that these were made into tea and told of the use to which each was put.

Tea from life everlasting was good for sore throat, that from the berries of the saw palmetto would cure a cold in the head, while sassafras tea was a good Spring tonic and would thin your blood for the hot weather of Summer.

Growing in the yard were other plants which he believed had medicinal value. The leaves of the castor oil bean *(Palma Christi)* made a poultice that would cool the fever and the beans could be pressed for the oil. To open up your head if you had a bad cold, put a handful of mullein leaves in a tea pot of hot water and breathe the steam from the spout.

His directions for the preparation of one of his best remedies gives full instructions on some details but neglects quantities: Take a handful of life everlasting, "blade and root," break it up and put it in the bottom of the pot. Sift some oak ashes and put these ashes in a cloth bag, tie the bag and put it in the pot on top of the life everlasting. Then take a handful of snake root (You want more life everlasting than snake root.) and put it in the pot. Next, chop some "fat light wood" (heart of long leaf yellow pine) into splinters and add to the other things in the pot, cover all this with water and boil "at a simmer" half a day. Strain and drink this tea. Charles said this would cure the flu, "crick" in the neck, cold on the chest, or fever!

[161]

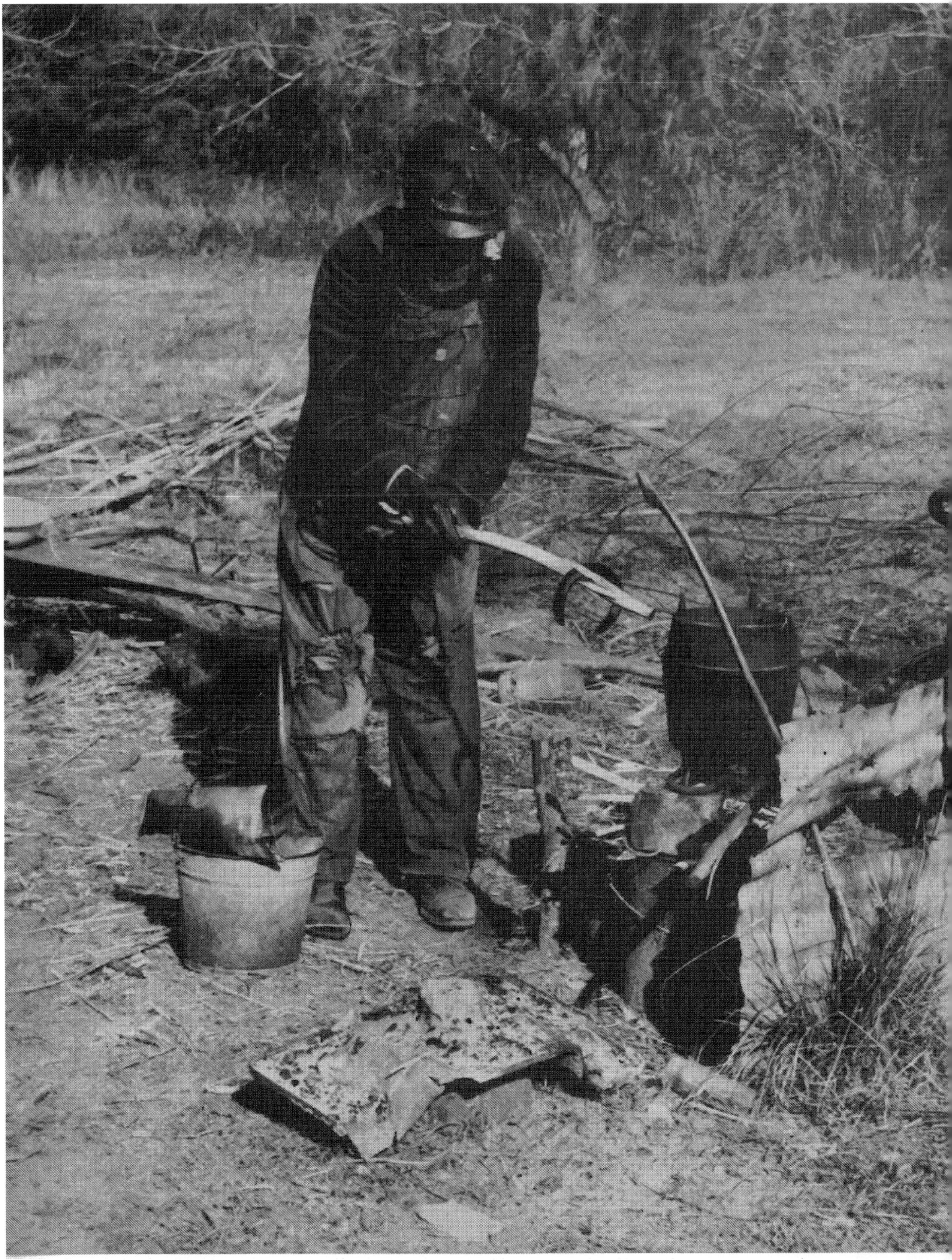

Charles Wilson and His Horseshoe

Though Charles cooked out-of-doors, sometimes he had a fire when there was nothing cooking!

In the foreground of this picture there is an iron door from the oven of an old wood stove. In this Charles built a fire to heat a horseshoe, believing if he kept the horseshoe hot the hawk could not catch his chickens. In fact, if the horseshoe was kept hot, the hawk could not close his talons on the chicken if he caught it! Furthermore, even the smoke from this fire which heated the horseshoe had special powers and no hawk could alight in a tree if this smoke was blown through its branches.

Charles was very serious about this and believed implicitly in the efficacy of the horseshoe. After many years of burning, his horseshoe wore out and broke in two pieces. He was in despair for he had young chickens that would be easy marks for the hawk. Finally, he got another horseshoe, built a fire, heated it and relaxed; his chickens were safe.

Of course Charles lost sight of the fact that in order to keep the horseshoe hot he had to stay out in the yard and keep the fire burning; the hawk saw him and did not come around to bother the chickens. But it *worked!*

Living alone and in a community of Negroes, Charles continued to practice these superstitions which he had learned from his parents long after they had been discarded by other Negroes. He was the last of the old Negroes to plant bene *(Sesamum)* at the end of every row of cotton, corn, etc. in the field. Bene was called the "good luck" plant and was said to bring a good crop.

When asked where he got his bene seed, Charles said he saved it; but when pressed to tell where he got his original start, he said his parents always had it and he was told "Dey brung it fum Africa." He said the "old folks" gathered the seed to use in cooking. They made bene cakes and, on special occasions, bene candy. Also, it was ground in a mortar to extract the oil, which was used as a shortening in the making of cake, oyster stew, or as a butter substitute.

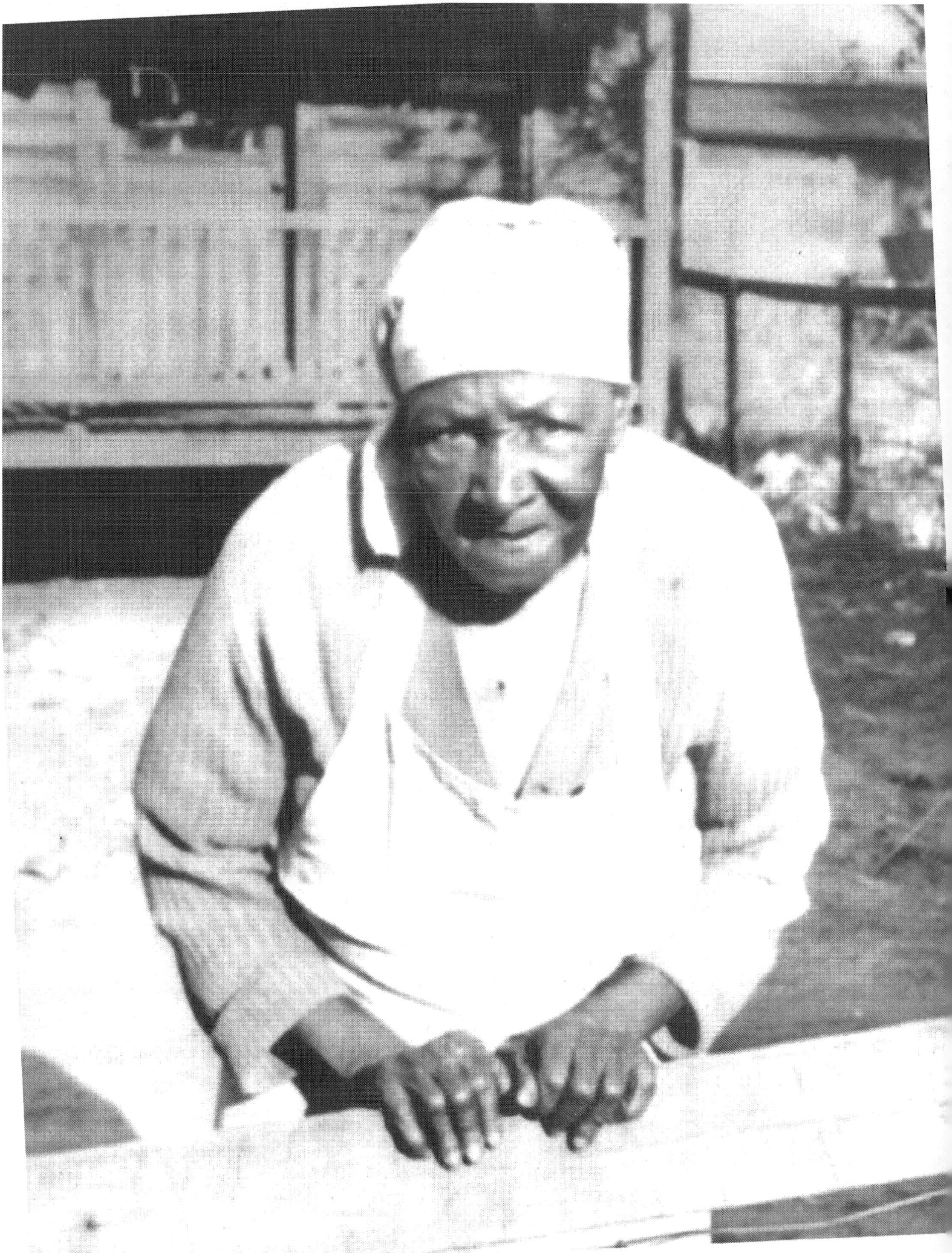

Mary Williams

Mary's parents belonged to the Robert Hazlehurst family who owned Anguilla Plantation. As Mary was born after "the War," she was not a slave; but she always proudly claimed she was "of the pure Hazlehurst stock."

Many years later, while her family was still living there, Anguilla became the property of Hardee M. Stafford, who built the old Anguilla house which became the Townsend home. Mary adopted the new owners of Auguilla as her "family" and, when the Staffords sold the plantation, she moved to Brunswick. However, this did not sever the bond and she continued to claim the protection of the Hazlehursts and the Staffords — her "white folks."

Anguilla Plantation, located on the mainland about fourteen miles west of Brunswick, took its name from the famous Sea Island cotton whose long silky fibres brought wealth to the plantations of this area for a century. This was a Persian cotton which had been developed in the British West Indies and was sent to St. Simons Island from the Island of Anguilla. For many years it was called "Anguilla Cotton"; later, it became known as Sea Island cotton since it was believed that it would grow only on the sea islands. However, the Hazlehursts, having planted it on their plantation, proved that it would grow on the mainland as well as the islands, and named the plantation Anguilla.

Anguilla and adjacent Marengo, the home of the Nicolau family, were among the plantations served by Georgia's first Post Road and oldest highway. Waynesville, located near this road, became a popular watering place in the 1830's when planters from the coastal area established summer homes there to escape the "miasma" of the dreaded night air which was thought to cause malaria fever. Beyond Waynesville and these Post Road plantations lay the "pine barrens" of the section known as "Wiregrass Georgia," with a way of life in sharp contrast to the plantation life of the coast. The Post Road marked the western boundary of this Coastal Culture.

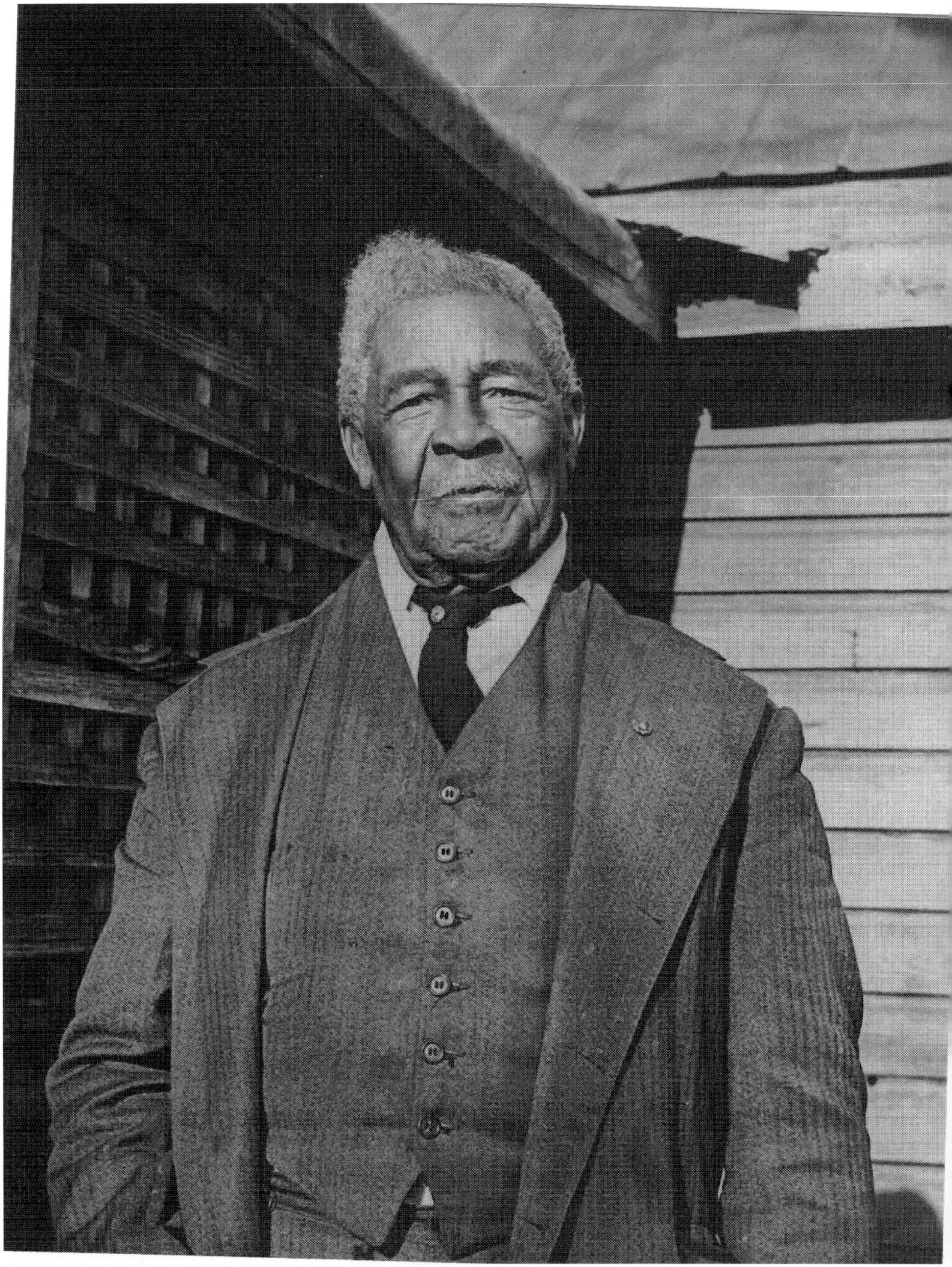

Reverend Elijah J. Rozzell

Reverend Elijah J. Rozzell has the distinction of having served one congregation for fifty-eight years. In 1895, he became the pastor of the Mt. Olive Baptist Church in Brunswick and continued in this capacity until his feeble health necessitated his retirement. His gentle voice and manner were what one would expect of his calling and his life and work in this community earned for him the respect of all who knew him.

Rozzell was not a local man and the story of his coming to Brunswick is interesting. He, his father and other members of his family, were among a group of 297 men, women and children who arrived here on February 23, 1893. They came from McCrory, Arkansas, having been prosperous farmers in Jackson, White and Woodruff Counties in that State. Beguiled by the tale of an unscrupulous man who promised to send them to Liberia, these people sold their farms and livestock to secure the money for the trip. Paying this man five dollars apiece for the voyage, they packed their household goods for the train trip to Brunswick, where they expected to board the vessel for Africa.

Arriving here, they found that the man had absconded with their money and there was no ship awaiting them. Transplanted into a strange community, with only their clothes, household goods, and some foodstuffs which they had brought from their farms, they presented a tragic picture. The people of Brunswick took them in hand, provided shelter, and offered work. Turpentine and lumber operators and farmers from all over South Georgia heard of them and came to Brunswick to offer them homes and work. Many found employment on the wharves which lined the harbor of Brunswick. Today, the descendants of these Arkansas Negroes live throughout this section and have proved themselves to be good citizens.

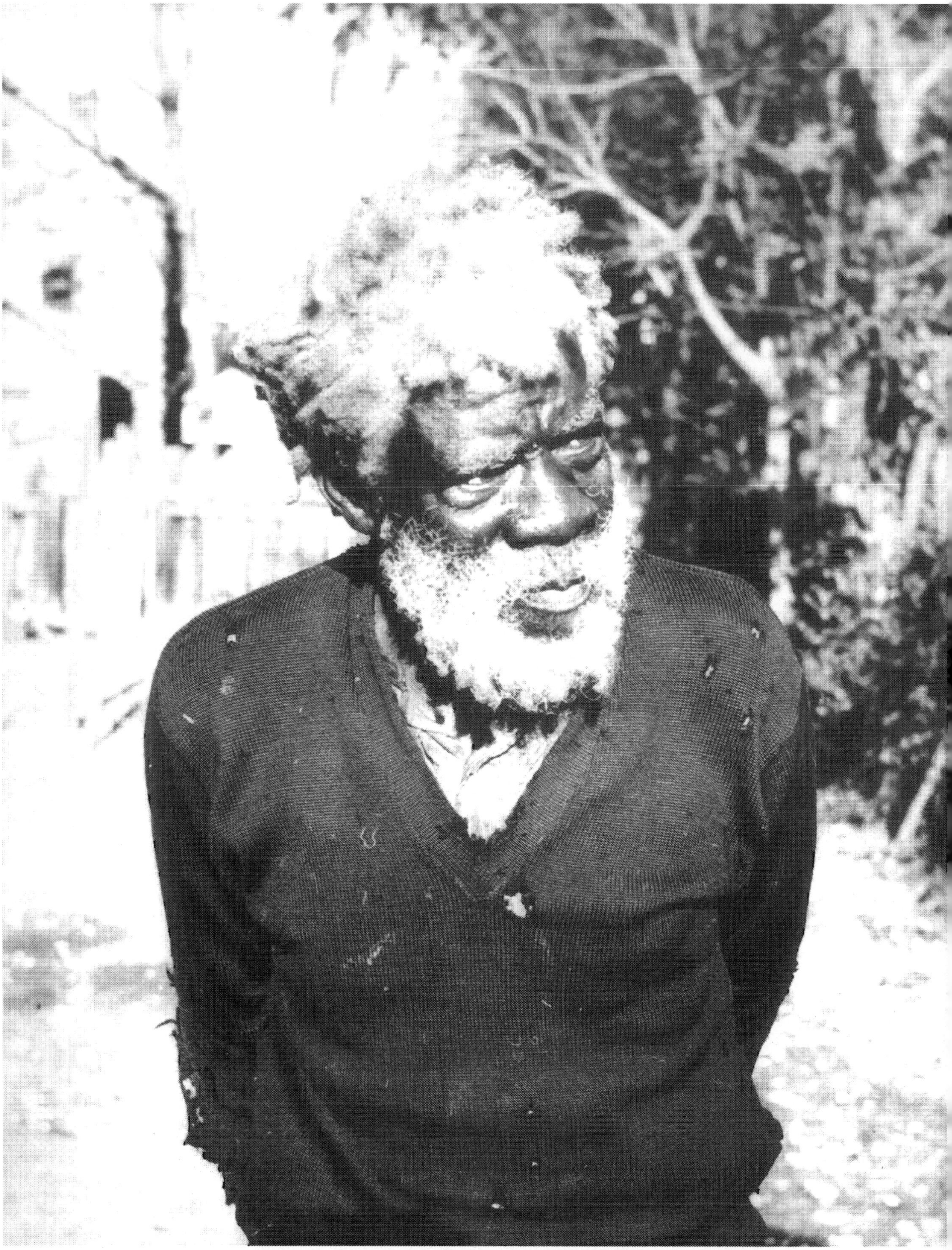

Dan Hopkins

Dan Hopkins was born on Cumberland Island "about ten years befo' de war broke out." He was the property of Robert Church and after the war he came to Brunswick where he lived with "Ole Missus" until she died. After that he started in as a deck-hand, finally, working up to the position of engineer on the various steamers that made regular trips from Brunswick to Darien and to St. Simons, Jekyll, and Cumberland Islands. He worked on the *Egmont, City of Brunswick, Hessie, Attaquin, Emmeline* and *Atlantic*.

In 1882 he was married to Lena Carter of Sapelo Island, the record of their marriage being carefully recorded in the Bible of the bride's family. Dan and Lena lived in Brunswick where they owned a comfortable home in Dixville.

In his old age as Dan's mind became feeble, his wife would not allow him to go on the street alone for fear he might get hurt. They had a big yard where he spent much time, talking over the fence with the neighbors and amusing himself for hours at a time.

A visitor who called to see Dan asked his wife where he was and was informed, "He's out in de yard."

Then came the question, "What does he do in the yard?"

The wife's answer was, "Oh, he picks up shells."

"What does he do with shells?"

"He polishes 'em off nice an' clean, puts 'em in his pocket an' brings 'em in de house."

"Then what do you do with them?"

Dan's good old wife's reply showed her understanding heart: "I puts 'em back in de yard so he kin pick 'em up agin."

She apologized for the appearance of his hair, saying he did not want his hair cut; and, if he did not want his hair cut, he did not have to have it cut. That was *his* business! And we agreed.

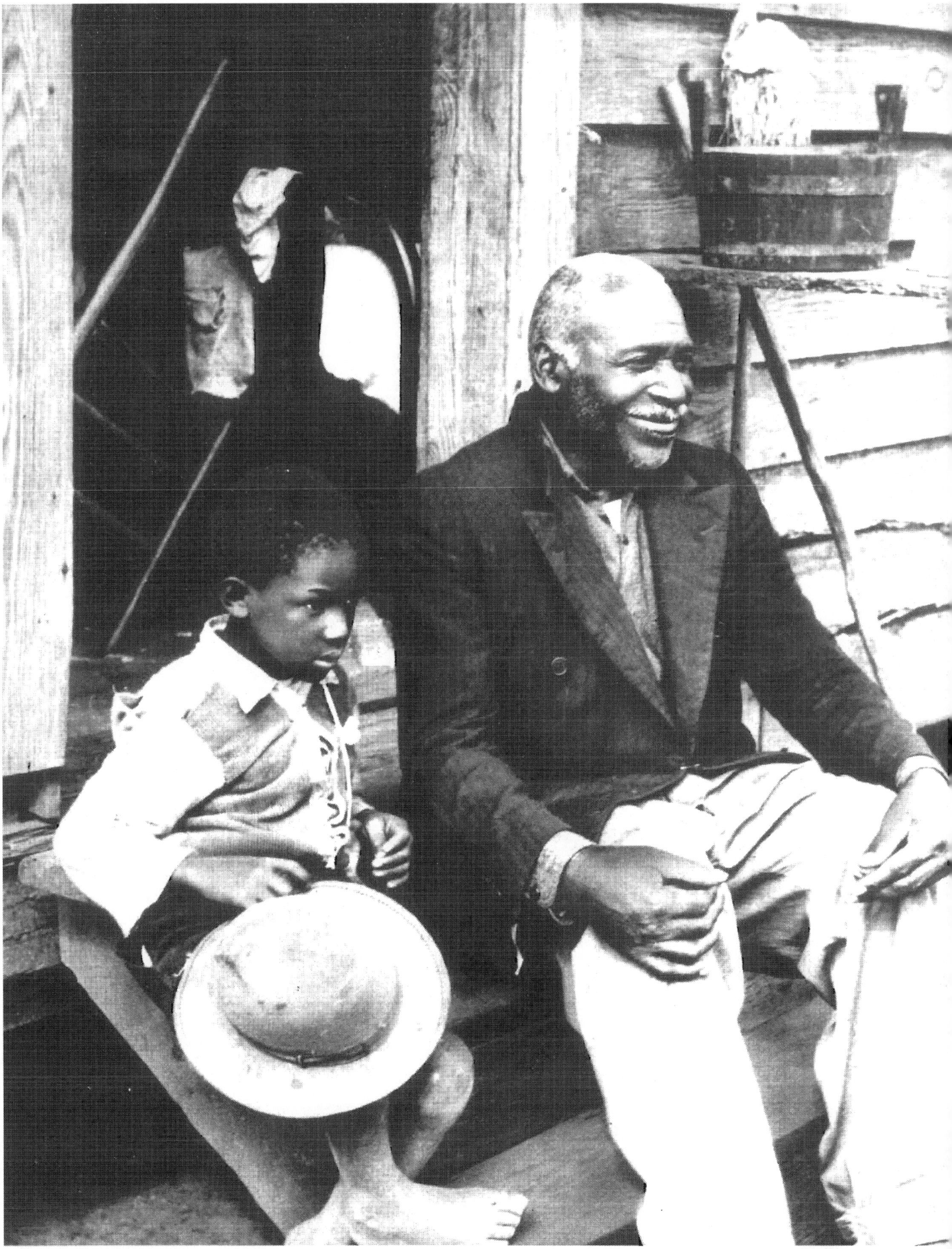

Rufus McDonald

Rufus McDonald lived in the Pennick section of Glynn County in a house that had belonged to his wife who had been dead many years. When talking about the house he referred to it as "heirs' property," meaning that it was not his house but would go to the children of his wife by a previous marriage.

Here, near the kitchen door, were the hoe and the mop, while the wooden tub held the supply of water within easy reach of the kitchen, with the water dipper and a bar of Octagon soap nearby.

Rufus lived to be eighty years old and in his last illness he said, "I won't be here much longer, but I aint tired o' being here yet!"

Rufus looked like "Uncle Remus" and it seems entirely proper that there should be a child in the picture with him. No doubt he *was* Uncle Remus to this child and told him the old stories which the Negroes brought from Africa and which have been handed down from generation to generation. Joel Chandler Harris preserved the folk tales of the Middle Georgia Negro while here on the coast where the dialect is entirely different, these old African tales were collected and published about a quarter of a century after the war by Georgia's eminent historian, Charles Colcock Jones, Jr., under the title, *Negro Myths from the Georgia Coast*.

This little boy was one of the "heirs" who would claim the property when Rufus was gone. While playing around in the yard, this child, like all people who live much in the open, was quick to notice the new moon which had appeared in the western sky. Turning to look at it, he clasped his hands in an attitude of prayer and said, "God bless the new moon!"

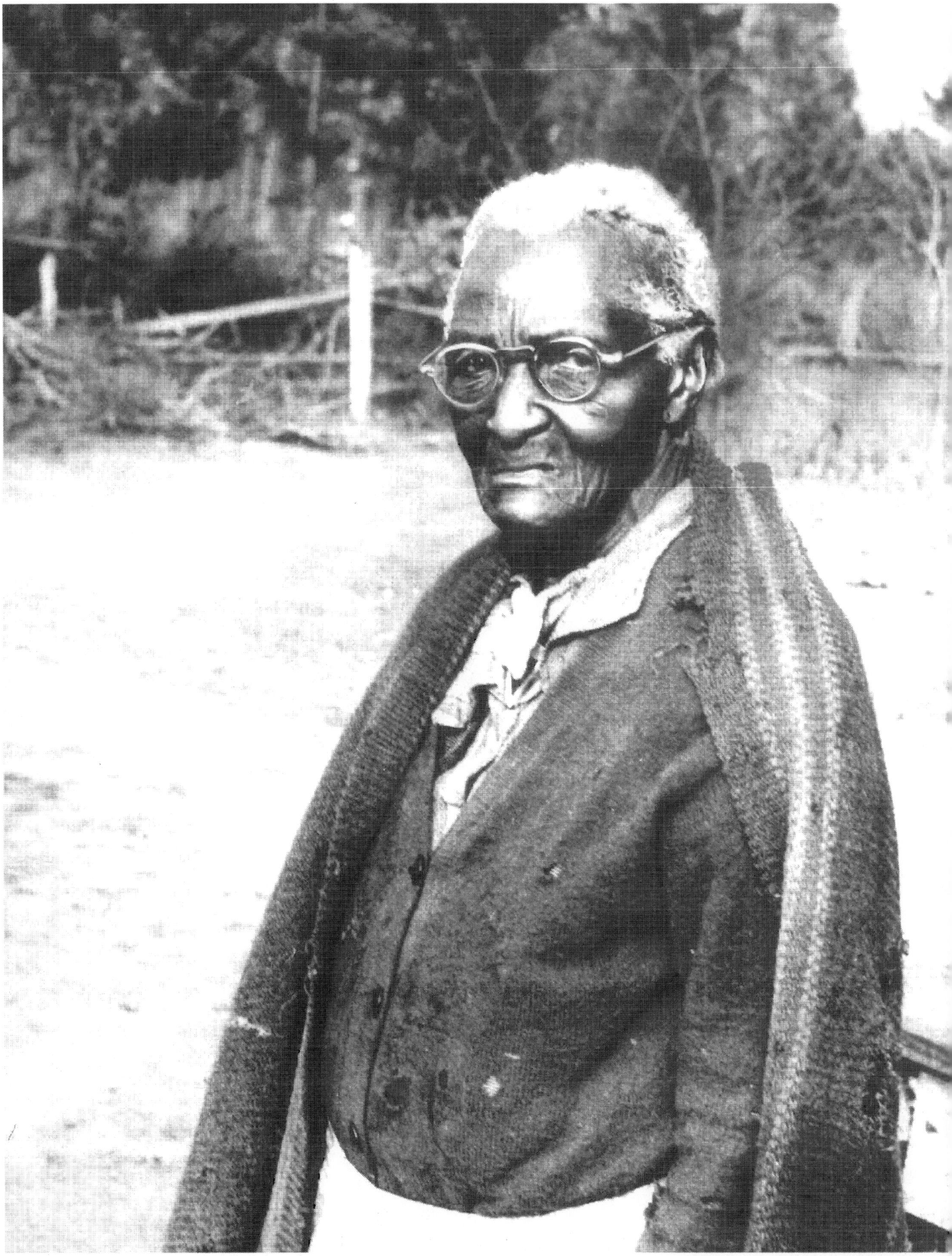

Ella Pinkney

Ella Pinkney, whose years rounded out a century, was very proud of the fact that she had been a house servant. When asked her age, she dated herself with the statement that she was a big girl waiting on the table at Mr. Berrie's house "When freedom come," which was her way of referring to the emancipation of the Negro.

Ella's pride in having been a house servant was typical of the attitude of slaves of the plantations. Among them there was a definite caste system, headed by the house servants — the butler, cook, maids, and children's nurses — and the artisans — the carpenter, blacksmith, seamstress, and nurses for the sick — who looked down on the "field hands." The Negroes trained for these special positions were chosen because of their superior intelligence. Many of these were Senegalese, who had a strong Arabic strain in their ancestry and were considered the most intelligent of the African tribes and, therefore, especially desired as house servants and craftsmen.

As would be expected for one of her great age, sometimes Ella was not well and had to stay in bed. On such an occasion she told a visitor, "De han' ob de Lord is on me, so I jus' keep quiet till He lif's it."

Her little vegetable garden with its straight rows, free of grass and weeds, brought forth the question, "Ella, who made your garden?"

"I made my own garden," she said.

The visitor protested, "But, Ella, you've just been telling me about the misery in your back."

Ella's reply expressed her wonderful philosophy of life: "O missus, yer got to resis' yer feelin's!"

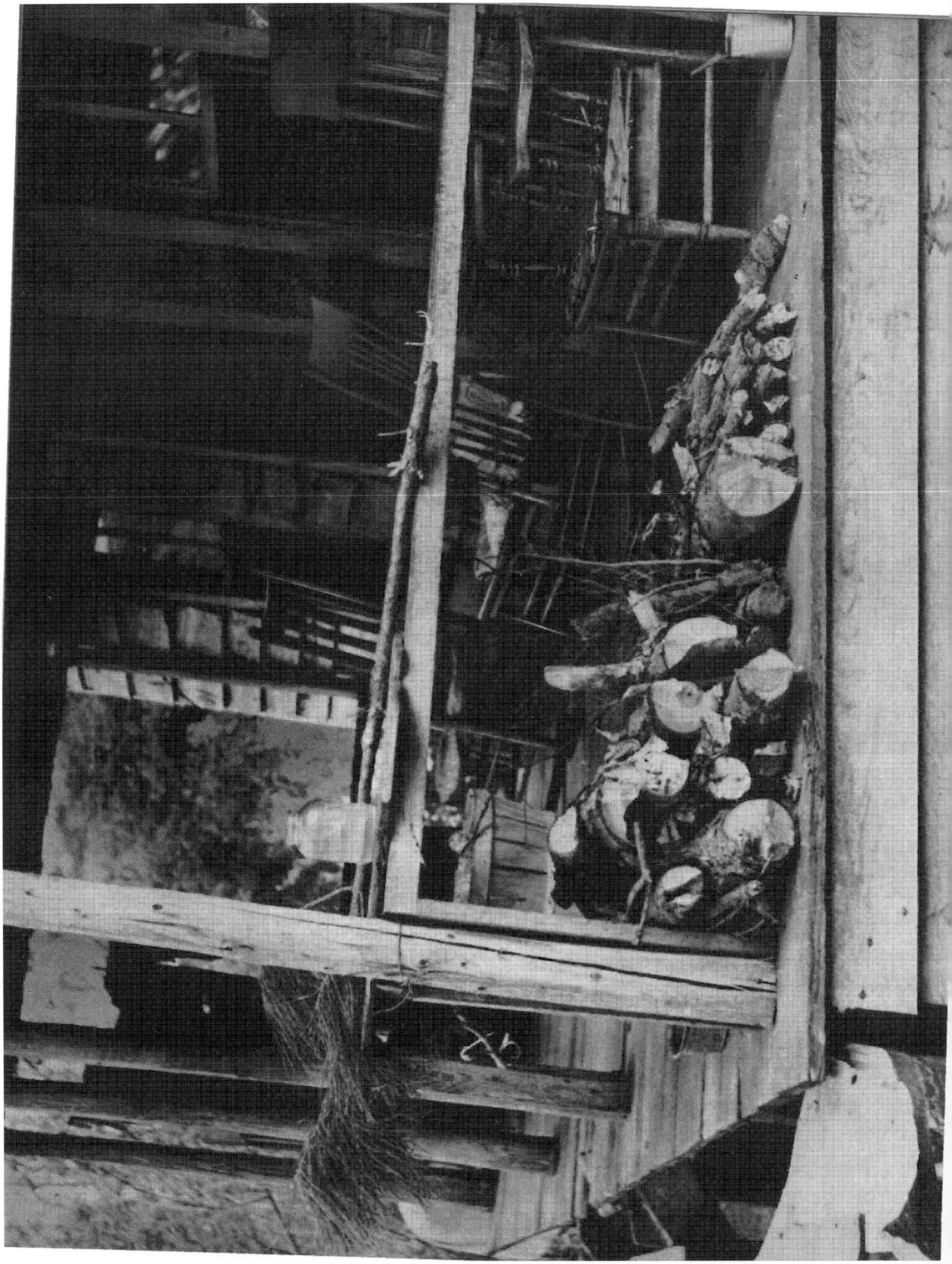

Ella Pinkney's Front Porch

Ella's plan of living was reduced to a simple formula and life centered on her front porch. Here she could sit and see who passed by on the road. If she had company, there were chairs for them also; if she wanted wood for the fireplace in the house, she did not have to go out in the yard to get the wood. The wash-tub was here, too, so that she could do the washing and still not miss the passerby.

The brush broom with which Ella swept her yard was lying on the banisters. Negroes always sweep their yards and never allow grass to grow in any part of them. Having fought to keep grass out of their fields, they want none of it in their front yards either.

The arrangement of the flowers in their front yards followed the pattern of the plantation garden, though on a greatly reduced scale. The walks and designs for small flower beds were outlined with sea shells These designs were small circles or diamond-shaped beds balanced on either side of the walk which led from the gate to the front steps.

In these circles or diamond-shaped beds were the cape jessamine, ribbon cane, moss or cabbage roses, japonicas, crepe myrtle, oleander, hydrangea, spirea, spider lily, and other flowers which they had gotten from their "white folks." The beds and walks were bordered with violets, hearts'-ease, snow drop, jonquil, and narcissus, and everywhere was clean white sand to be swept with the brush broom.

These Negro houses were built a foot or two off the ground and rested on wooden blocks or brick pillars. This allowed circulation of air under the house which was insurance against termites, besides providing a storage place for many odds and ends!

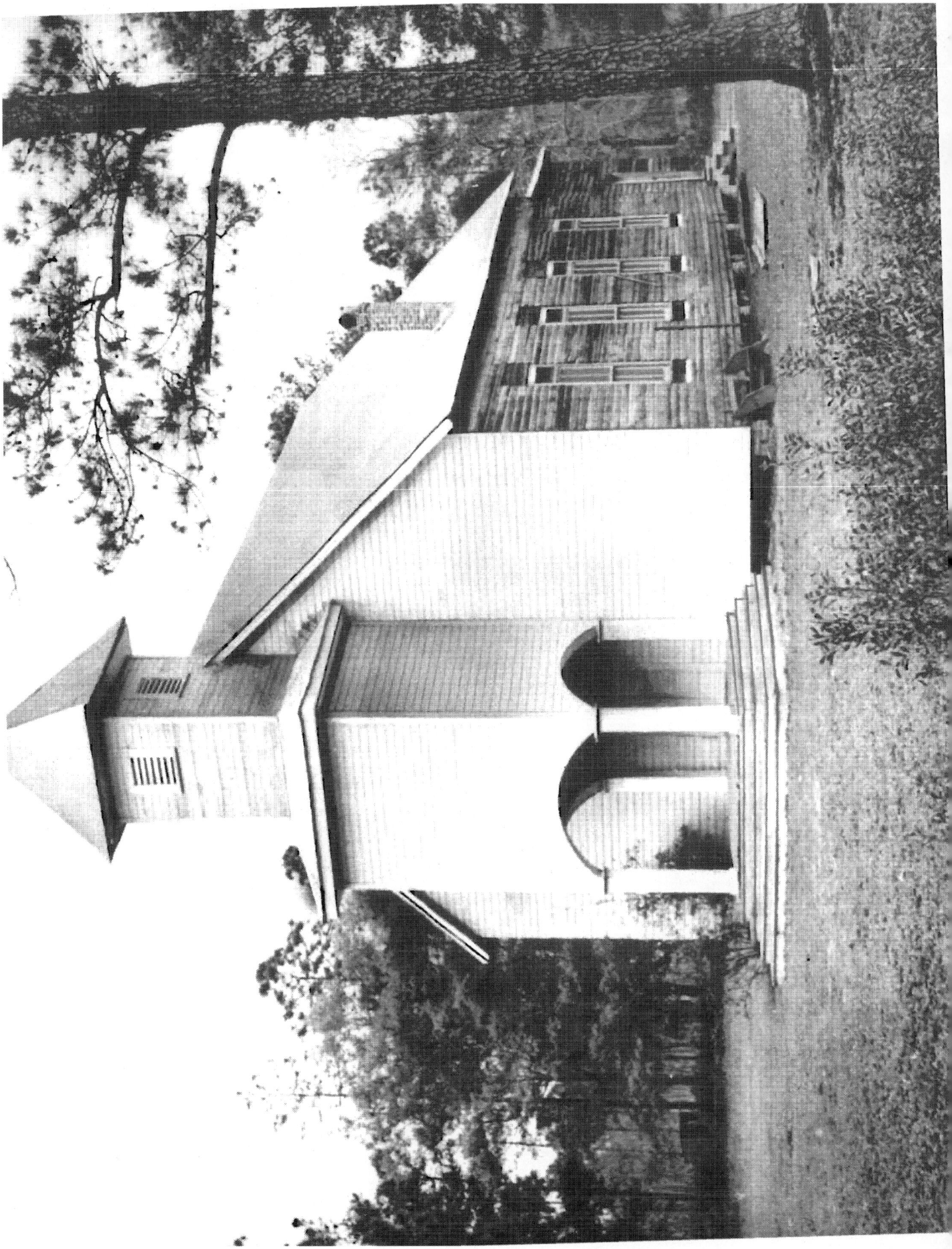

Salem Baptist Church

This Negro Baptist Church located near Sterling serves the Negro population for many miles around. Its congregation is made up of families of former slaves from the various plantations nearby, many of them being from the rice fields. Up until the organization of this Salem Baptist Church, these Negroes had worshipped in the Broadfield Baptist Church; but in 1874 eighty-four members of the Broadfield Church asked for letters of dismissal from their old church and organized the new Salem Church.

The Baptist Church is very popular among the Coastal Georgia Negroes to whom the baptismal ceremony is an important event. Though most modern churches have pools built into the building, the time-honored custom of the early churches was to baptize in the river.

Marching from the church and singing as they marched, the entire congregation formed the procession. Led by the minister and the deacons and followed by the candidates robed in white, the group proceeded to the bluff where the ceremony was to take place. The deacons and the minister walked cautiously into the water, measuring the depth with a staff and picking out a safe place for the baptism. This was carefully timed so as to take place at "high water" just after the tide had turned and was on the ebb, for the water must be going out in order to take away the sins of the newly baptized members. If the tide had not turned, the water might bring the sins back and it was important that they be carried away by the outgoing tide.

For a half century after it was built this building went unpainted. Then the members found the money to paint the front, and for a quarter of a century it stood with only that part of the building painted. Being a thrifty people and knowing how hard it is to pay a debt, they hesitated to obligate themselves. A visitor hearing their story and admiring the spirit of people who could do without that which they could not afford, gave the paint for the entire building and the members did the work themselves. This new coat of paint called for other improvements and repairs, so that now in the last quarter of its first century this old building has taken on new life.

[177]

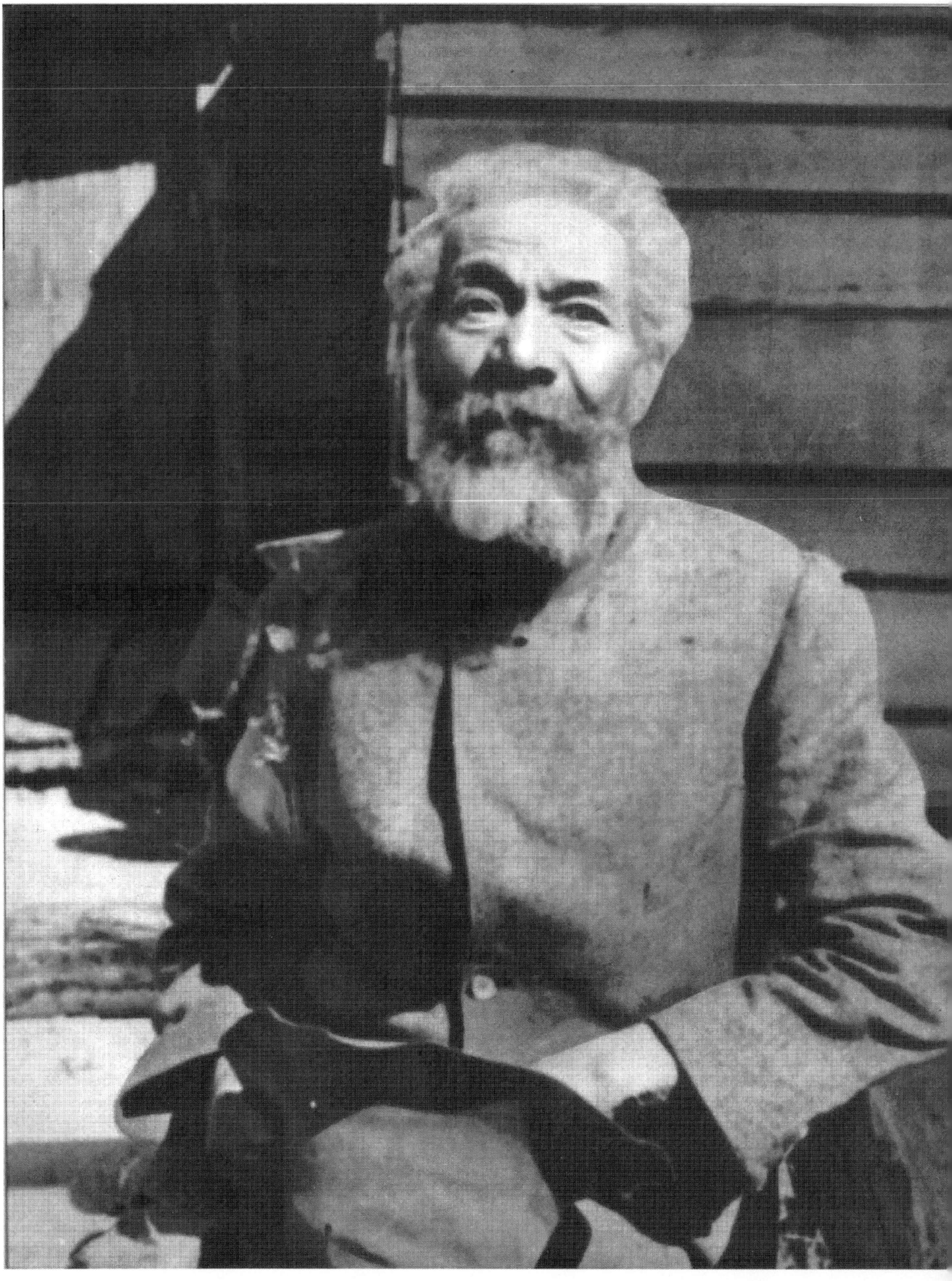

Charles Alexander

Charles Alexander was born at Butler Point on St. Simons Island the first year of "the War." Since he was born before the emancipation of the Negro, he always said he was born a slave even though he knew nothing of slavery.

His mother, Minta, belonged to the Butlers and Charles said she lived for a time in Philadelphia, where the Butlers had one of the finest residences in that city. Speaking of her, Charles said she was a "valuesome" woman.

One of his brothers bore the name of their old master, being named Pierce Butler Alexander, and Charles had a grandson with the same name; however, they wrote it as they spoke it, "Pace Butler Alexander."

Charles had gone to school when he was young; he said he went through the blueback speller four times. He was one of a large family of children, all of whom were outstanding in the community in which they lived.

His brother, John Ellison Alexander, worked out a unique method of keeping up with the days of the week. He nailed seven nails in a row and moved a looped wire from nail to nail for each new day. When he reached the last nail in the row the looped wire was then moved back to the first nail and a new week was ushered in.

These men had a sister who became a deaconess of the Episcopal Church and operated a school in their neighborhood, a settlement known as Pennick. Deaconess Alexander earned and held the respect of all who knew her. Her influence for good in the lives of the children who came under her guidance is her monument.

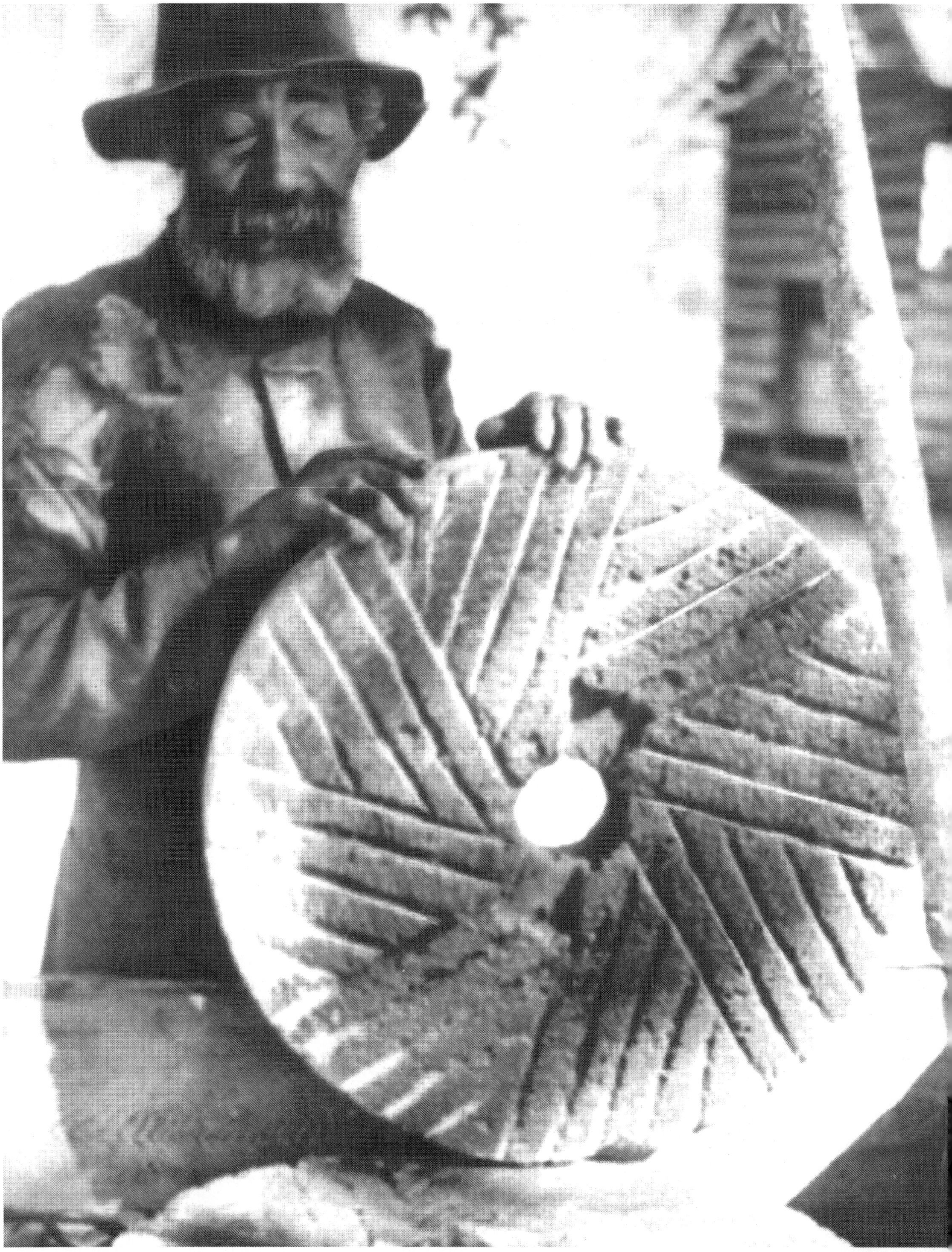

Charles Alexander's Mill

This old mill had been used by four generations of Charles Alexander's family to grind corn into meal and grits. He explained, however, that he did not use it any more for now he bought his meal and grits at the store.

This mill was made of two round stones about two feet in diameter and four inches thick. The lower, or nether, stone was fixed in the box which housed the mill, while the upper stone, known as the "runner," was turned on the nether stone.

The inside surfaces of these stones were cut with grooves or "furrows." In such mill stones the pattern of these furrows varied greatly but always the furrows were arranged so that they threw the ground grain out into the box from which it was collected.

The smooth surface of the stones between the furrows was known as the "land."

The grain to be ground was poured into the "eye" or hole in the center of the runner, while the oblong depression in the middle and around the eye of this upper stone, or runner, was called the "bosom" and was made to hold the "frog," which held the two stones apart and made it possible to turn the runner on the nether stone.

A long pole, which went through a hole in the horizontal timber above the mill and rested in a socket near the outside edge of the runner, was used to turn the stone. Two people, standing on opposite sides of the mill, grasped the pole and turned the runner.

Here, Charles is showing the inner surface of the runner, the furrows of which make a pleasing design.

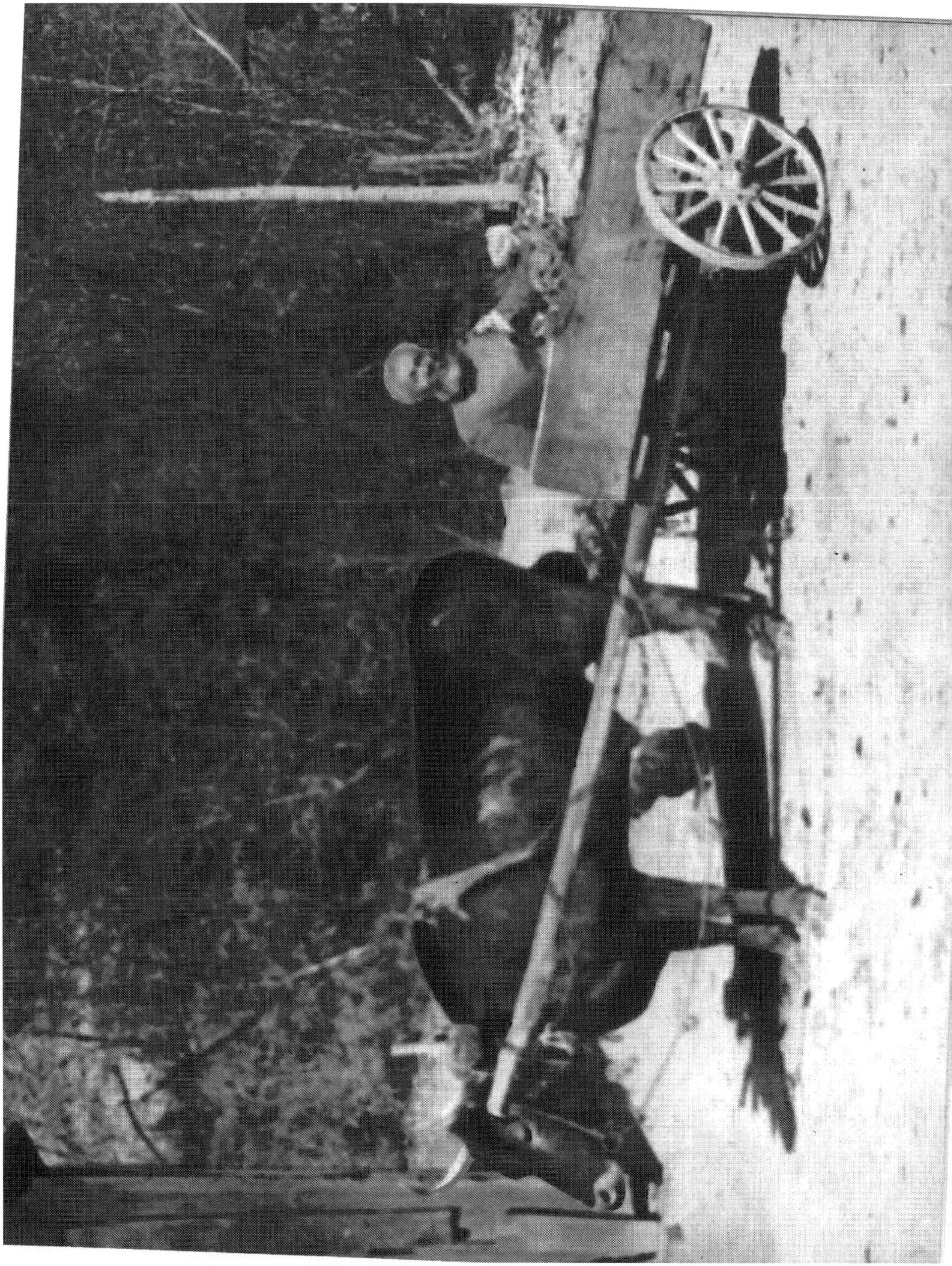

Charles Alexander's Ox Cart

Seeing the cart in the yard at Alexander's home in the Pennick section of Glynn County, the visitor inquired, "Charles, do you have a critter?" (A critter being a horse, a mule, an ox, or anything that does the work.)

The reply was, "Yas'm, I got a critter." He then got his critter out of the woods and hitched it to his cart to show how he would ride down the road to the store. He said it took all day, but it was better than walking! We wondered.

Some of the harness was crocus sack and did not look very substantial; but perhaps it was safe, for it did not seem probable that this steed would have any inclination to run away!

Though Charles used a yoke to hitch up his ox, he "drove" with plow lines as reins instead of guiding his ox with the "gee" and "haw" commonly used for such animals.

The small wheels put the cart close to the ground and made it easy for Charles to crawl into the cart for his slow ride down the road. Evidently he was like the man who told his son to *ride* always and never walk if he could help it: "Ride a horse if you can get it; if you can't get a horse, ride a mule; if you can't get a mule, ride an ox — but *ride!*"

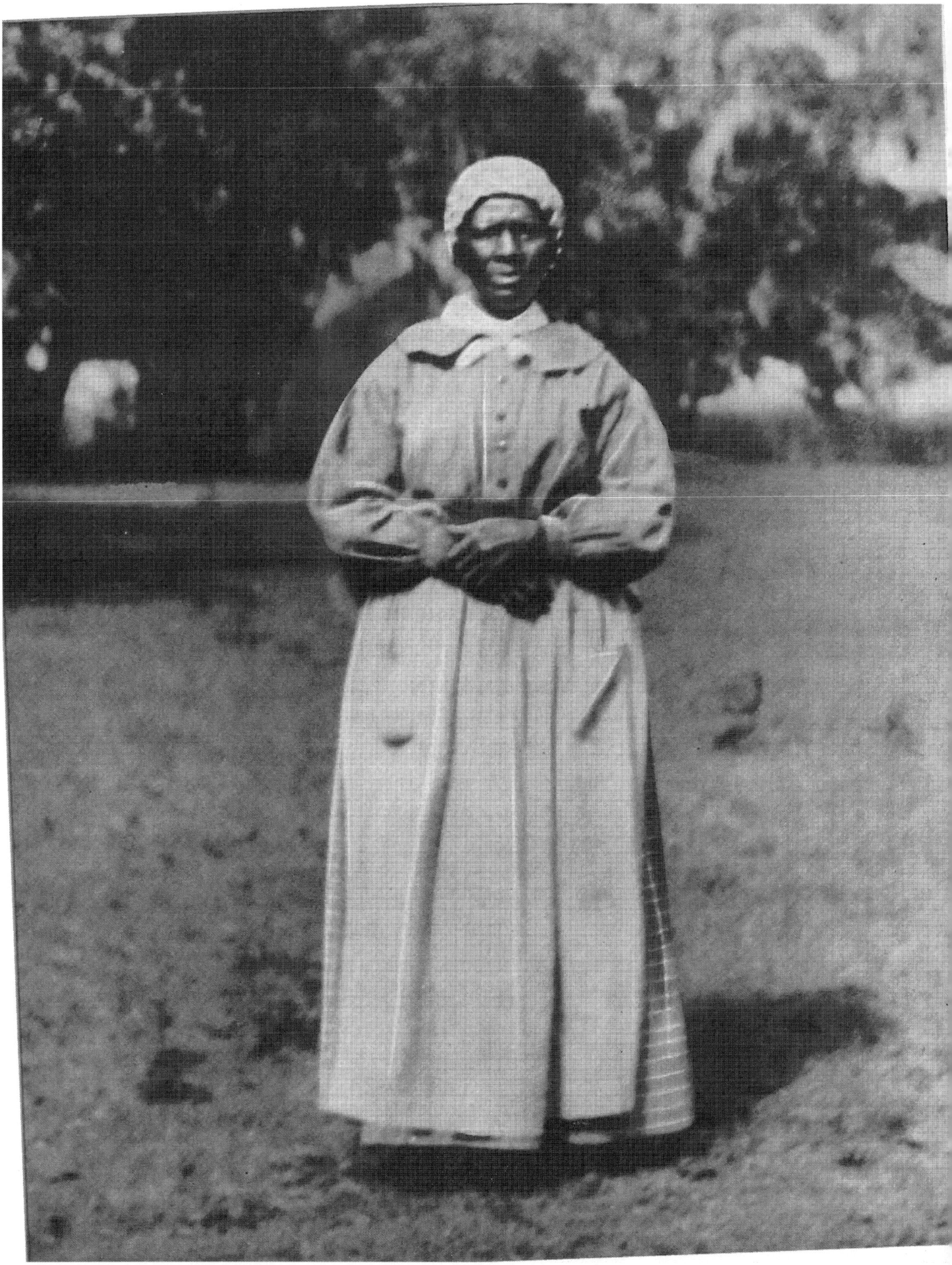

Tyrah Wilson

Tyrah Wilson was the mantuamaker of Mrs. George C. Dent, née Ophelia Troup, of Hofwyl Plantation. Trained as a seamstress, Tyrah was in charge of the sewing room and of a group of women who worked under her direction and whose task it was to make the clothes for the Negroes of the plantation. Measuring and cutting the cloth under the direction of the mistress of the plantation, the sewing room workers were a busy group.

Old plantation record books are filled with individual entries that tell of the purchases of supplies for this department, such as ten pounds of thread, one hundred needles, and hundreds of yards of Osnaburg, grey cloth, Kersey, and linsey woolsey, as well as homespun, linen drill, and bleached shirting.

This old picture shows the correct dress of a house servant of the plantation. The gingham dress consists of a shirt waist with long sleeves and and high neck finished with a collar, while the skirt is ankle-length and made of several widths of cloth gathered to the waist band.

The white apron, with two big pockets, covers the front and reaches almost to the bottom of the skirt. In these pockets, no doubt, Tyrah carries the keys to her work rooms since she would be responsible for the materials kept there. Keys were considered a badge of authority and the person who carried them was a trusted servant.

The kerchief at her neck and the cap on her head complete this perfect picture of an old-time servant.

The pride in her bearing tells of her knowledge that, in the world in which she moves, she is a person of importance.

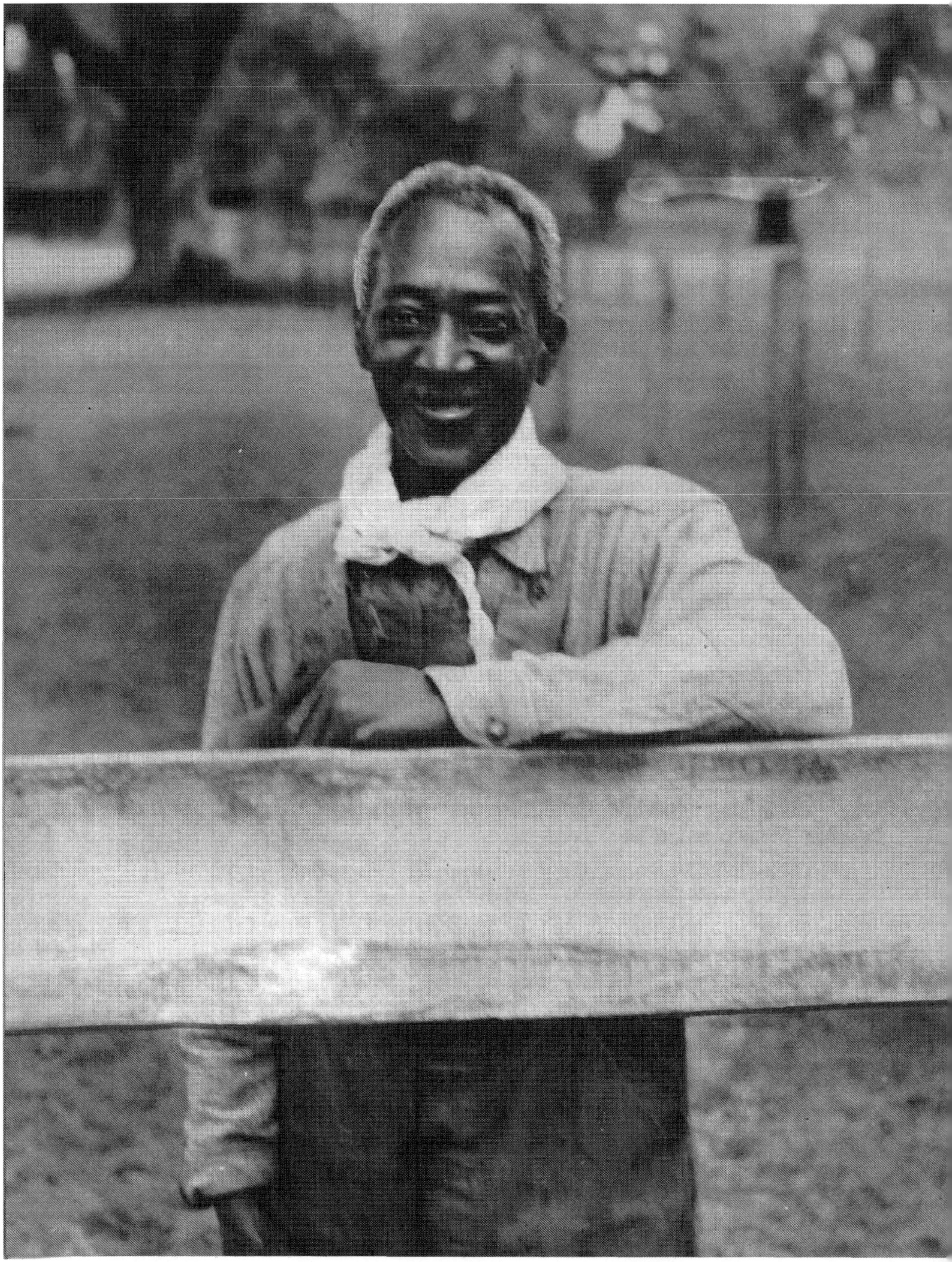

Morris Polite

From the time he was old enough to work until his death at the age of eighty, Morris Polite worked on Hofwyl Plantation and for three generations of one family. At his funeral the preacher commented on this, saying, "That speaks well for Morris and speaks well for the family, too!"

As far back as anyone knows this Polite family has belonged to Hofwyl Plantation or Broadfield Plantation, Hofwyl having once been a part of Broadfield. Since "the War" Morris' grandfather, his father, Morris, his sons, and his grandsons — five generations — have worked on this same plantation where their slave ancestors toiled.

Morris lived in a settlement known as Petersville, which was formerly a part of the Broadfield-Hofwyl tract. Here he owned a small plot of ground where he built a modest cottage in which he and his wife, Joan, raised a family of thirteen children. In this Petersville settlement many of Morris' children, grandchildren and great-grandchildren still live; so that, slave and freedman, the members of this family have lived in an area not more than two miles square for about a century and a half.

This family of Negroes still live up to the reputation of their ancestor who took the name "Polite" after the emancipation of the Negro. Morris' grandfather, who adopted the name, was noted for his politeness. Of him it was said, "He always had his hat in his hand and was bowing and scraping."

Morris' features show his descent from those African tribes who had superior intelligence, being of the group who were trained as house servants or for specialized work — never as field hands.

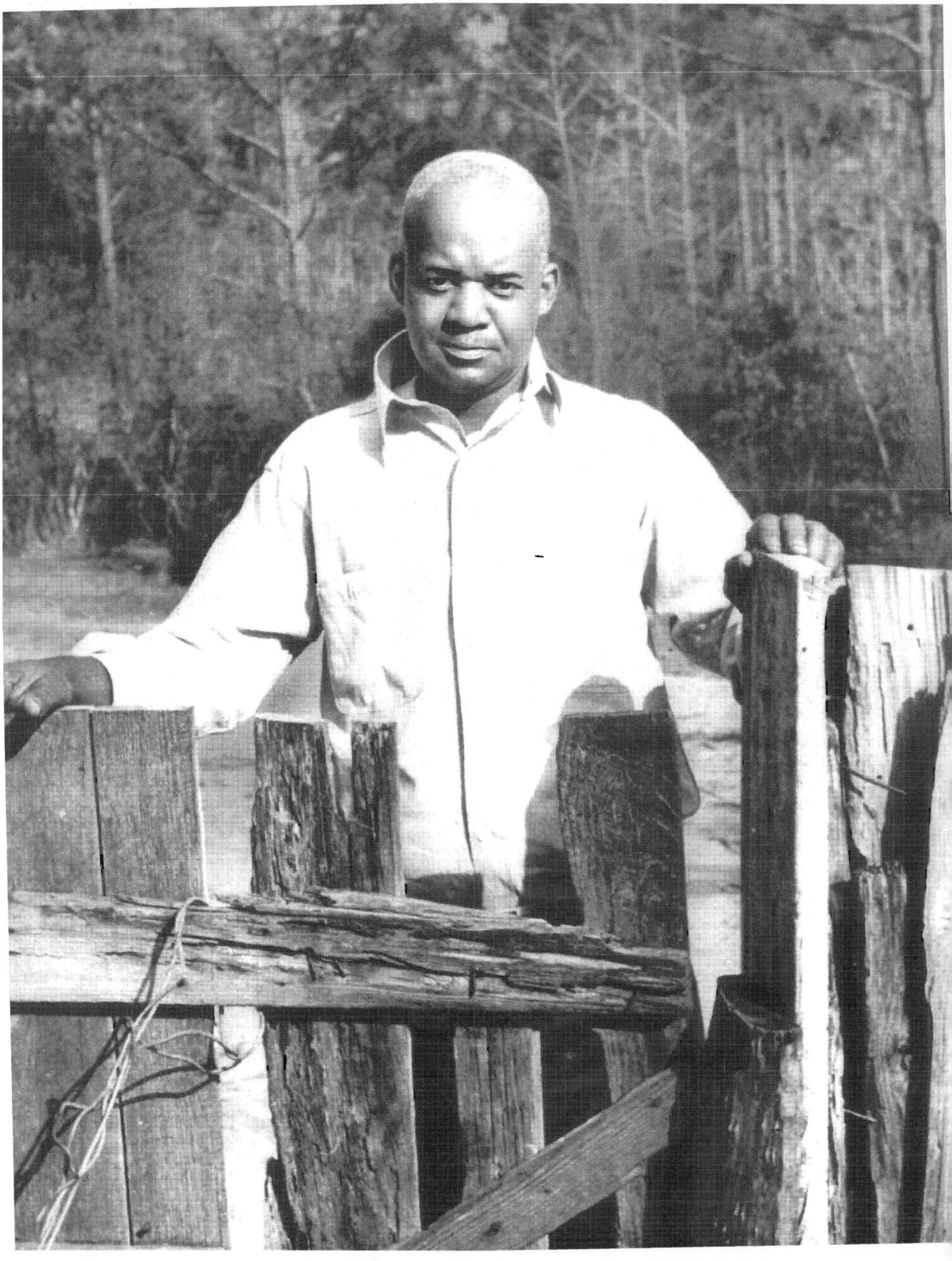

London Polite

London was Morris' oldest son and in many ways was like his father. However, Morris was sober and sedate while London always found something to laugh about. His happy disposition made him a favorite with children who liked nothing better than to be with him.

London had charge of the Cate farm, Touchstone Ridge, for twenty-six years and was a faithful, loyal servant. His wife, Mamie, was sick for a long time and he attended her every need to the very end.

When Mamie died, London was discussing affairs with the "Missus" who asked, "London, have you ever been married before?"

"Oh yes, Missus, I got a wife right her in Brumsick."

"Oh! Then you were divorced."

His reply was a trifle startling for he said, "Missus, de guvment 'vorce me."

His "Missus" asked, "Well, London, how was that?"

London's reply was a full explanation: "Well, you know, Missus, I was drafted in de fust World War an' dey tol' me ef I wuz libin' wid her dey wouldn't sen' me to France; an' I tol' dem dey could sen' me to war, I wouldn't lib wid dat woman no mo'. Dey didn't gib her none o' my 'lotment and dat wuz all de same as a 'vorce!"

The Missus' reply, "O, yes!" might have seemed slightly skeptical to London, for he further bolstered his defense with this statement:

"But, Missus, dat wouldn't uh made no diffunt. I married her in Darien an' I married Mamie in Brumsick!"

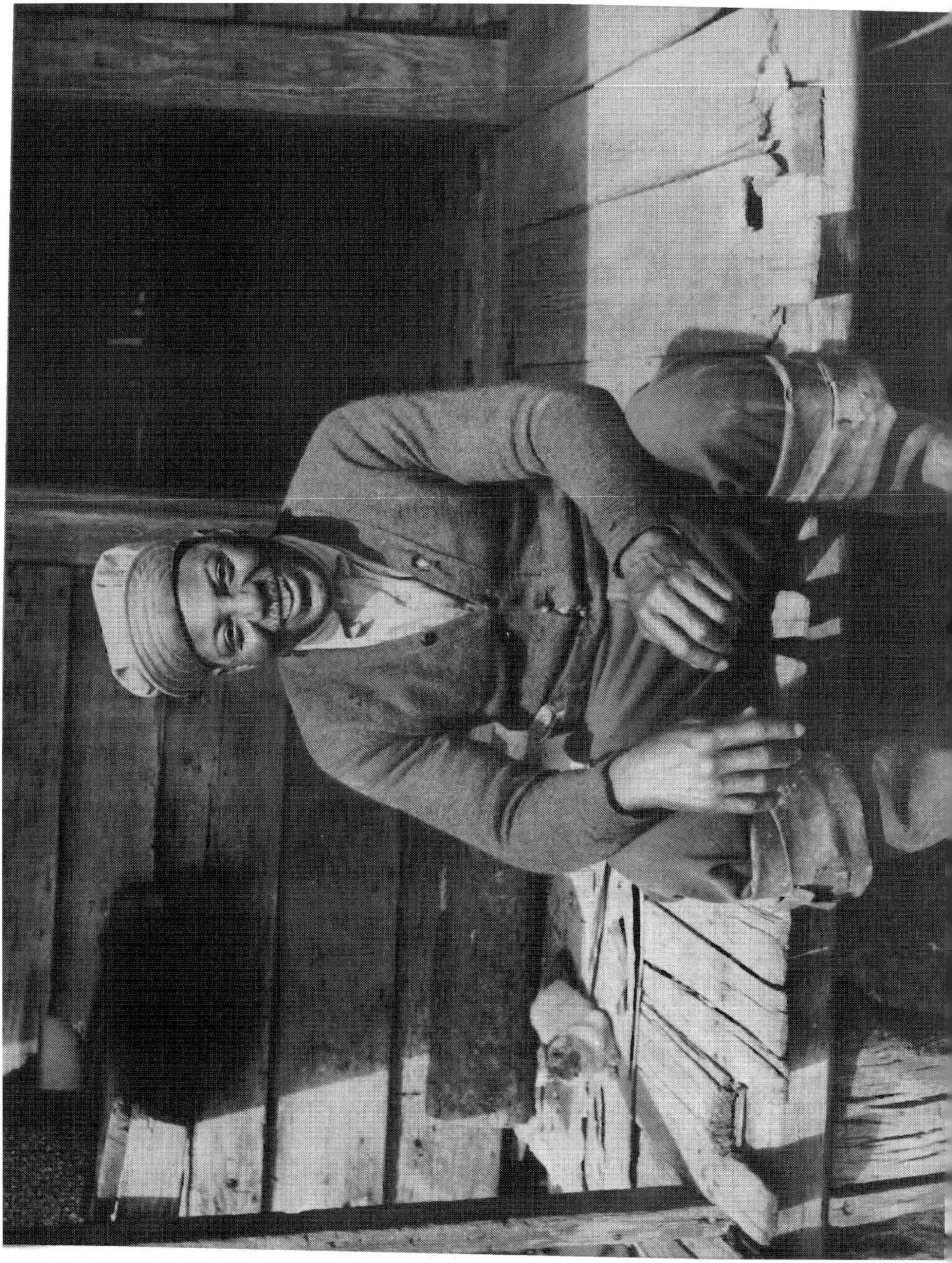

Jerry Harris

For a man to live his life in one community, to raise a large family and send his children through high school, to operate his own business, to use his influence for good, and to become a leader in his community, thus, earning the respect of his fellowman, is all that could be expected of anyone — and Jerry Harris has done all of these. One would think that all this would be sufficient to say about Jerry but something else could be added: in addition, he has a happy disposition and so has his wife, Leola, the daughter of Morris Polite.

Like the Polite family, Jerry's ancestors belonged to the Broadfield-Hofwyl Plantation. He, too, lives in Petersville and can claim the same distinction that goes to the Polite family in that all the generations of his family who have lived in America, as far back as anyone knows, have spent their lives in this small area. In fact, there are no "displaced" persons in Petersville; all of them belong there.

After the Civil War the Negroes who had lived on the Glynn County rice plantations located on the south bank of the Altamaha River — Hopeton, Altama, Elizafield, Evelyn, Grantly, Broadfield, Hofwyl and New Hope — settled themselves in communities nearby. Here, they acquired small tracts of land, built their little cabins and continued to work on the same plantations where they had labored as slaves.

Petersville was one of these communities, having taken its name from an old man named Peter who lived there. Another settlement was Needwood, so named because of a shortage of "fat light wood" (heart of the long-leaf yellow pine). Still another such community bore a name which needs no explanation, Freedman's Rest!

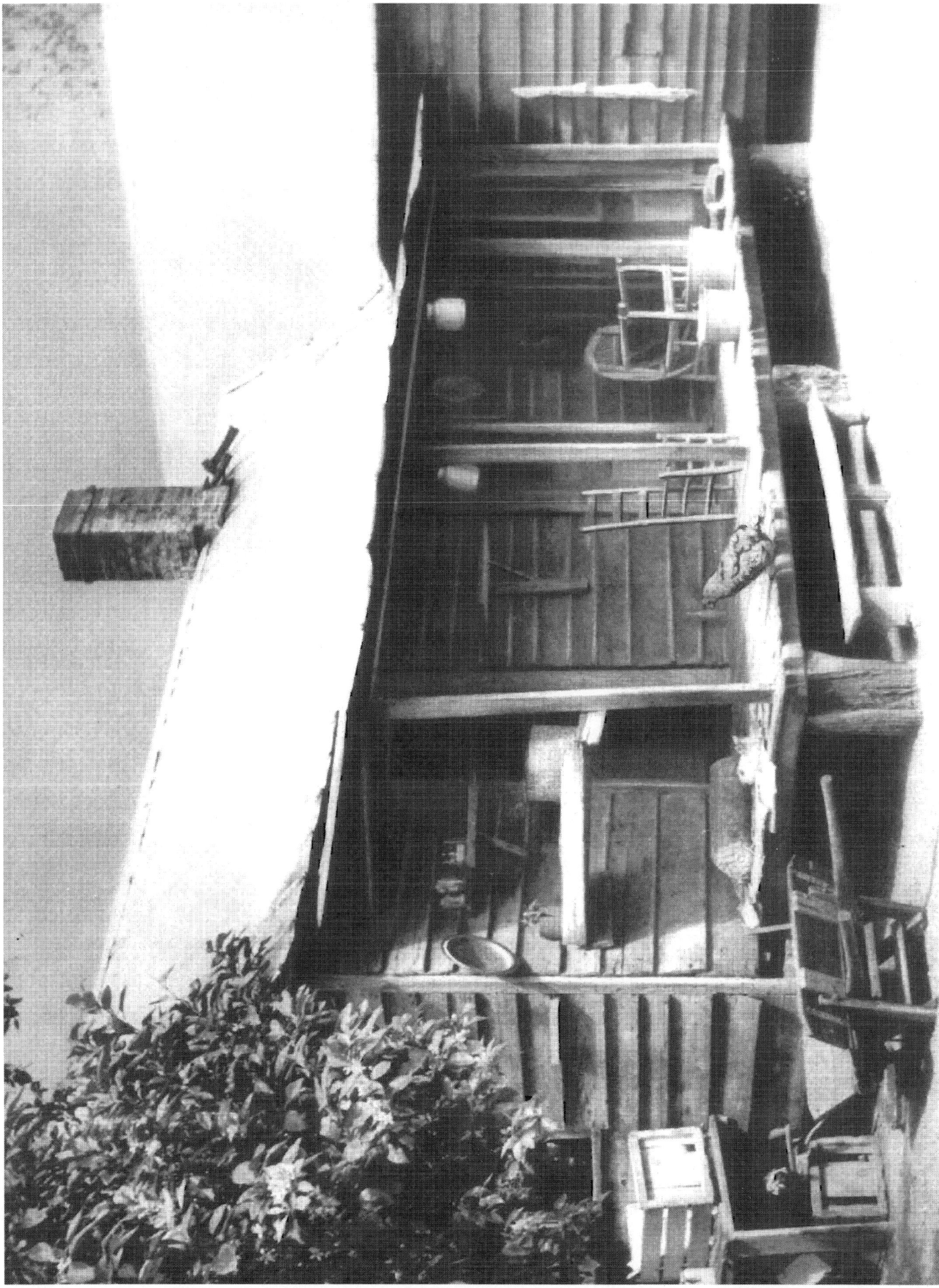

Jerry Harris' Back Porch

This house has seen a lot of living, for here Jerry Harris and his wife, Leola (Polite) Harris, have raised a large family. This picture speaks of their way of life.

The milk cans are hung within easy reach for their trip to the barn, wash tubs are placed at a good height, and chairs await the worker who has time for resting. On the shelf at the end of the porch sits a large pot, the lid hanging nearby. The wheelbarrow stands where its load of wood was discharged and the cat sleeps contentedly in the patch of sunshine.

Through the open door of the kitchen can be seen the kitchen cabinet, while the electric refrigerator stands just beyond. The absence of a pump or a bucket of water tells you that this house uses water from an artesian well, which is piped into the kitchen.

The box on a shelf just outside the kitchen window has in it a nest to which the chicken that has just hopped up on the porch is making her third trip. She first flew up on the porch, walked into the kitchen, hopped up into the window and down into the box. Finding something not to her liking, she flew to the ground, then hopped back up on the porch, into the kitchen, up into the window, down into the box and out again. On this third trip she seems satisfied to settle down on the nest and get on with her work of laying an egg.

The beautiful sour orange tree shading the kitchen, gives a delightful fragrance when in bloom and furnishes fruit for drinks and for marmalade. Leola's love of growing plants and flowers is seen in the "cutting" which is being rooted in the tin can on the shelf.

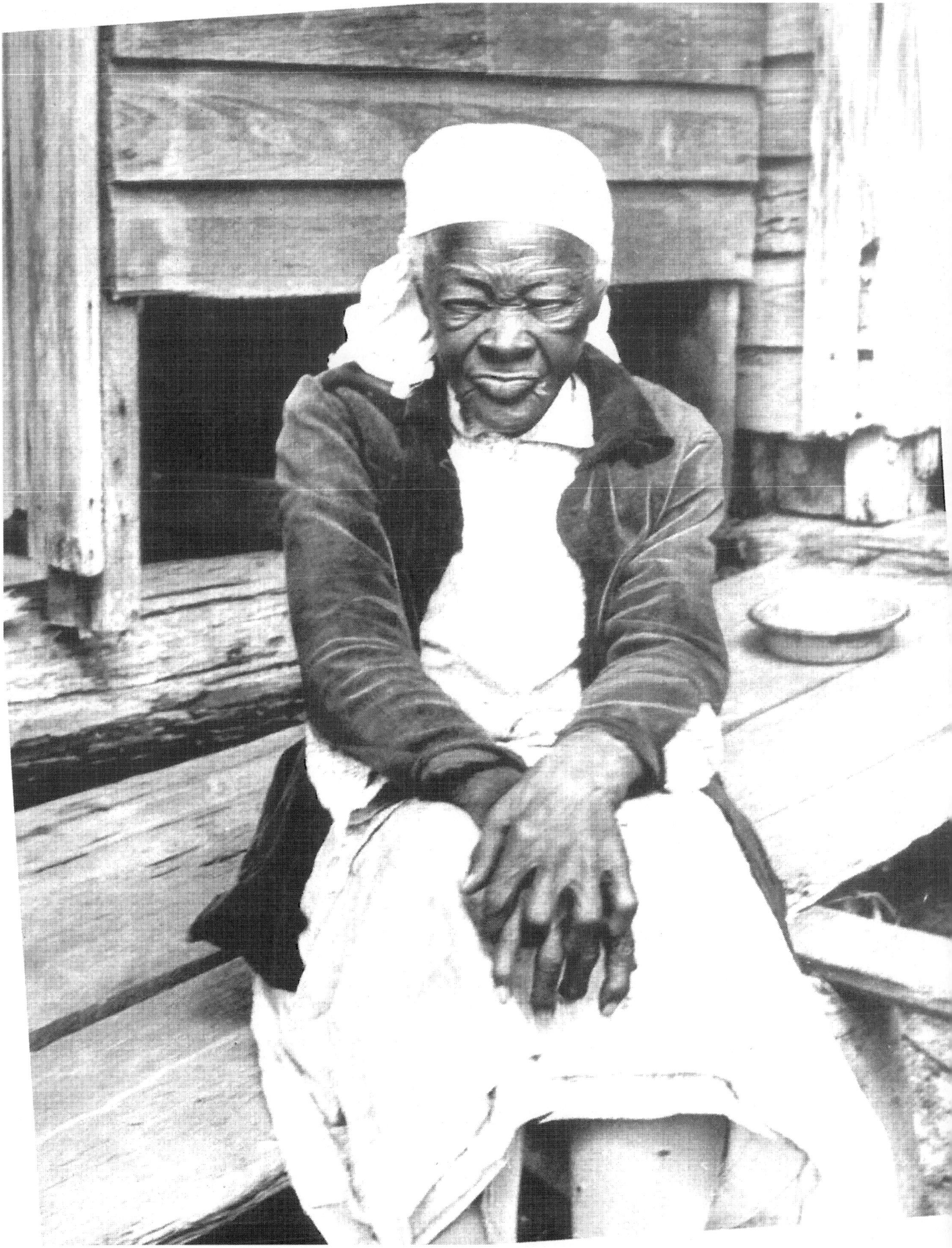

Sibby Kelly

Old Sibby Kelly was a "granny woman," or midwife, who lived in a Negro settlement known as Petersville, about fifteen miles from Brunswick.

Sibby served her people well. It is believed that she brought more babies into the world than any white doctor who ever lived in Glynn County. When asked how many babies she had "birthed," she replied that she "didn't keep no count." But when asked how many she had lost, she was positive in her statement, "Ain's los' none; some ob 'em die but tain' my fault!"

She would never talk about the "birth beads" and the use of a knife or other sharp instrument which was put on the floor under the bed in the belief that it would cut the pains. Those were her secrets and she guarded them jealously.

Fashions come and go, but Sibby never changed from the old-fashioned method of tying up her head. A piece of white cloth folded smoothly above the forehead and tied in the back with the ends hanging down on the back of the neck was the proper method and she stuck to it.

Sibby lived alone in her little cabin. The Welfare Director, who administers the pensions these old people receive, tried to persuade her to move down the road and live with some relatives who could cook for her and wait on her, but Sibby would have none of it. She backed up against her little cabin and said, "Here I libs; here I dies!" And there she died, just as she wished, in her own house. She did not want to live in the house of someone who could boss her, tell her when to get up, when to go to bed, what to eat. Sibby kept her independence and was her own boss!

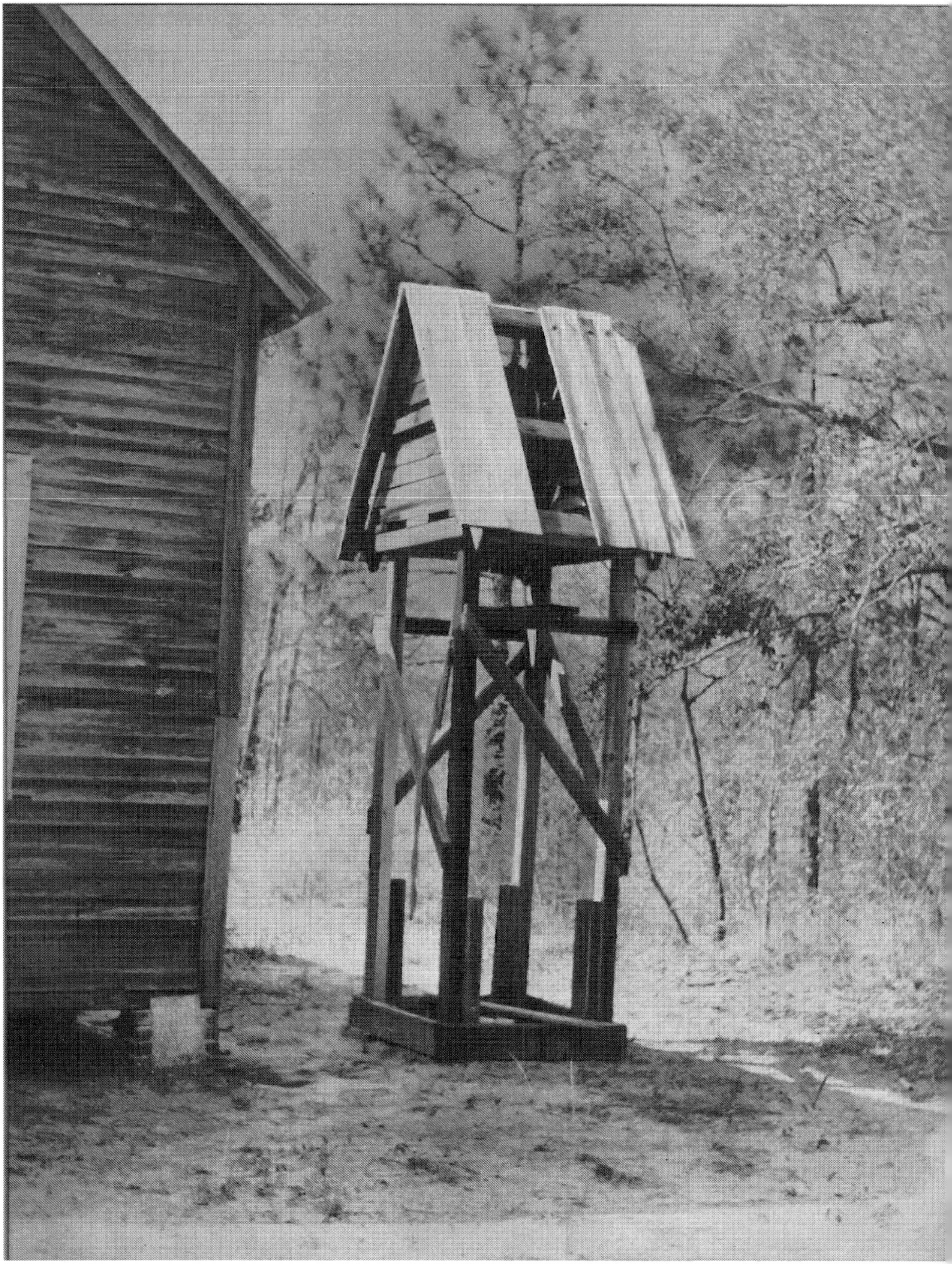

Bell Tower of
the Petersville Baptist Church

The members of the Petersville Baptist Church felt that their church would not be fully equipped unless it had a bell. Building a steeple to house the bell would have been an expense beyond their means, so they erected this simple structure near by. Here the bell was mounted where it could ring out its summons just as effectively as though it had been installed in a steeple above the church.

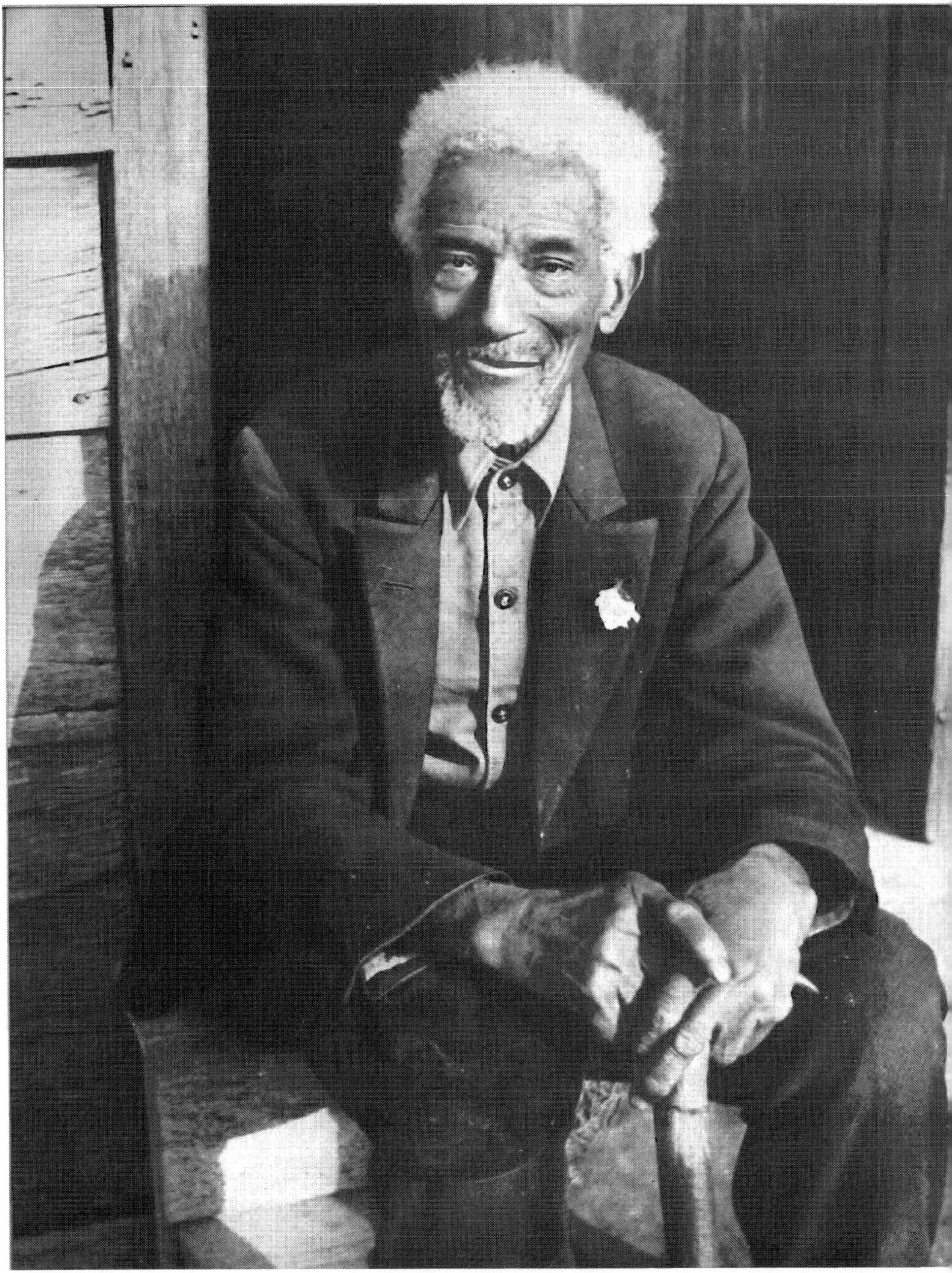

Liverpool Hazzard

Liverpool was the last of the Butler slaves. The Pierce Butler holdings in this section were Hampton or Butler Point, the Sea Island cotton plantations at the north end of St. Simons Island; Butler Island, the rice plantation in the delta of the Altamaha River; and Hammersmith, a tract on the mainland. At the height of their prosperity these plantations were peopled with almost a thousand slaves.

Born in 1828, Liverpool lived until 1938. One hundred and ten years is a long time to live! Yet his mind was clear to the last and he was a most valuable source of information on the life of another era. Furthermore, he was able to be up and around and to enjoy life.

When he was 107 years old, an enterprising Georgian built a fence around him and charged admission to his home. However, Liverpool stipulated that his friends, white and black, should not be charged for seeing him. Though he lived three years longer, the age painted on the fence in figures a yard high was never changed; on the fence he remained 107 years old.

During the Civil War, Liverpool was the cook for a company of Confederate soldiers commanded by Capt. William Miles Hazzard and stationed at Camp Walker, on the mainland in Glynn County. Though he was a Butler man and proud of it, after the war he took the name Hazzard for, as he said, that was the last white man who was his boss while he was a slave.

Liverpool delighted in telling of his experiences during the war. The soldiers of the company which he had served were his especial interest. He maintained contact with these men, their children, and grandchildren, feeling almost as if he, too, had been a Confederate soldier.

One of the tales which he told small boys was of the time when he and some of the soldiers hid the horses down in a swamp so that they would not be found by the Federal troops who were in the neighborhood. The Confederates held their hands over the mouths of their horses for fear they would neigh when they heard those of the enemy. Thus, they prevented detection. It seemed to please Liverpool very much that he had a part in this scheme which saved the horses from capture.

[199]

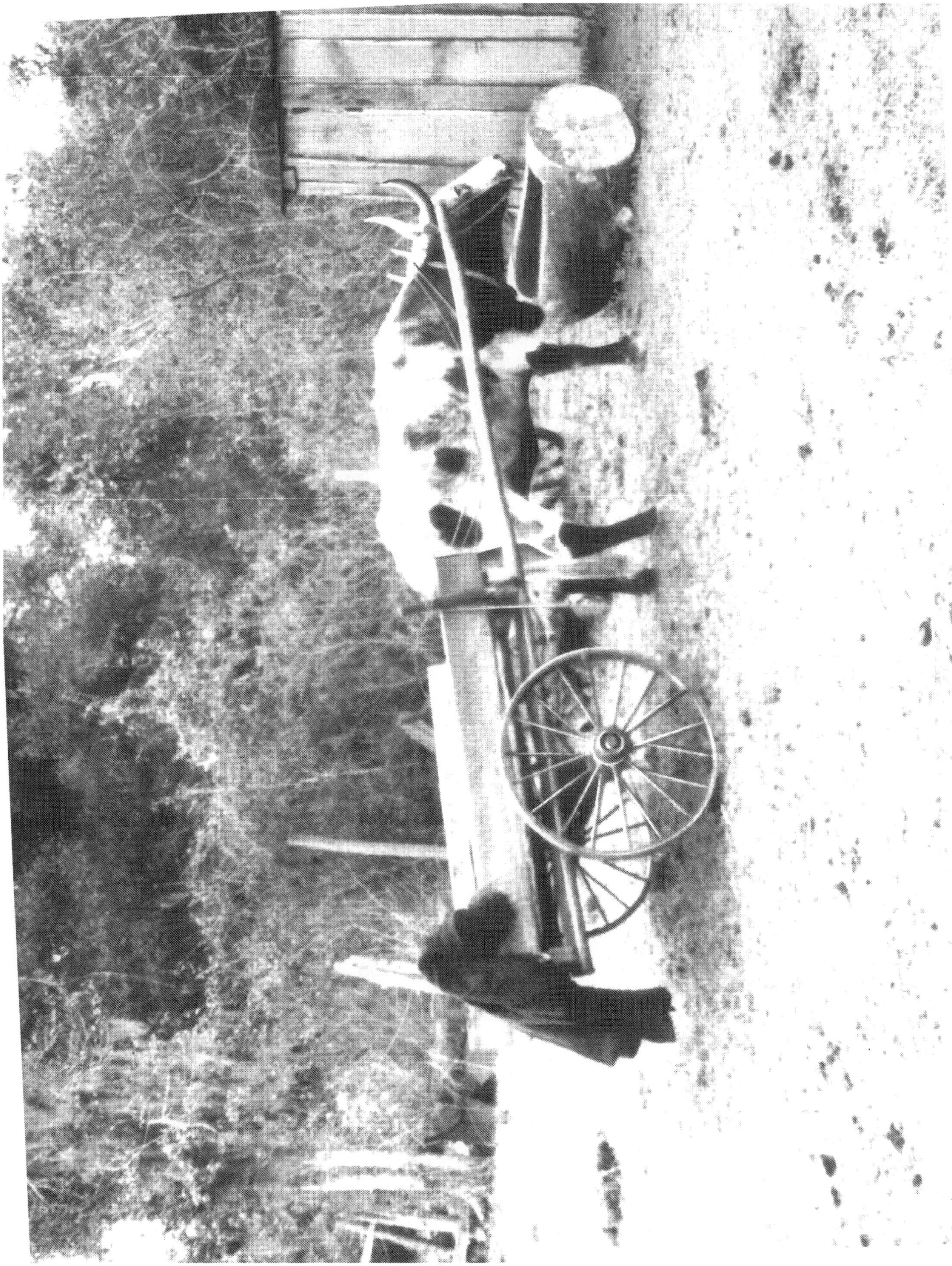

Liverpool's Ox Cart

For many years Liverpool lived alone in his little cabin in Darien. A granddaughter who lived nearby cooked for him and took care of his needs. He rode around Darien in his cart and seemed not to mind the pace of his steed, though it must have taken all day to get anywhere. He and his ox had been together a long time and seemed to understand each other.

Both before the war and after, Liverpool's work was on Butler Island. Here he was an oarsman, one of a crew who rowed the plantation boats. These boats were built from a single cypress tree, hollowed out much as the Indians built their canoes. After wet sand was placed around the edge of the boat, the middle was burned and worked with tools until it was of the right thickness. Finished to a polished smoothness on the outside with a drawing-knife, these boats were "streamlined" and moved smoothly through the water. Equipped with outriggers of iron to increase the leverage of the oars, the boats were manned by four to ten oarsmen and ranged in length from thirty to as much as forty-eight feet.

As they passed up and down the waterways, the boatmen sang, their oars keeping time with the rhythm of the song. Each plantation had its own songs and, if a boat passed in the night, it could be identified by the songs.

Such craft, a necessity on the plantations in this section, were in constant use, being the popular means of transportation. In addition, they provided the plantation masters with a means of entertainment. Boat races were a popular sport and drew enthusiastic crowds.

The gentlemen gave fanciful names to their craft — *Comet, Swan, Flea, Lizard, Leopard, Star, Minerva, Sunny South, Goddess of Liberty, Devil's Darning Needle, Lady of the Lake* — and painted them and costumed the crew accordingly. The *Goddess of Liberty*, a six-oared boat, thirty-two feet long and three feet, eleven inches wide, was painted white, with a blue band in which there were twenty-four stars (for the twenty-four states of the Union), while the crew was dressed in red. The *Devil's Darning Needle* was painted black and the crew dressed in green. The crews, trained to a high degree of perfection, frequently covered the half-mile course in two minutes, twenty seconds.

[201]

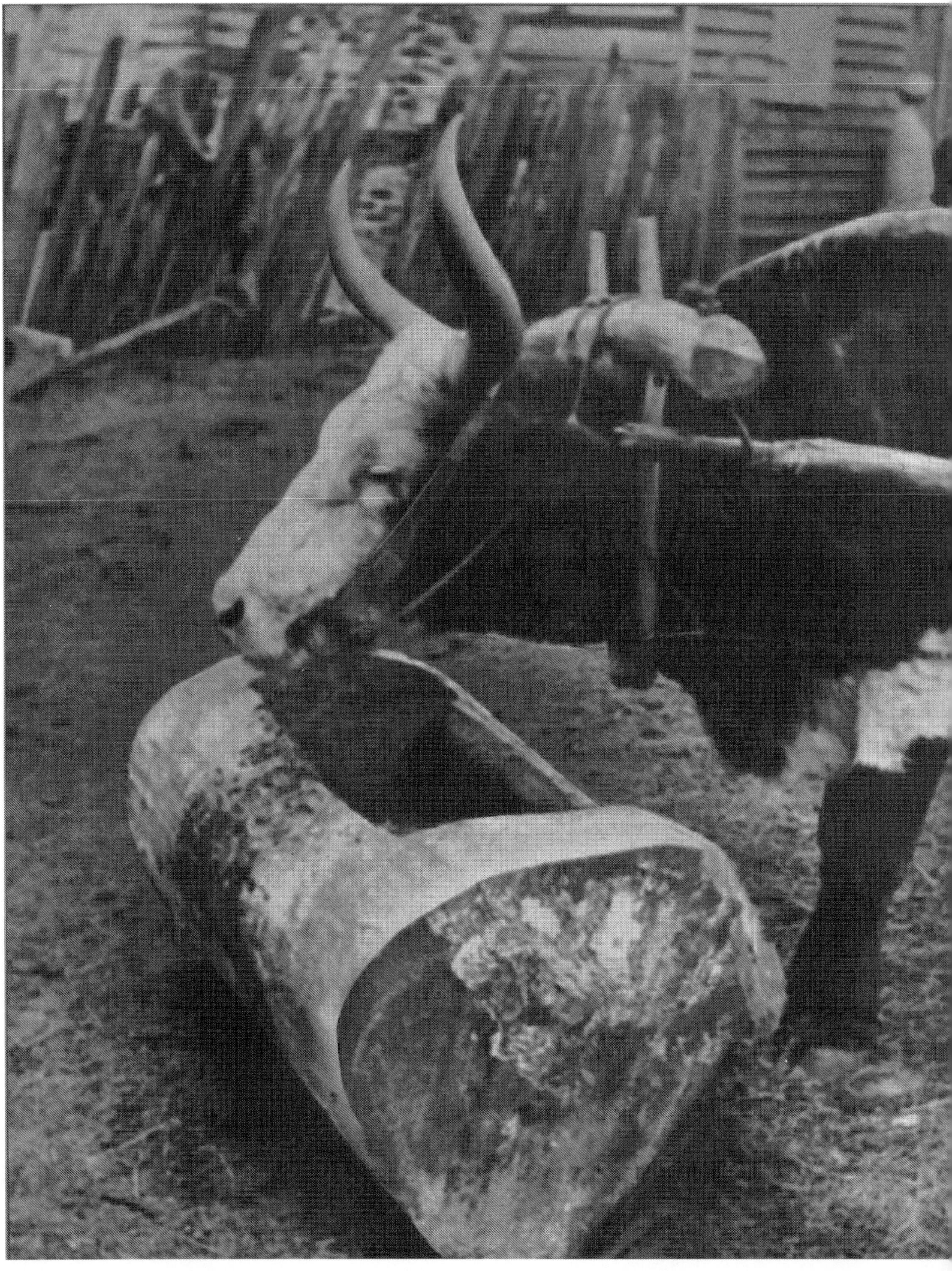

Liverpool's Ox Cart and Trough

Liverpool was quite modern in many ways, learning to enjoy a cigarette when he had always been accustomed to a pipe. However, in most instances he clung to the ways of his youth, as in his use of this trough used to water the ox. Typical of those used in this section for many generations, such a trough was made of oak or long-leaf yellow pine and hollowed out with tools and by burning. Since it was made of durable materials, it would last a lifetime, or even be passed down from one generation to another.

Liverpool was the type to have been used as a household servant and, when not used as an oarsman, that was his work. When Pierce Butler, Fanny Kemble's husband and Liverpool's "Massa," was stricken with malaria fever, Liverpool rowed him to Darien for medical attention. Mr. Butler died and was buried in Darien, but later his body was removed to Philadelphia.

After the death of Pierce Butler, his daughter Frances, who became the wife of the Rev. James W. Leigh, lived here and operated the Butler Plantations for some years. Her book, *Ten Years on a Georgian Plantation,* gives a picture of life during Reconstruction. Liverpool continued as the oarsman for the Leighs and took part in the races held on the river, though these races were among the craft in this particular area and not between the plantations up and down the coast.

The Leighs had an only child, Alice, who married a distant relative, Sir Richard Pierce Butler. Lady Butler often visited Georgia and kept in touch with these Butler Negroes. On these visits she would give a party for them and their descendants, who came from over the area to see their "Missus." One one such occasion, in thanking her for the party, the speaker said, "Dis festival will long be remembered. It will be remembered by the *offsprings* when de *foresprings* is done dead an' gone!"

Lady Butler gave Liverpool a monthly allowance which enabled him to live. Henry Ford also assisted in caring for him, so that he was comfortable in his last years.

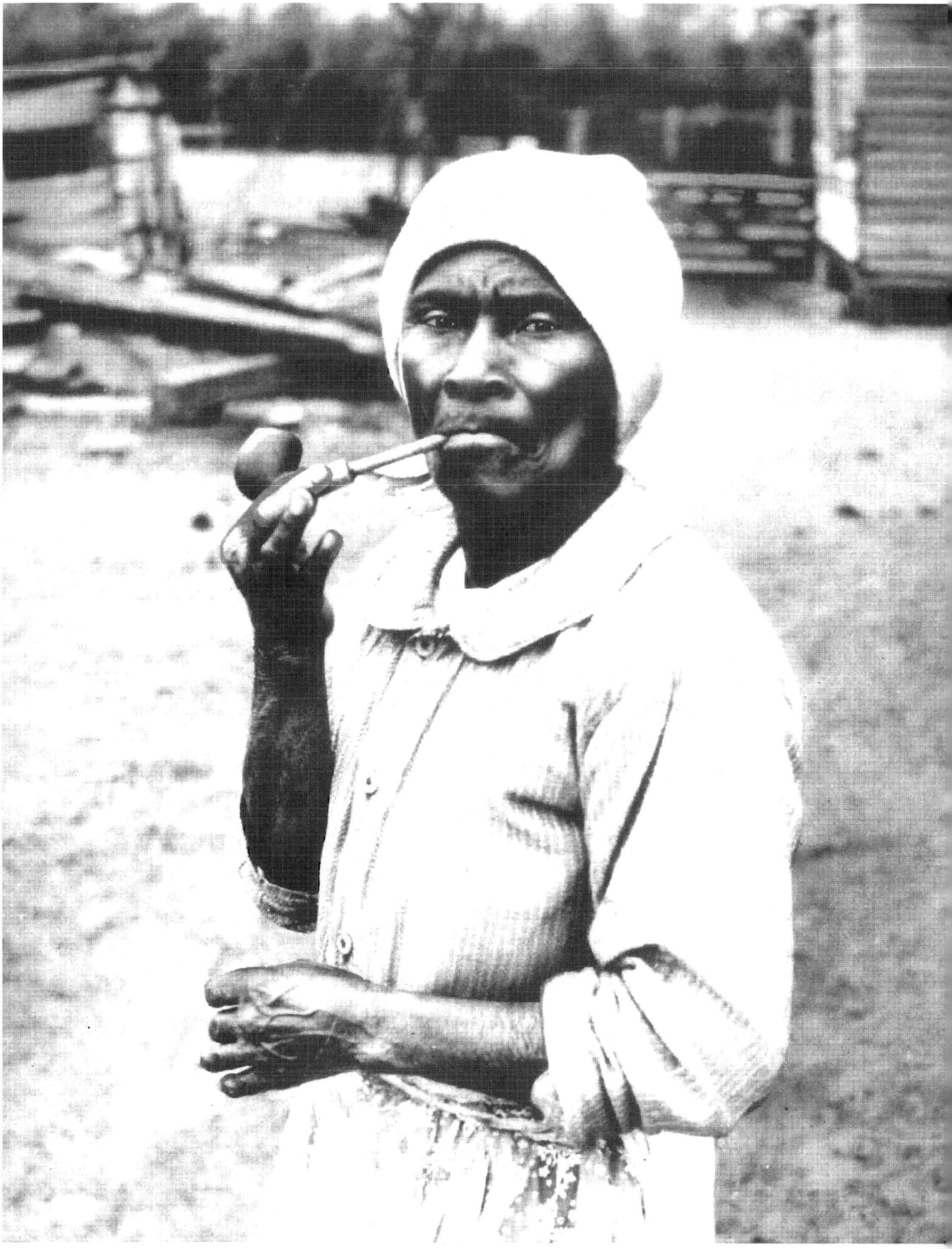

Old Jane

Jane was raised on a rice plantation and was what was known as a "Gee-chee" from the Ogeechee River which was noted for its rice plantations. In South Carolina she would have been called a "Gullah" from the African tribe, Angola.

These terms were used to designate Negroes who spoke a very poor grade of English. Living on these large rice plantations, they saw very little of white people since the plantation master and his family, in an effort to escape malaria fever, left the plantation in summer. The Negro, with his immunity to malaria, could live in an area that would have meant death to the white man. Because of this lack of contact with white people, these rice-field Negroes developed a jargon all their own which bore little resemblance to the English language and which, to a stranger, is like a foreign language.

Jane supervised the work of the children who were tying chickens to send them to market. She made the children count aloud so they would be certain to tie *three* chickens — not *two,* nor *four* — in each bundle. This is what they said, "Dis'n un; dis'n narru; dis'n tied pun top ur tarruh. Now, dem foots all tie tergurruh!" Translated, this would mean, "This is one; this is another; this one that's tied on top is the other. Now, their feet are all tied together!"

Jane was a McIntosh County woman and lived her last years in Darien just across the road from Liverpool Hazzard. When people went to see Liverpool — and paid admission for the privilege of seeing a man who was more than a hundred years old — Jane would meet them and fuss because they did not pay to see her for she claimed to be as old as Liverpool.

She was one of the fortunate recipients of Henry Ford's bounty. When Mr. Ford was living on his Richmond Hill Plantation in nearby Bryan County he became interested in the old Negroes and helped them to live more comfortably. He had Jane's house repaired, supplied furniture and equipment, paid a woman to take care of her, and made a monthly allowance to meet current expenses.

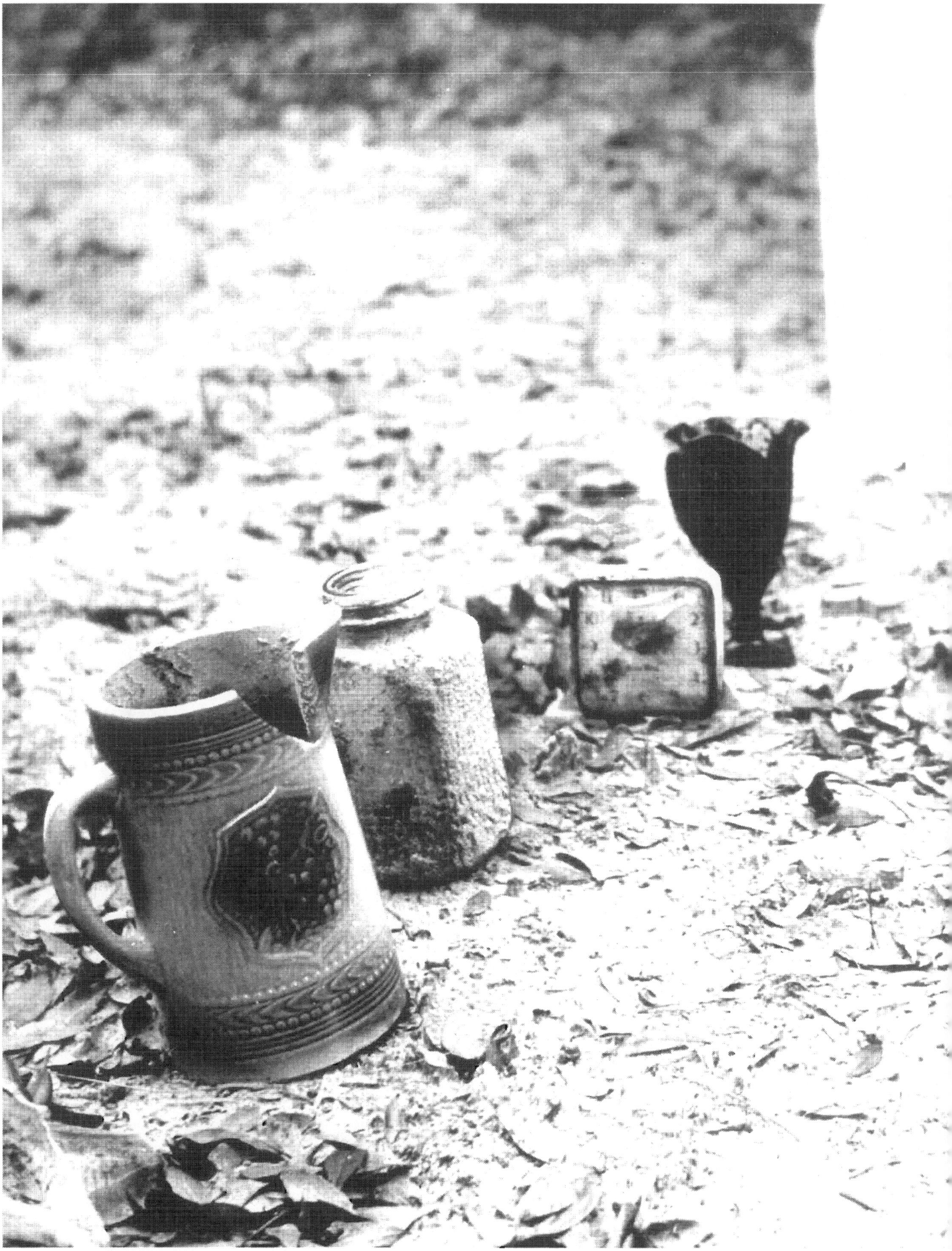

Negro Graves

In old Negro burying grounds the grave is outlined with various and sundry items. In some cases there is a board at the head and another at the foot of the grave with these articles placed along the ground between these two boards.

The articles on the graves include every kind of container or utensil — sea shells, salt and pepper shakers, pickle bottles, shaving mugs, moustache cups, piggy banks, the interior mechanism of a radio, alarm clocks, lamps, automobile head lights, electric light bulbs, flash lights, combs, cold cream jars, plates, cups, saucers, ash trays, milk bottles, and chamber pots. Everything on a Negro grave is broken. To them this is symbolic. Life is broken; the vessel is broken.

No doubt many of the articles used to decorate these graves had been broken accidentally and were then brought to the grave, but some of them are broken deliberately. In fact, this is standard procedure at a funeral. After the grave is filled and the earth shaped into a neat mound, the flowers are placed on the grave. If any of these are in a vase or other container, this container with its flowers is knocked against a stump, or some other object, and a hole broken in the bottom of the vessel before the vase and flowers can be placed on the grave. The same treatment is given a potted plant, the bottom of the pot being broken before the pot with its growing plant is placed on the grave.

Years ago Negroes put these broken articles on all their graves; but, today, one finds them only in isolated communities far removed from the influence of the white man's culture. To seek them out, one must leave the paved roads and search in remote areas where the Negro still keeps alive his African culture and practices those customs handed down from generation to generation.

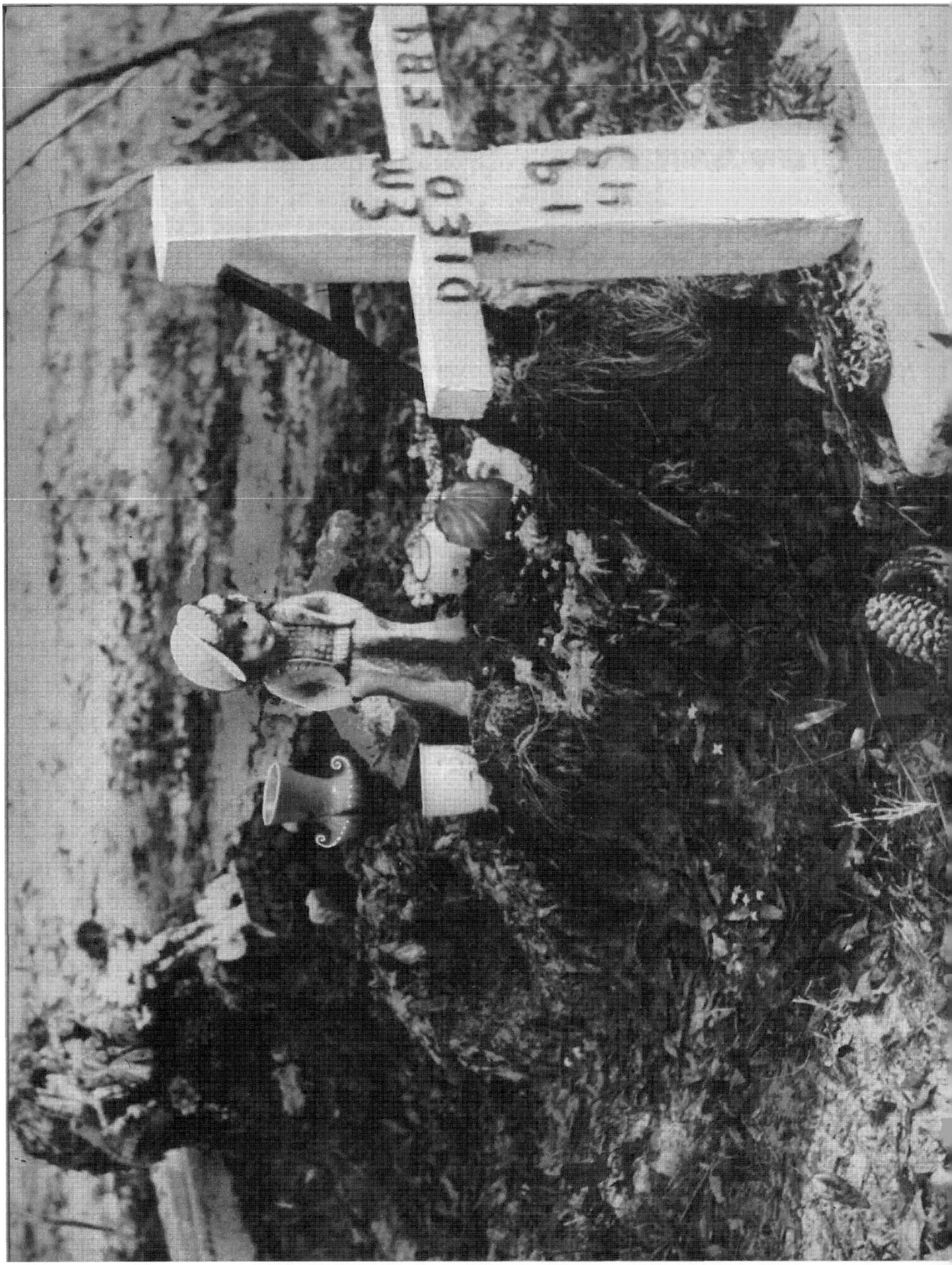

Jackie Coogan

Though the decorations on the graves usually follow the same general pattern, being items attractive to the Negro and, perhaps, articles which had been owned by the dead, yet, sometimes there are things that are most unusual. Such is this figurine of Jackie Coogan in the role that made him famous when he played with Charlie Chaplin in *"The Kid."* About fifteen inches high and made of bisque, this figurine withstood the ravages of the weather for many years.

Jackie Coogan stands near a shaving mug marked in gold paint with the number "6" and amid a collection of vases and jars of every description. Behind him lies a papier-mache cross decorated with a wreath and all around there are such things as dishes, pine cones, the remains of a wreath from a florist shop, and a wooden ladder-like arrangement which was used to hold the floral offerings at the funeral.

Even when it was first put on the grave, this Jackie Coogan statue was broken and had to be pushed down into the earth so that it could stand up.

Some of the Negroes believe that these broken articles will keep the "ha'nts" from walking on the grave; to them this is important, for they feel that the dead should be allowed to rest in peace undisturbed by these evil spirits.

These pieces of broken glass, lying in the sand and exposed to the weather, undergo a chemical change and take on beautiful amethyst tints. However, the Negroes believe this change in the color of the glass comes about because of its having been on a grave.

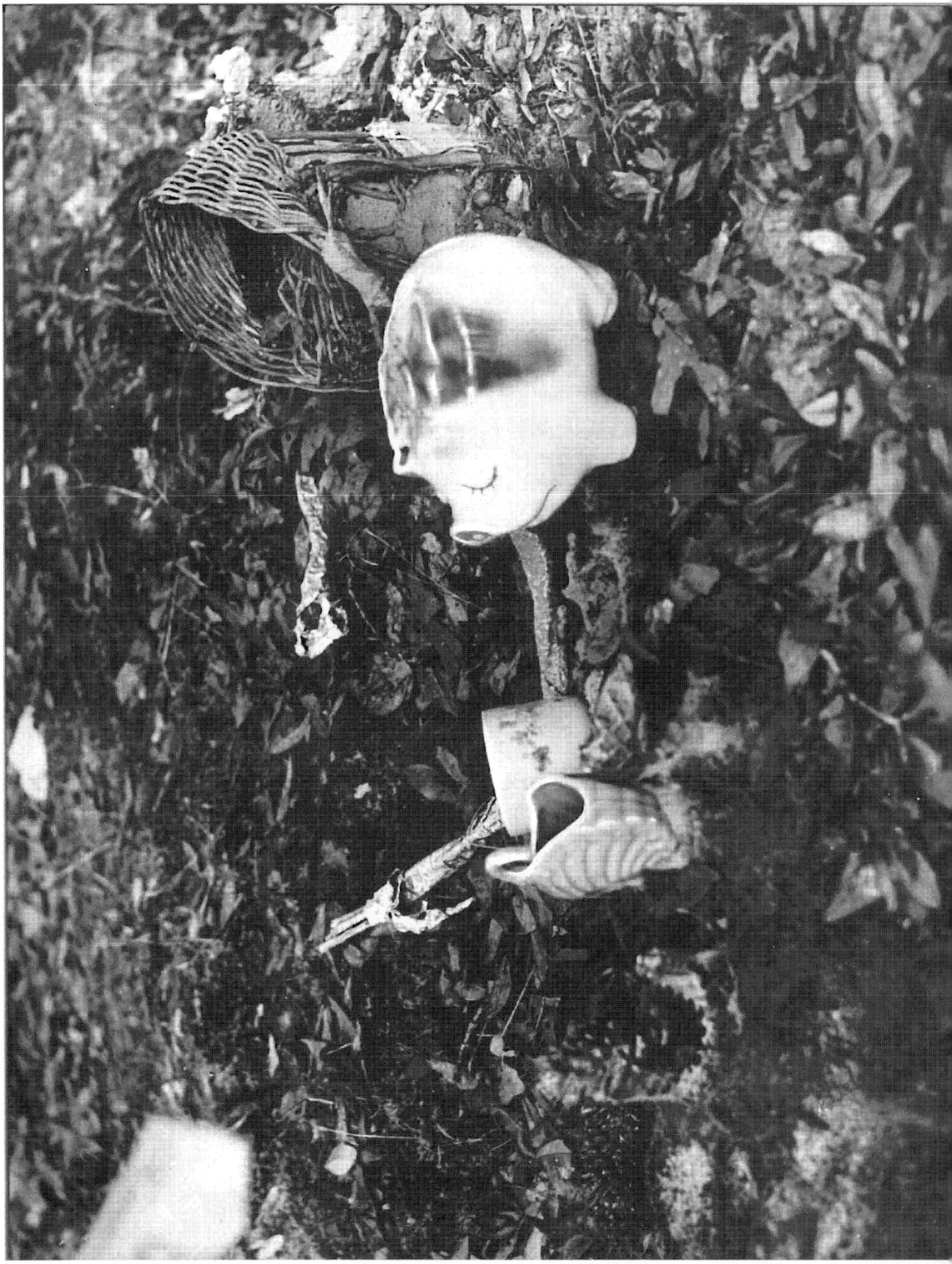

A Piggy Bank

Though there is little doubt that much of the material used to decorate these Negro graves is put there when the grave is new, still articles are added from time to time.

This crockeryware piggy bank is on the same grave which at one time was decorated with the bisque figurine of Jackie Coogan that crumbled after some years. Now, with his long eyelashes and turned-up nose piggy stands in Jackie's place!

These queer practices are so much a part of the life of the old-time Negro that they do not seem strange or unusual either to the Negro or to those white people who knew the Negro. Many other practices which are tied in with their African inheritance were continued by the Negroes. For instance, they would not sweep the floors while a corpse was in the house. Neither would they wear clothes that had belonged to a dead person, for that person might come back in search of his apparel.

If a ha'nt did come back and try to catch you, it was a good plan to pour whiskey on the ground. The ghost would stop to drink the whiskey and you could get away safely.

A broom across the door would keep the ha'nt from coming through the door, for every straw in the broom would have to be counted. A sieve or wire screen served the same purpose for the number of holes in the sieve or screen must be determined.

The old Negroes were greatly concerned with luck. They studiously avoided bad luck and carefully cultivated those things that brought good luck. Among these good luck items rice was most important. When one moved into a new house, a few grains of rice were thrown on the floor in each and every corner of the house. Many years ago Mrs. Maxfield Parrish built a new cabin in which the Negroes could sing. Visitors on the opening night well remember the ceremony with which Julia Armstrong threw rice in each corner, thus asuring good luck for the singing of the Negroes.

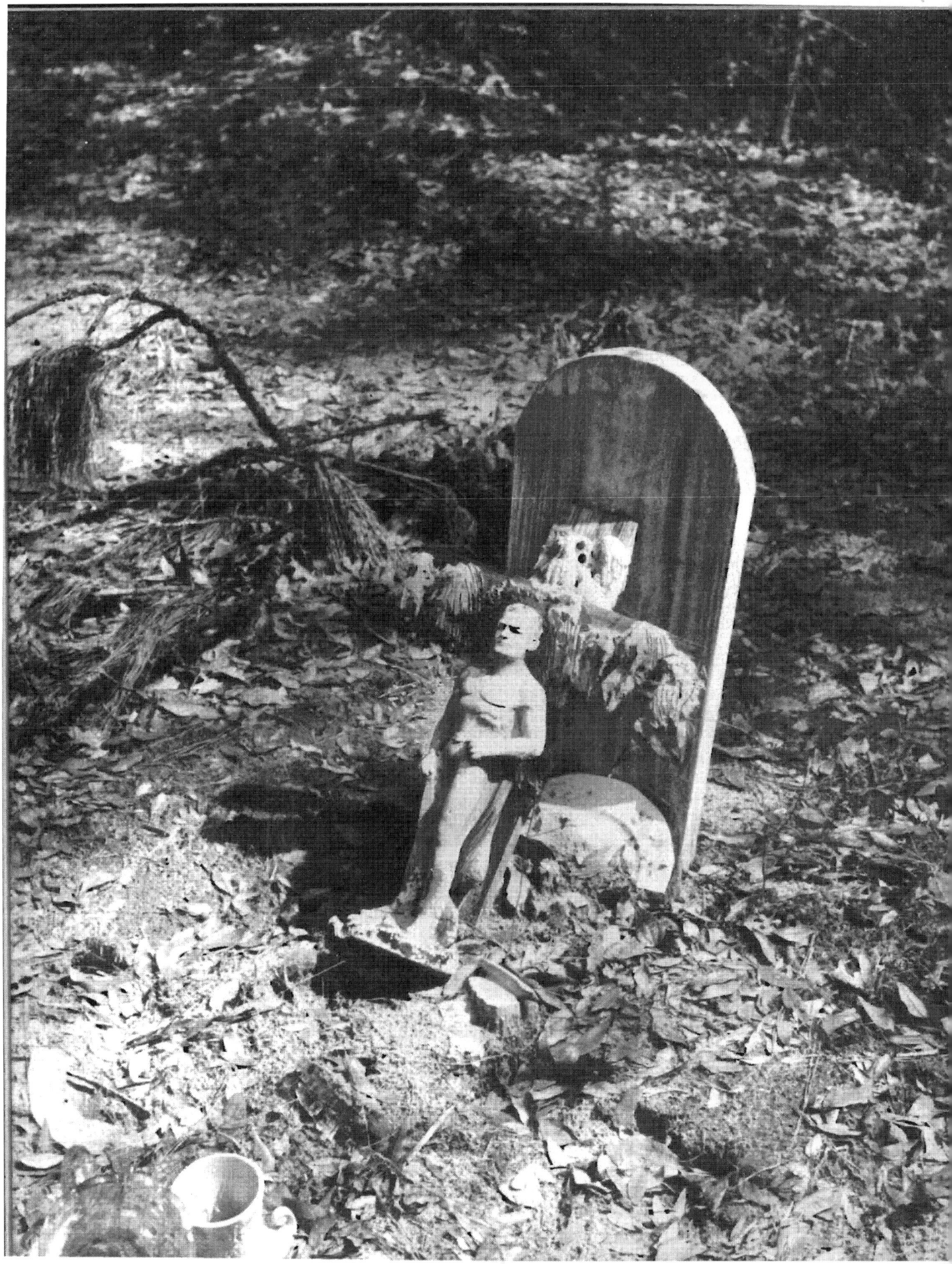

Superman

On a grave near that which had the Jackie Coogan statue stood Superman. Dressed in some sort of garment that looked like a yellow unionsuit, he had a red scarf draped over his elbows in much the same fashion that women wear a stole.

Superman was not able to stand alone and so he was leaning against a wooden cross which had been decorated with large crepe paper flowers. A visit to these graves several years later showed that the papier-mache figurine had not been able to withstand exposure to the weather and Superman had crumbled!

Each Negro settlement has its own burying ground, following the practice of the Plantation Era when each plantation had a burying ground for its slaves. Many generations of the old Negro families of this area have been buried in these old slave burying grounds and they continue to bury their dead in these same old cemeteries. The belief is strong among the Negroes that your body must lie with those of your ancestors. Sometimes this meant that a husband and wife were buried in different cemeteries, the woman being buried by her parents in one burying ground while the husband was laid with his family in another. Even today when Negroes die elsewhere their bodies are brought back from great distances that they may rest with their own people.

In these old Negro graveyards one never sees shrubbery planted to beautify the area or fresh flowers kept on the grave, as is the custom in white burying grounds. However, the Negroes always carried flowers to the funeral and placed them on the new-made grave.

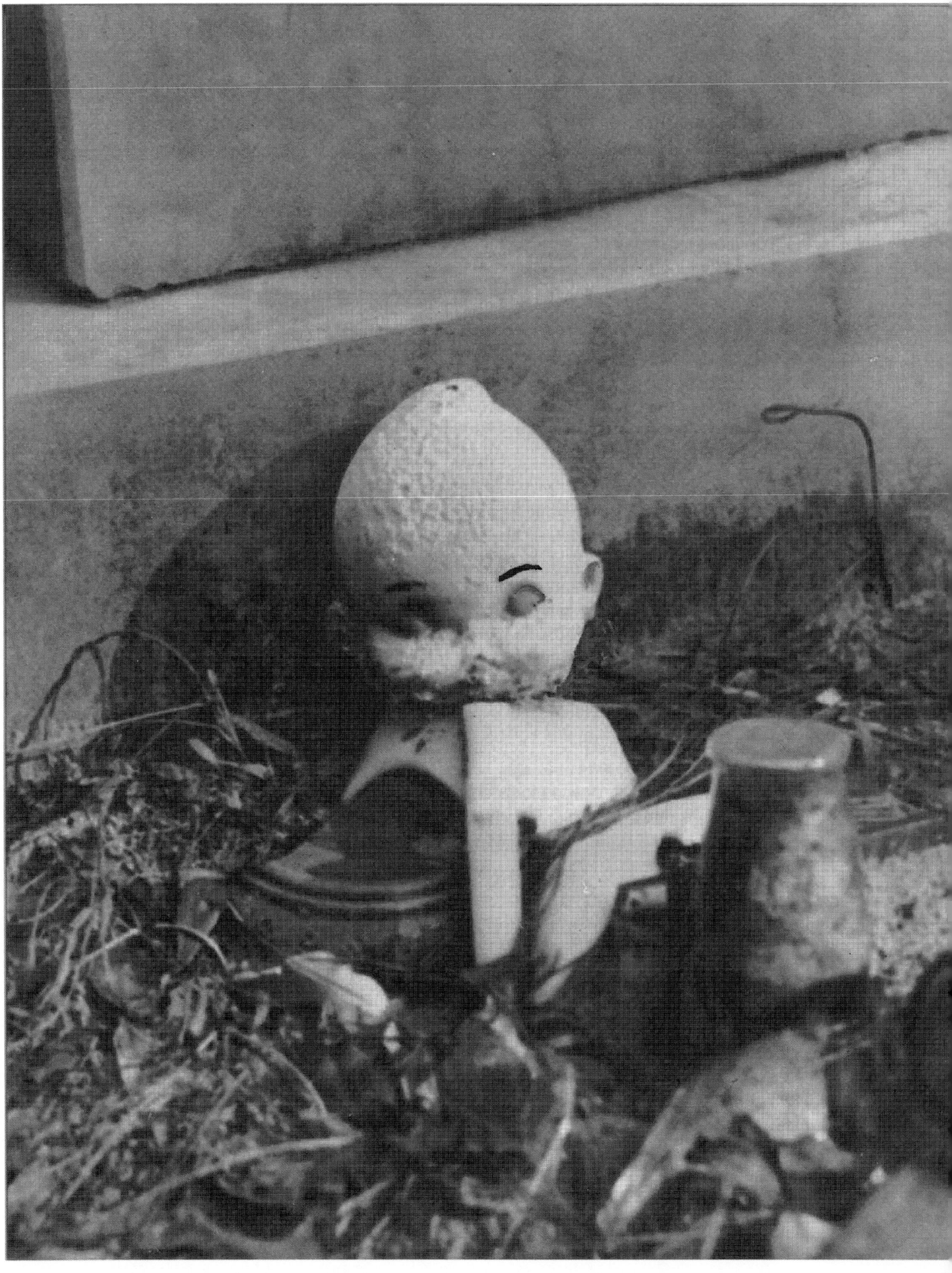

Doll's Head

Near the graves with figurines of Jackie Coogan and Superman was this doll's head with the bluest of blue eyes. The body of the doll was missing and the bisque head had already begun to show the effect of wind and weather, but the blue of the eyes was not dimmed as the head of the doll leaned against the headstone amid the mass of broken articles which marked the grave.

The Negro has many superstitions about the dead. At funerals they pass before the coffin and pause to look on the corpse, perhaps saying a few words to it, and laying a hand on the body; for, if you do not lay your hand on the corpse to tell it goodbye, it will "ha'nt" you! Even small children and babies are held up to view the remains, the parent taking the child's hand and placing it on the dead body so that the child will not be tormented by the "ha'nt."

Since they believe that the spirit of the dead hovers over the body until the body goes into the ground, they want to be sure they have made their peace with this spirit so that it will not come back and bother them.

At funerals the Negroes sing the deeply religious songs of their people and at no time do these songs prove more impressive than on such occasions. Typical of the funeral songs are these: "I Want to Die with a Staff in My Hand," "Low Down the Chariot and Let Me Ride," and "My Soul Be at Rest."

During the Plantation Era funerals were sometimes held at night, the Negroes marching to the burying ground carrying torches of "pine knots" to light their path. Gathering around the grave, they held their torches until after the funeral, when they threw them behind them. In these burying grounds were many of these pine knots lying all over the ground, for no Negro would ever move them.

[215]

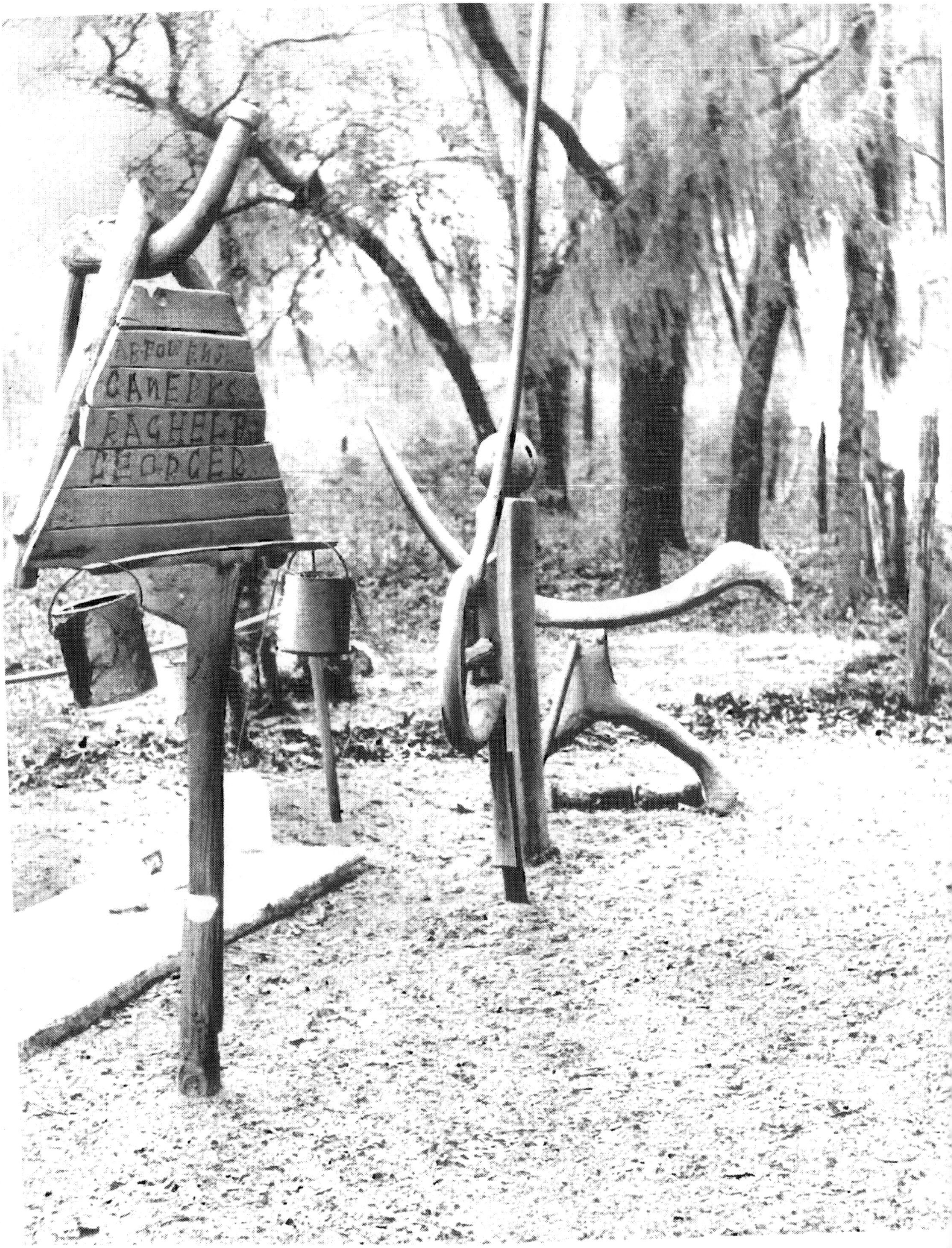

Bowens' Family Burial Plot

At the Baptist Church in the Trade Hill section of Liberty County, Georgia, there is a typical Negro burying ground where the graves are decorated with all sorts of broken articles. Adjoining this regulation burying ground there is a small plot fenced off as the private graveyard of the Bowens family.

Enclosed within a wire fence so as to set it apart from the large cemetery, this family plot contains some of the most unusual arrangements made of wood, of iron, or of brick and cement. The man who constructed these arrangements found queerly shaped pieces of wood and put them together to create these original designs. Indeed, it would seem that he might be credited with having inaugurated the fad for driftwood arrangements.

In this picture, far to the right, is a modernistic design of a bird or, perhaps, it is intended to represent an animal. On the left several pieces of wood have been joined together to hold up the sign board on which are carved the names of some of the persons buried in the enclosure. The piece of wood in front of the sign board holds two tin buckets — one on either end — in which at one time flowers may have been growing.

These strange pieces stand in a row on the edge of this family plot and on the side next to the public road. This may have been done so that they would be seen or, it has been suggested, that it may have been an effort to protect the graves from the evil spirits that might come from this open road. No matter what the purpose may have been in this, the fact remains that they are unique!

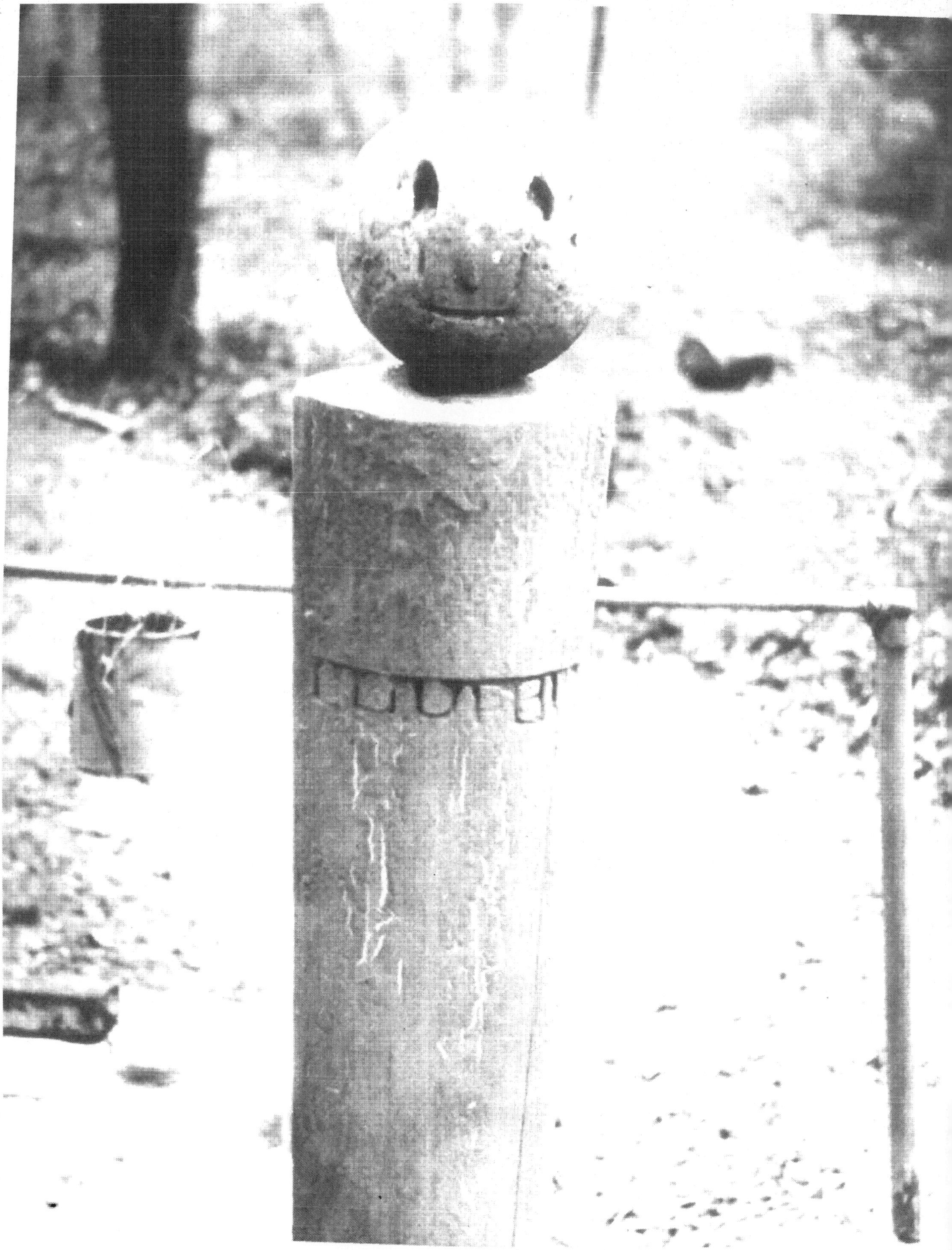

The Bowens Marker

This post, which is the central marker of the Bowen's Family Burial Plot is unique. The head on top represents pure voodoo, while the letters carved a few inches below spell B O W E N S.

Among the Negroes the belief in "conjur," or voodoo, is strong and conjur doctors, witch doctors or voodoo men, as they are sometimes called, still practice their profession. Their "bag of tricks" contains a remedy for any and every ailment. With the use of certain ingredients a conjure doctor sets himself up to cure any disease or condition and, what is more important, he professes to be able not only to *cause* but also to *cure* any sickness. He will fix a concoction that will cause a person to get sick even though that individual is many miles away.

Now that automobiles are in general use, persons travel hundreds of miles to secure the services and purchase the wares of these practitioners. If the conjur has taken effect and the person is already sick and it is desired to remove the cause of this sickness, it is necessary to take the sick person to the voodoo man so that he can practice his magic.

Though many of the items used in making voodoo remedies consist of roots of various flowers and shrubs (and for this reason these men and women are sometimes called "root doctors"), there are other items which have to be purchased from a drug store. These include brimstone (burnt sulphur in sticks), alum, cream of tartar, Epsom salts, Rochelle salts, saltpeter, potassium iodide (which they call "idine potassa"), senna and manna, slippery elm (el um) bark, and gum guaiac (gum bo-wackum).

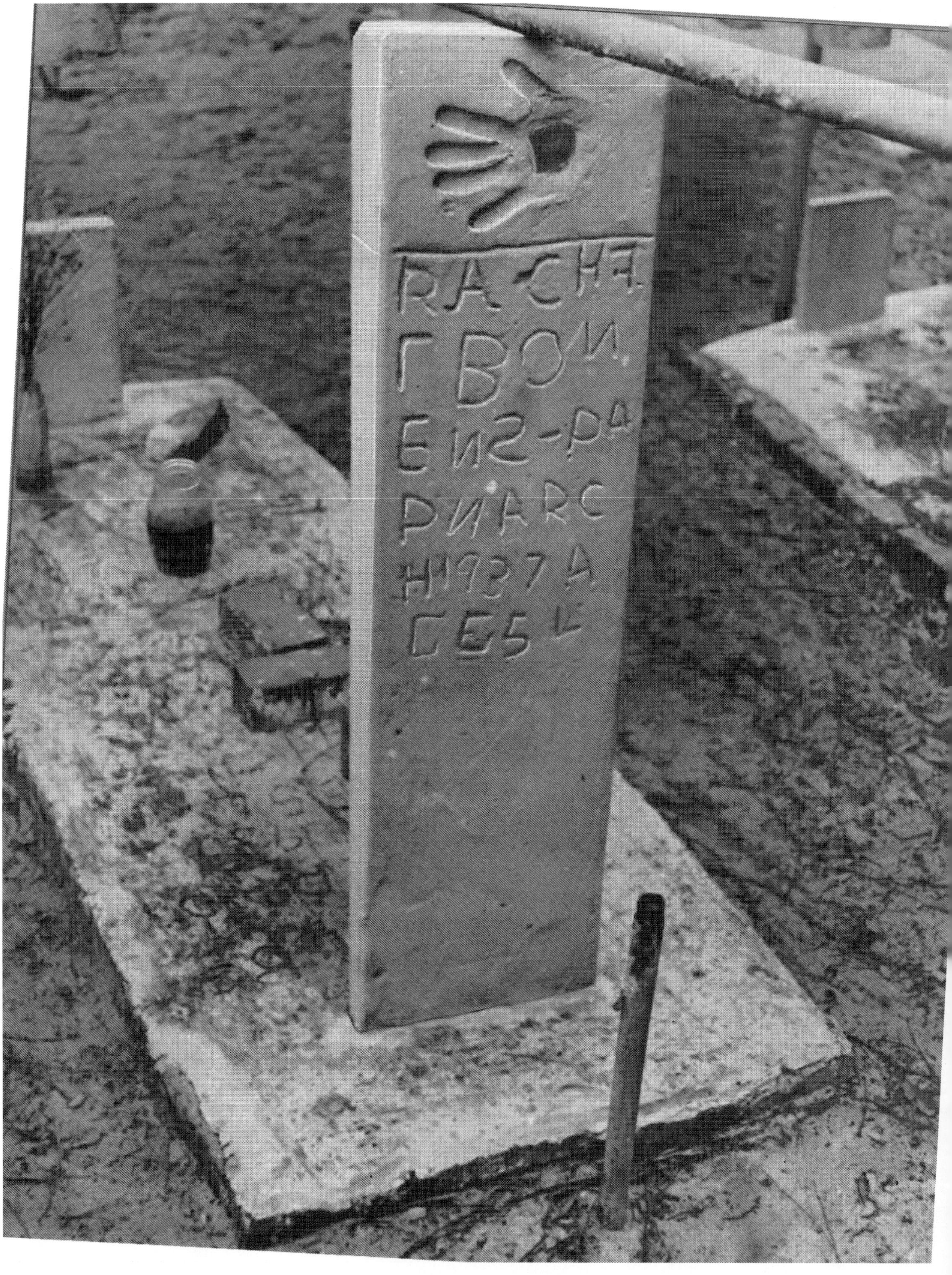

The Grave of Rachel Bowens-Pap

The graves in this Bowens' Family Burial Plot are well built of brick and cement. The tombstones are of cement with the inscription made and decorations applied while the cement was still damp.

This tombstone marks the grave of Rachel Bowens-Pap. At the top there is the imprint of a hand embedded in the palm of which is a piece of looking glass.

The inscription is difficult to decipher. On the top line is RACHE, the E written backward, and the L is on the next line and upside down, to spell RACHEL. Next comes BOW, though the W was not finished, and on the next line ENS to finish BOWENS. A hyphen follows and PA with another P on the next line to spell PAP. Next, 1937 with A on one line and, on the next line, GE to spell AGE while the 54 completes the inscription.

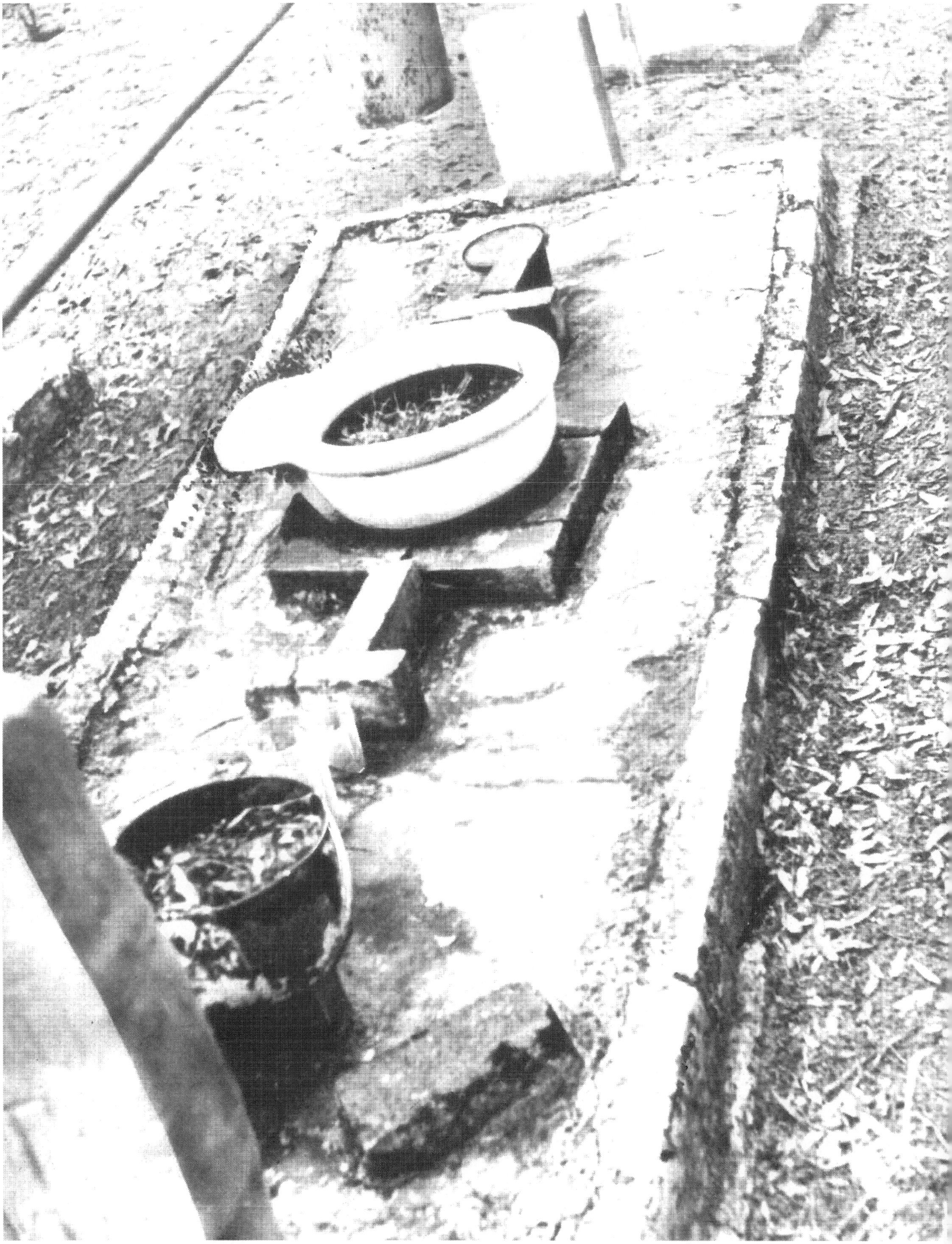

The Grave of the Reverend Aaron Bowens

This is the grave of the Reverend Aaron Bowens. The entire grave is covered with brick and cement to form a slab in the middle of which a toilet bowl has been installed.

Just what it means why it was put there no one seems to know, but no doubt the manufacturer would have been surprised if they had known where their bathroom fixture would be installed.

The Historical Background of
St. Simons Island

The earliest known inhabitants of this area were Indians of Muskhogean stock whom the Spaniards called Guale Indians. Several Indian villages were located on St. Simons Island. From one of these, excavated on the site of Malcolm McKinnon Airport in 1936, were unearthed many interesting artifacts which reveal much of the life of these people.

On practically every bluff on St. Simons are shell banks which are the refuse heaps or "kitchen middens" of these Indians. They contain oyster and clam shells, broken pottery, bones of animals eaten by the Indians, bowls, drinking vessels, hoes and tools fashioned from conch and whelk shells, awls and other tools made of animal and bird bones.

Although France, Spain and England laid claim to the land which is now the State of Georgia, France was the first to start colonization. In 1562, French Huguenots, led by Ribault, made a settlement at Fort Royal in South Carolina, which was soon abandoned. Two years later another settlement, led by Laudonierre, was made on the south bank of the St. Johns River in Florida and called Fort Caroline.

These settlements aroused Spain who sent her ablest seaman, Pedro Menendez de Avilles, to rout the French and hold the lands for Spain. Menendez founded St. Augustine in 1565 and destroyed the French.

The following year he explored the coast of Georgia and of South Carolina. He brought Jesuit priests to found missions among the Indians; later, the Jesuits were replaced by the Franciscans who established a string of missions reaching as far north as Port Royal, South Carolina. Three of these mission settlements were located on St. Simons Islands, one of them, San Simon, giving the Island its name. For more than a century Spain colonized this land. The missionaries worked to Christianize the Indians and to teach them agriculture. However, Indian raids and British depredations took their toll. Step by step Spain receded and in 1686 removed all of her settlements north of the St. Marys River. With Charlestown, S. C., as Britain's most southerly settlement and with the Spaniards south of the St. Marys River, the area which is now Georgia was an abandoned land and for half a century remained so.

The founding of the Colony of Georgia in 1733 was Britain's challenge to Spain's claim, and the building of a string of forts along this Georgia coast gave proof that the British planned to make their claim hold. Fort Frederica and Fort St. Simons on St. Simons Island, with Fort St. Andrews and Fort William on Cumberland Island, as well as other batteries and outposts on the mainland, formed this Southern Frontier for Britain's Colonies in North America against the Spaniards in Florida.

Fort Frederica, built in 1736 by British settlers under the direction of Gen. James Edward Oglethorpe, the most expensive fortification built by the British in North America, became the military headquarters for this line of defense. A regiment of British soldiers brought over in 1738 manned these fortifications.

In the town of Frederica the settlers built their houses of brick, tabby, or wood and practiced their trades and professions. It was a thriving village—a little bit of Old England transplanted here in America.

In order to prevent the Spaniards from landing on any of the many bluffs on St. Simons Island, Oglethorpe settled soldiers of the Regiment and some of the Frederica citizens on these sites.

At the northwest point of St. Simons he located nineteen soldiers with their families. They called the place Newhampton, which soon became Hampton. Here each settler was given a fifty-acre grant of land, which he farmed.

South of Hampton, on Frederica River "from whence they can see vessels a great way to the Northward," Oglethorpe set up a "Watch House" in charge of Richard Pike, one of the indentured servants who had been maimed in the public service. Pike and his wife, the daughter of a freeholder at Frederica, lived on this site which became known as Pike's Bluff. A corporal's guard was stationed there and the soldiers were rotated weekly.

At West Point, Capt. Albert Desbrisay of the Regiment and others had plantations.

On Dunbar Creek, John Terry, the Recorder at Frederica, established his plantation. Here he built a substantial house and planted hundreds of orange trees, giving the place its name, Orange Grove. He made other substantial improvements which he stated were worth seven hundred pounds, and operated a silversmith's shop; however, he will be remembered best as the writer of letters which told of the life of the people of that day.

Hawkins Island was the plantation of Dr. Thomas Hawkins, the doctor at Frederica as well as the surgeon of the Regiment, and the man whose wife made life so miserable for John and Charles Wesley.

At Gascoigne Bluff, Capt. James Gascoigne of H. M. Sloop-of-War, *Hawk,* maintained headquarters for the vessels of Georgia's first Navy. He had a storehouse for supplies, as well as a careening ground for repair of the ships. He was granted five hundred acres for his plantation and built a substantial house and several outhouses.

South of Gascoigne Bluff, at the site which came to be known as Retreat Plantation and which is now the Sea Island Golf Course, was the home of John Humble, the first pilot to bring vessels into this harbor.

At the South End of St. Simons, surrounding Fort St. Simons, were the houses built for the soldiers of the Regiment stationed there. These clapboard houses, built along regularly laid out streets, presented a neat appearance.

On the northeast point of St. Simons a grant of land was made to Daniel Cannon and the place became known as Cannon's Point. Cannon, a carpenter, with his two sons, Joseph and Daniel, was one of the first settlers of Frederica.

John Lawrence and Archibald Sinclair, both Frederica settlers, had grants of land on the western shore of St. Simons and these tracts of land still bear their names.

Below these was the tract occupied by a group of German Lutherans, knowns as Salzburgers. These families made their living by planting and fishing, selling their wares to the Frederica settlers and to the officers of the Regiment.

Capt. Raymond Demere of Oglethorpe's Regiment made his home below the German Village tract and called it Harrington Hall in honor of Lord Harrington under whom he had served at Gibraltar.

Capt. George Dunbar's plantation was located on the bank of the creek which bears his name.

In 1738 the Anglo-Spanish conflict flared into open warfare. Spain drew first blood, killing two Highlanders on Amelia Island. Oglethorpe led a force into Florida to learn what preparations the Spaniards might be making for an attack on Georgia. The British burned Fort Picolata and captured Fort St. Francis de Pupa on the St. Johns River.

Returning to Georgia, Oglethorpe planned to lay seige to St. Augustine. He set out in May, 1740 with a force consisting of the soldiers of his Regiment, the Highlanders from Darien, Indian allies, and a considerable number of soldiers from South Carolina under Col. Vanderdussen.

In this Florida campaign Oglethorpe destroyed seven forts and a year later wrote Newcastle that the Spaniards had not been able to rebuild any one of them. While the invasion did not accomplish its purpose of capturing St. Augustine, it did keep the Spaniards busy and thus delayed their expedition against Georgia while it gave Oglethorpe time to prepare his defenses.

In 1742 Spain assembled a great fleet of fifty-one vessels and three thousand men and sailed against Georgia. Entering St. Simons Sound on July 5th they succeeded in passing the guns of Fort St. Simons and sailing on up to Gascoigne Bluff, where they landed. Oglethorpe abandoned Fort St. Simons and concentrated his forces at Fort Frederica. The Spaniards occupied the abandoned Fort St. Simons, making it their headquarters. On July 7th, 1742, an engagement between these forces, known as The Battle of Bloody Marsh, was a complete victory for the British. The Spanish forces hastily withdrew and never again did Spain attempt to regain control of this territory. This was the turning point in the struggle between Spain and England for this southeastern section of our country. This Spanish Invasion of 1742 is a part of the struggle which is generally known as the War of Jenkins' Ear and was ended by the Treaty of Aix-la-Chapelle in 1748. The following year Oglethorpe's Regiment was disbanded and St. Simons Island was practically abandoned. It was not until after the Revolutionary War that settlers came again to occupy the Island.

In 1786 James Spalding of Retreat Plantation received the gift of a package of seed of a Persian cotton which had been developed on the Island of Anguilla. From this small beginning there was developed a staple crop which was to bring wealth to this coastal area. For many years this variety was known as Anguilla cotton; later, it was called Sea Island cotton. The invention of the cotton gin about this time brought about the development of great cotton plantations.

St. Simons had fourteen plantations, ranging in size from a hundred to three thousand acres and with thousands of Negro slaves.

Hampton Plantation became the property of Major Pierce Butler, who came to America in 1766 as a Major of the 29th British Regiment. His grandson, Pierce Butler, married Fanny Kemble, noted English actress and violent abolitionist. Fanny Kemble accompanied her husband to Georgia in the winter of 1838-39 and spent two unhappy months at Hampton, or Butler Point, as it is now called. While here she kept a journal, which was published in 1863 under the title, *Journal of a Residence on a Georgian Plantation, 1838-9.* This "Journal" is said to have caused more criticism of the South than any book that was ever written except *Uncle Tom's Cabin.*

Pike's Bluff and West Point became the plantations of two brothers, Dr. Thomas Fuller Hazzard, and Capt. William Wigg Hazzard. The Hazzard lands extended east to join those of the Wylly family, whose plantation occupied the lands of the German Village, now known as The Village.

The Demere family moved to the South End of St. Simons where they built a home known as Mulberry Hall and called their plantation The Grove.

James Gould of Massachusetts, who, in 1808, had built the first St. Simons Lighthouse and then stayed to become its first keeper, established a plantation at Rose Hill and then moved to Black Banks.

The Cater family lived at Kelvin Grove, which included the site of the Battle of Bloody Marsh. The marriage of Ann Cater to James Postell brought this plantation into the Postell family.

James Bruce had located at Orange Grove and the marriage of his daughter, Rebecca, to Major Samuel Wright brought this property into the Wright family.

At Retreat Plantation, Major William Page and his wife, Hannah Timmons Page, trained their only remaining child, Anna Matilda, in the duties of operating a plantation. Anna Matilda married Thomas Butler King of Massachusetts, who became the local Representative in the United States Congress and, later, Collector of the Port of San Francisco. Mrs. King's operation of the plantation was so efficient that it became one of the finest on St. Simons and her Sea Island cotton brought top prices in the markets of England.

The Lawrence family continued to operate their plantation and Major Pierce Butler now owned Sinclair, which was used by the plantation owners as the meeting place for their social organization, "The Agricultural and Sporting Club of St. Simons."

Two friends and partners in business, John Couper and James Hamilton, settled on St. Simons—Couper at Cannon's Point and Hamilton at Gascoigne Bluff. Hamilton prospered greatly and finally removed with his family to Philadelphia, where his home was one of the finest of its day. When he died in 1829 he was rated as one of the few millionaires of the country. Hamilton Plantation is now the site of the Methodist Center, Epworth-By-The-Sea.

John Couper and his son, James Hamilton Couper, developed at Cannon's Point one of the finest plantations in the South. In an effort to diversify his crops, John Couper brought in dates from Persia and olives from France. Cannon's Point has been called "Georgia's First Agricultural Experiment Station."

During the Civil War St. Simons was abandoned by the plantation owners. The men were in the Army of the Confederacy and the women and children refugeed on the mainland at Waynesville and, later, at Waresboro. The Negro slaves remained on the plantations and many of the men joined the United States Army, enlisting in a regiment commanded by Col. Thomas Wentworth Higginson, the first Negro regiment in the United States Army.

When the war was over, most of the owners, as well as their former slaves, returned to the plantations. They had no other place to go and it was hard for them, both master and freedman, to realize that their former way of life had ended. The master had his plantation; the Negro had nothing. It was a hard life for both, but they soon adjusted themselves to new conditions.

Lumber mills which came to Gascoigne Bluff in the 1870's, provided employment for both the plantation master and his former slaves.

It was during the mill days that the resort era began on St. Simons. At first steamers brought excursion parties from Brunswick and from Darien, landing at the wharf at Gascoigne Bluff, but in 1887 a wharf was built at the South End, near the lighthouse, where grew up a summer colony.

In 1924 a causeway was built connecting St. Simons and Sea Island with the mainland. Visitors in automobiles explored the beauty spots on St. Simons and Sea Island, many returning to make their homes. Thus was brought about a new era in the history of these islands.

Index

CPSIA information can be obtained at www.ICGtesting.com
Printed in the USA
LVIW011806020519
616415LV00007B/75